The Hours of
RICHARD III

The Hours of
RICHARD III

ANNE F. SUTTON &
LIVIA VISSER-FUCHS

Front cover: Richard III's Hours, Lambeth Ms.474, f.15. Annunciation and the beginning of the Hours of the Virgin.

First published 1990
First published in paperback 1996
This paperback edition first published 2024

In association with the Yorkist History Trust

The History Press
97 St George's Place, Cheltenham,
Gloucestershire, GL50 3QB
www.thehistorypress.co.uk

ISBN 978 1 80399 632 5

Typesetting and origination by The History Press
Printed and bound in Great Britain by TJ Books Limited, Padstow, Cornwall.

MIX
Paper from
responsible sources
FSC FSC® C013056
www.fsc.org

Trees for LYfe

Contents

Illustrations

PLATES

FIGURES

12. Bodleian Library, Ms. Lat. liturg. f.2, f.79v. Funeral.
13. Bodleian Library, Ms. Rawlinson liturg. d.1., f.59. Funeral.
14. Blackburn Museum and Art Galleries, Hart Ms. 21018, f.49. Funeral.
15. British Library, Additional Ms. 42131, f.46. Funeral.
16. Executors of Major Abbey Ms. JA.7398, f.75. Requiem mass.
17. Pierpont Morgan Library, New York, M.893, f.60. Requiem mass.
18. British Library, Additional Ms. 65100, f.193v. Requiem mass.
19. British Library, Harleian Ms. 2887, f.80. Funeral.
20. Bodleian Library, Ms. Rawlinson liturg. d.1, f.40. Christ in Judgement.
21. Blackburn Museum and Art Galleries, Hart Ms. 21018, f.35v. Christ in Judgement.
22. Executors of Major Abbey Ms.JA.7398, f.57.Christ in Judgement.
23. Pierpont Morgan Library, New York M.893, f.44v. Christ in Judgement.
24. British Library, Harleian Ms. 2887, f.68. Christ in Judgement.
25. Bodleian Library, Ms. Rawlinson liturg.d.1, f.110v. Portrait Heads.
26. Lambeth Ms. 474, f.1. Collect of St. Ninian.
27. Edinburgh University Library Ms. 42, f.72v. St. Ninian.
28. Lambeth Ms. 474, f.7v. Calendar page: October.
29. Lambeth Ms. 474, f. 181. First page of 'the prayer of Richard III'.

Acknowledgements and thanks for permission to reproduce illustrations are due to Lambeth Palace Library for plates 1, 2, 3 and figures 26, 28 and 29; to the Abbot of Altenburg for plate 4; to the Trustees of the National Library of Scotland for figure 1; to the British Library for figures 2, 4, 8, 9, 11, 15, 18, 19 and 24; to the Bodleian Library, Oxford, for figures 3, 12, 13, 20 and 25; to the Trustees of the Berkeley Muniments for figure 5; to the Conway Library, Courtauld Institute of Art, for figures 6, 16 and 22; to Blackburn Museum and Art Galleries for figures 7, 14 and 21; to The Pierpont Morgan Library, New York, for figures 10, 17 and 23; and to the Edinburgh University Library for figure 27.

Acknowledgements

We are deeply grateful for the help of many people given so generously during the course of this work.

Above all the informative and mild comments of Dom Eligius Dekkers, O.S.B., of the Sint Pieters Abbey, Bruges, on 'Richard III's prayer' and 'litany' and the assistance of Mr. Nicholas Rogers on all aspects of the book have been invaluable. Without their encouragement we would have found the worlds of art history and liturgy much more hazardous.

Assistance on specific points has been generously given by the Abbot of Altenburg, Brother P. J. Berkhout, O.S.B., of the Sint Adelbert's Abbey, Egmond, Professor L. M. de Rijk, Dr. L. E. Boyle, O.P., Prefect of the Vatican Library, Mr. Gregory Clark of the Pierpont Morgan Library, Dr. Mirjam Foot of the British Library, Dr. Lynda Dennison, Dr. Christopher de Hamel, Mr. Michael Orr, Miss M. Pemberton and Dr. B. C. Barker-Benfield of the Bodleian Library, Madame M.-H. Tesnière of the Bibliothèque Nationale, Paris, Dr. Rowan Watson of the National Art Library, Victoria and Albert Museum, Miss Helen Young of the Palaeography Room, University of London Library, Mrs. Andersson-Schmitt of the Universitetsbibliotek, Uppsala, and Mr. David Smith of the Gloucester Record Office.

We are most grateful to Lambeth Palace Library and its librarian, Mr. E. W. Bill, for facilitating the study of the Hours and its publication, and to his assistant, Miss Melanie Barber, for her help.

Encouragement has been gratefully received from Mr. and Mrs. P.W. Hammond, Mr. Jeremy Potter, Dr. Rosemary Horrox and Dr. Caroline Barron of the Richard III and Yorkist History Trust (now the Yorkist History Trust), which has made the publication of this book possible.

Thanks are also extended to Mrs. Sue Haylock for her typing, to Michael Berlin, and to the staff of the following: the British Library Manuscripts Department, the Fitzwilliam Museum, the Royal Library, The Hague, the Bodleian Library, the municipal libraries of Carpentras, Châlons-sur-Marne, Le Mans and Rennes, the libraries of the Catharijneconvent, Utrecht, and the Rijksmuseum Meermanno-Westreenianum, The Hague, the National Library of Scotland, the Edinburgh University Library, the Glamorgan Archive Service, Blackburn Museum and Art Galleries, the college libraries of Sidney Sussex, Gonville and Caius, Corpus Christi and Trinity, Cambridge, and University College, London.

Denique familiae pro tolerantia.

The Yorkist History Trust

The Yorkist History Trust is a charity founded in 1985 to advance and disseminate research and education related to the history of late medieval England (and in particular the reign and life of King Richard III). We fulfil these aims by offering research grants to scholars working on the period, by offering publication grants to titles of relevance, and by publishing critical primary source editions, volumes of collected essays, and academic monographs. Recent publications include Peter Fleming's *Late Medieval Bristol: Time, Space and Power*, an edition of *The Lordship of Middleham in 1465–66 and 1473–74*, edited by Livia Visser-Fuchs, Jonathan Mackman, and Anne F. Sutton, and the late Dr Sutton's magisterial *The King's Work: The Defence of the North under the Yorkist Kings*.

Future projects include editions of the executors' accounts of Sir Ralph Verney, the probate accounts and inventories of Sir Thomas Charlton, documents relating to the Smithfield Tournament, and London's Common Council Journal covering the reign of Richard III, as well as a monograph on the chronicler Robert Fabyan. We have recently funded projects on the gentry of the fifteenth century and the Brewers' Company of London. We welcome applications for editions and monographs to be published by the Trust and to support other publications and research on the fifteenth century. To submit an application, or for more information, please see our website: www.yorkisthistorytrust.org.

List of Abbreviations

The following abbreviations are used in the notes. Full citations for the works thus abbreviated, and for other works referred to by short titles, will be found in the Bibliography.

AH	*Analecta Hymnica Medii Aevi*
Antidotarius	Salicetus, Nicolaus, *Liber meditationum* …
BL	British Library
BN	Bibliothèque Nationale, Paris
Darmstadt	*Die Handschriften der Hessischen Landes- und Hochschulbibliothek Darmstadt*
Horae Ebor.	Wordsworth, Chr., *Horae Eboracenses*
LH	Leroquais, V., *Les Livres d'Heures*
Lyell	De La Mare, A., *Catalogue of the Collection* … *bequeathed* … *by James P.R. Lyell* (the numbers refer to the list of *incipit* of Latin prayers on pp. 366–400)
PL	Migne, J. P., *Patrologiae cursus completus. Series Latina*
RH	Chevalier, U., *Repertorium hymnologicum*

ONE

General Introduction

A study of the Hours of Richard III is justified more by his ownership than by any other single factor: his ownership and the addition of certain prayers for his use as King make the manuscript unique.

Lambeth Ms. 474, here styled the Hours of Richard III, was not made originally for the King. As demonstrated below, it was produced in London about 1420 for an unknown owner, possibly a cleric. It is a text of unusual length and some distinctive features. At some date after 6 July 1483, the date of his coronation, Richard III chose to use this text as his personal book of hours. He made four additions to it:

1. His birth-date in the calendar (f.7v).
2. A collect of St. Ninian (f.1).
3. A long, fairly common prayer, the history of which is here studied for the first time. It is called 'Richard III's prayer' because it has been so often and mistakenly asserted that it is unique to Richard and has been used to draw unfounded conclusions about his personality (ff. 181–183).
4. A long devotion, perhaps a litany, which was apparently composed for him personally and which may reflect his interest in the crusading 'movement', such as it was, in his day (ff.184–184v).

Richard III (1452–1485) is one of the most controversial figures in medieval history. In 1483 he succeeded his brother, Edward IV, on the throne of England, setting aside his nephews who were declared illegitimate. To establish himself he had to execute several opponents and crush one rebellion. During the two years of his reign his only son and his wife died. In administrative terms his rule was not unsuccessful but its full potential was never realised for he failed to defeat an invasion led by Henry Tudor, the future Henry VII, losing his crown and his life at the battle of Bosworth on 22 August 1485.

Criticism of Richard III centres on the murder of his nephews. Other crimes of which he has been accused and of which Shakespeare's play is a constant reminder include the murder of Henry VI, Edward IV's predecessor, his own wife, and his brother, the Duke of Clarence. These charges, however, are rarely now considered worthy of attention by serious historians. The disappearance of his two nephews, who are not known to have been seen again after the first few months of his reign, remains a constant theme of debate: did he murder them or not? Richard's personality can still be described in the most pejorative of terms as a consequence.

As a man's religious convictions can be considered fundamental to his character and behaviour Richard's piety has naturally provoked comment, and conclusions have been made linking his piety with his crimes and a need to atone. Some of these theories have drawn on material in the Hours, especially 'his' prayer, but none have been based on any real inspection or understanding of the manuscript or of the prayer's text and purpose. A study of the Hours is therefore long overdue and should contribute to a better appreciation of what are the facts about Richard III and his piety to be found in the Hours. A caveat must be entered, however, on the more general issue of whether the piety of a king of the fifteenth century, or indeed of any individual, can ever really be known. In the authors' opinion the enigma of Richard III cannot be solved by looking at his Hours.

There are other reasons to study this second-hand book of hours chosen by Richard III for his own use, and each of these may incidentally contribute to our understanding of why he chose this manuscript. It is a long text, longer than many other hours, and stuffed with individual prayers presumably all chosen by the first unknown owner of the book – these are set out and explained folio by folio in the 'Analysis of Contents'. Despite this wide choice of prayers offered to him in the book Richard III still felt impelled to add others that were important to him. The liturgical texts of this Hours justify a study in their own right.

In its decoration the Hours is a comparatively modest one. It is not like the more lavish ones so often owned by royalty. If Richard III owned any such magnificent hours, and princes often had more than one, they either do not survive or all signs of his ownership have been expunged by a later owner (Henry VII is known to have superimposed his arms over those of Edward IV in some books). Although Richard's Hours is plain it is nevertheless a good example of a fine period of London illumination. By its illumination it is also possible to date the manuscript.

Both its liturgical contents and its decoration presumably appealed to Richard III. The text shows the preoccupations of a devout man of the fifteenth century and its decoration puts it in the context of the development of London manuscript illumination in the same period. Richard III chose a very useful, solid, unflamboyant and English manuscript for his daily use – one that can be shown to be entirely in keeping with the other books he owned. He seems to have chosen his books for their contents.

Books of Hours

A book of hours, or primer, was the private book of devotions of the layman in the later Middle Ages and the Renaissance. It was the result of a long development towards a more personal expression of religious feeling.[1]

The 'hours' referred to are not the sixty-minute hours of the clock as we know them, but recall an older division of day and night marked by the position of the sun and varying with the season. Since very early times and in many religions people have felt the need to pray to their god at frequent fixed intervals. In the Christian faith not only the moment but also the content of each devotion soon became highly formalised. As early as the third century AD the faithful were expected to worship at the 'natural' times of midnight, cockcrow and sunset, and also at the third, sixth and ninth hour of the day. They were to express their faith by reading certain parts of the Bible and singing designated psalms and hymns at each of these occasions. This was the duty of laymen as well as of priests and monks.

In the ninth and tenth centuries the renewal of religious zeal led to an extension and elaboration of the official daily devotions, or Divine

Office. By the year 1000 the most important 'extras' were the Gradual and Penitential Psalms, the Litany, the Office of the Dead and the special offices of the Virgin, the Trinity, the Holy Cross and the Holy Spirit.[2] Many of these came to be regarded as integral parts of the older devotions, but unlike them they were not related to the festal days of the saints and hardly changed with the church's year. The laity found these offices more attractive and convenient than the long complicated devotions of the clergy: their objects, such as the Virgin or the Passion, appealed, and their format was brief and almost invariable. These offices were at first added to the existing layman's devotional book, the psalter,[3] but also came to lead a separate life by about 1400.[4]

The main and most distinctive item in a book of hours is the Little Office of the Blessed Virgin Mary (*Officium Parvum Beatae Virginis Mariae*).[5] Its prayers, lessons and psalms, read and sung in honour of St. Mary, were spread over day and night, each part to be said at its appointed 'hour'. The names of the hours or offices changed in the course of the Middle Ages, but by Richard III's time Matins (*matutine,* from the Latin *matutinum,* 'morning') was the first and began at midnight or shortly after. Together with Lauds (*laudes matutinales,* 'morning praises', because originally it always ended with psalms 148, 149 and 150 in praise of God) it formed one long office said during the night and early morning. The next four, shorter, offices, Prime, Terce, Sext and None, at the first, third, sixth (noon) and ninth hour, filled the day. Between Terce and Sext, Mass was celebrated. Vespers (*vespere,* 'evensong') started at sunset or earlier. Compline (*completorium*) completed the cycle and was said before going to bed.[6]

The text of the Hours of the Virgin was usually preceded by a perpetual calendar listing the saints and feasts of universal and local importance, set passages from the Four Gospels, one from each, and the Passion according to St. John.[7] After the Hours themselves (and there could be included not merely those of the Virgin but the Hours of the Cross, the Holy Ghost etc.), followed the Seven Penitential Psalms with the Litany of Saints and The Office or Vigil of the Dead. Several other items are common to most books of hours and will be discussed below in so far as they are included in Richard III's manuscript.

In specific details the books vary according to the diocese or monastic order in which they were used.[8] Among the better known 'uses' are those of Rome, Paris and Utrecht on the continent, York and Salisbury (Sarum) in England. Franciscan, Dominican and Augustinian use are also found. Analyses of the variations in the short devotional texts that accompany the psalms sung at each hour and of the saints in the calendar, as well as the precise texts of hymns and prayers, help to establish a manuscript's origin or the market for which it was made. This is of importance to the art historian studying book illumination and painting.

As the popularity of books of hours grew their contents gradually eluded clerical control and their quality deteriorated. The Latin they were written in came to contain many errors because of the ignorance of the copyist, and items were added, mostly prayers, of which the contents bordered on, and often trespassed well into, the realm of superstition.[9] These additional devotions, however, can also provide evidence of sincerity and faith. Some are very old and may be found in collections already existing in the time of Charlemagne. Most were anonymous, many were ascribed to saints and fathers of the church and some were credited with miraculous origins and equally miraculous powers.[10]

The contents of books of hours were very familiar to every literate person in the later Middle Ages and their influence on imagination and speech and thus on contemporary prose and verse was considerable.[11]

TWO

The Manuscript, Its Scheme of Decoration and Status

Lambeth Ms. 474 is a book of hours according to the use of Sarum. It is now in a mid-sixteenth century binding, with some gold tooling, which has recently been rebacked. The binding was executed in the workshop of the King Edward and Queen Mary Binder which was active in the 1540s and '50s doing work for Henry VIII, Edward and Mary as well as less illustrious customers.[12] Unfortunately it is not known who commissioned this rebinding. All edges are gilt. The lining sheet from a fourteenth-century service book with music is visible. Two brass clasps with catches survive, hinged to the front cover, but the bottom hinged bar is missing.

It now has 184 vellum folios with two unruled flyleaves at the end, blank except for some erasures; several leaves are missing and there are no unruled flyleaves at the beginning. Most of the twenty-six gatherings have eight leaves, the first is of two only, the third of six. In the twenty-first gathering, between folios 151v and 152 there is a neat stub. Of the twenty-fourth the seventh leaf is lost (the one that contained the beginning of 'Richard III's prayer'). The twenty-fifth gathering has two leaves and after these (that is, after the end of the same prayer) at least three ruled folios have been crudely cut out. The twenty-sixth gathering consists of the leaf on which is written the surviving portion of Richard III's 'litany' – it is of a different, rougher vellum, comparable to that of the concluding two flyleaves. All gatherings and all folios have been numbered in pencil, presumably by M. R. James when he collated the manuscript.[13] In two instances only, the Calendar and the instructions of the seasonal variations of the Hours of the Virgin, do the major sections of the text correspond with the physical divisions of the manuscript.

Devotional pieces were added to the original text for the use of Richard III and there are minor inscriptions by or about other persons. All these, as well as the damage or erasures, will be dealt with below in the discussion of the contents, under the appropriate folio, and in the section on ownership.

Without its binding the book now measures 193 by 140mm. It was originally much larger. If the proportions of the decoration of the Annunciation page are considered and if comparison is made with other manuscripts, closely related to Richard III's Hours in date and style, which survive in their first binding after only one careful cropping, an original size of at least 236 by 173mm. is arrived at.[14] Such a size would have left about 10mm. of space between the decorative sprays of the full border of the Annunciation page and the edge of the page. The sixteenth-century binder, who for some reason had to rebind the Hours, overcut the book, but he must be a little excused for his destruction of the Annunciation border for here the artist had painted far more in the upper margin than did the artist of the other two full borders. The binder certainly resewed the manuscript because some letters of the addition of Richard III's birthday in the October Calendar now disappear into the spine.

The text is in one column throughout and is in what M. R. James described as a 'tall narrow English hand,' a *gothica textualis quadrata formata*. A full page has eighteen lines ruled in brown ink, the text space measuring 83–83.5mm. by 117–117.5mm.[15] The devotional additions made for Richard III imitate the hand of the original book.

The manuscript is decorated simply but richly. There are historiated initials (that is, decorated with a picture) for the three key divisions of the text: the Hours of the Virgin (Matins; f.15), the Penitential Psalms (f.55) and the Vigil of the Dead (f.72). The initial of the second has been cut out. All these have full vinets, that is to say a border decoration extending around all four sides of the text.[16] There are no other pictures in the book; the rest of the decoration is composed of elaborate, formal foliage patterns of demi-vinets and champs (initials decorated in colour on a gold ground with ornamental sprays in the margin).[17]

The size of the introductory initials suit the importance of the individual offices, psalms, prayers, and so on down to the responses. Thus, a nine-line historiated initial and a full vinet opens Matins and six-line historiated initials with full vinets open the other key items in the book; a nine-line decorated initial introduces *Salve virgo virginum* (f.152), while eight-line decorated initials are suitable for the beginnings of Lauds (f.25), Prime (f.37v), Terce (f.41), Sext (f.43), None (f.45), Vespers (f.47v) and Compline (f.49) of the Hours of the Virgin, as well as the Psalms of the Passion (f.101) and the *Confiteor* (f.124), and the Fifteen Oes (f.145). Seven-line initials are sufficient for the Commendation of Souls (f.90v), the first of the *Miserere* psalms (f.109), and the Psalter of St. Jerome (f.112v). There are no six-line initials, apart from the two superior, historiated ones, and only one five-line initial, the one introducing the Seven Joys (f.162v). Four-line initials are frequent, for example one opens the first stanza of *Omnibus consideratis* (f.131v), the prayer of the Venerable Bede (f.136v), the *O intemerata* (f.156v), the *Obsecro te* (f.158), the Five Sorrows of Mary (f.168), and the *Stabat mater* (f.173). The status of the initial I is often not immediately clear as they curve down the margin and have no space left for them in the text, but most of them rank as four- or three-line initials (eg. ff.25v, 35v, 95v, 122v, 129v, 131, 151v).

The majority of prayers rate three-line initials and as these appear towards the end of the book, the book gives the appearance of 'running out' of decoration in its second half (especially ff.168v–180), as do other books of hours, for the same reason. The last, or rather the last surviving, prayer of the original book, to St. Julian, is introduced by a one-line initial (f.180v).

Subsidiary sections of the longer items are similarly marked by initials of different sizes. Two- and three-line initials introduce hymns, chapters, psalms and prayers throughout the Hours of the Virgin, and one-line initials introduce most minor items. Subsidiary initials for the Seven Penitential Psalms are all two-line ones, as are those for the *Commendationes Animarum* and Psalms of the Passion. The Vigil of the Dead is also served by two-line initials, except for one four-line initial at the beginning of the *Dirige* (f.74v). After an introductory eight-line initial for the first of the Fifteen Oes each subsequent one is marked by a three-line one.

One-line initials perform a great variety of functions: these are in gold or blue alternately and are decorated with pen flourishes in blue for the gold ones and red for the blue. None are remarkable. The lowest level in this hierarchy of attention marks is represented by the pale stroke of ochre paint through certain capitals in the text.

Titles and rubics are in red, sometimes heavily abbreviated, such as those indicating verses or responses. Paragraph signs are also in red (eg. f.36) and line fillers are in blue and gold.

The pages of the Calendar have little decoration: the one champ of the KL at the head of each month has alternately red and blue as its main colour and always has two stiff sprays of foliage jutting out from it. The painter seems to have considered decorating the outer margin of January with other sprays and tentatively sketched in a few, but he thought better of it and went no further. Red, blue and black mark the days and feasts in the usual manner, with one-line initials as described above. (See also in the Analysis of Contents for the Calendar).

The champs introducing the textual additions made for Richard III are in the London style, as it had become in the 1480s: their prolongations are like solid fern fronds rather than the curling tendrils of the decoration of the original book. The one-line initials are in the style of the rest of the book.

The time expended on decorating a book indicates something of its status and relative cost in the absence of precise details of its commission and price. Clearly the Hours of Richard III, with the scheme of decoration indicated above, is in a very different class of manuscript from the lavishly illustrated hours commissioned by such as the Dukes of Berry and Bedford. Nor does it have the status of a book of hours with a long sequence of historiated initials and miniatures such as the Nevill Hours, called after its first known owner, Richard III's cousin George Nevill, Lord Abergavenny.[18] It is, in its turn, superior to hours that have no historiated initials and call for no representational skill from the decorator, such as Lambeth Ms. 459 made in London 1470–90, which has plenty of crude foliage-decorated initials, or Bodley 113, an unpretentious Sarum hours similar in style and date to Richard's and made in London 1425–50 with a plain vinet for the Hours of the Virgin, demi-vinets, champs, all unelaborate and with little gold.[19] Closest to the Hours of Richard III but sufficiently different in small details to show effectively the range of books of hours produced in the same workshop, probably within months of each other in this case, is manuscript AB 6 C 4 of the Benedictines of Altenburg, Austria.[20] This has a full vinet and one historiated initial of seven lines for the Hours of the Virgin, using the same model as Richard's Hours, and its Vigil of the Dead and Penitential Psalms are introduced by demi-vinets with seven-line initials composed of foliage. The last are so similar to those in the Richard III Hours they might have been done for it. Subsidiary decoration is in the same manner, with no decoration at all for its plain Calendar. Everything in the Altenburg manuscript is slightly less lavish than in the Lambeth manuscript: its highest point is the one seven-line historiated initial for Matins; its subsidiary illumination is less extensive and its demi-vinets have less variety, but its style and colouring are the same. The Altenburg manuscript was the cheaper of the two commissions.

THREE

The Illumination: Style, Workmanship and Date

By the time Richard III's Hours was produced the illumination of books of hours had become subject to several conventions. These conventions imposed an overall order and both facilitated and standardised the tasks of the scribes and painters, speeding up the production of what has been called the best-seller of the middle ages: for example, the method of differentiating saints by their emblems was universal, even if the saints included might vary, and the labours of the months and later the signs of the zodiac became the usual way of illustrating the Calendar. The Hours of the Virgin were illustrated either by scenes from her life, concluding with her heavenly coronation, or by a sequence showing the Passion of Christ, the latter being usual in England. There were regional differences among these conventions, just as there were for the local use or custom of the diocese which affected which prayers, offices and saints were included, and different workshops added their own characteristic decoration. Bruges and Paris were noted centres of production with their own styles, and so was London in the early fifteenth century.

The illumination of books of hours was as much part of the humanisation of the church's offices and the personalising of devotion as the text. Each manuscript differed in some respects from every other manuscript, although the more expensive the commission the more unique the book might be as a work of art. The purchaser's wishes and purse affected the decoration, particularly as regards quality and quantity:

whether pictures were to be included, how much gold was to be used and whether personal motifs such as coats of arms were to be added. The decoration also depended on certain priorities dictated by the text and its contents: attention was first paid to the opening of the Hours of the Virgin, secondly to the Penitential Psalms and thirdly to the Office of the Dead.[21]

Only these three sections are historiated (given pictorial illustration) in the Hours of Richard III; the rest of the illumination is purely decorative, to please the eye, indicate the divisions of the text and help the reader to find his way about the book. The original owner did not make any discernible impression upon the artist's work (though he did on the contents). It is, however, an expensive product of a good workshop. The first page of the Hours of the Virgin has a border of the best quality English illumination of the time, and few openings lack pattern, colour and gold. The restrained reaction of commentators[22] hardly prepares one for its bright, clear colouring and its warm attractiveness. The last quality is partly due to the particularly pleasing combination of orange and gold, a softer combination than the blue and pink or harsh red that so often dominate similar manuscripts.[23] It is a book for use, for its owner to carry around and take to church, and to add new items to for personal devotion. It is not a showpiece designed primarily for its pictures – if Richard III owned such hours (and many rich people did own more than one), they are not known. This book was the service book he chose to use personally as king.

English Illumination in the early Fifteenth Century
From the end of the fourteenth century a marked change in the style of illumination (the art of decorating or 'lighting up' a manuscript with gold and colours) took place in England. A linear, flat and decorative style with little modelling of figures gave way to one that aimed at a three-dimensional and realistic quality, with solid figures and a liking for portraiture. This change is considered to have been the result of communication between English artists with their several native traditions and the continental schools of France, the Low Countries and Germany.[24] Artists had their own workshops, mostly small family based units with a few apprentices. They tended to congregate in one area, such as Paternoster Row in London. They were frequently employed

by middlemen, for example stationers of London, who handled and financed the commission and put out the work. They taught apprentices; they copied each others' work, they collaborated on large projects under one master or supervisor and they often specialised in one type of work, such as borders or miniatures; they moved around to find work, influenced each others' styles and models, borrowed themes; they were attracted or repulsed by foreign fashions and developments. For all these reasons the work and style of individual artists in early fifteenth century London are almost impossible to identify or distinguish, particularly when more than one worked on a book, a gathering or even on one page, and, as so often happens, when the talent of the painter was unremarkable and no details are known of the commission from documentary sources.[25]

To identify the artists who worked on Richard III's Hours, or at least locate them, in this web of workshops and styles, it is necessary first to describe the known illuminators and their circumstances in the early fifteenth century, as well as the manuscripts they produced. Secondly, the main decorative features of Richard's Hours need to be related to similar features in those manuscripts found to be closest to his Hours in character, paying particular attention to *dated* manuscripts. The main features are the historiation, the portrait heads and the subsidiary decoration of the borders and initials. The fluid interchange of styles and the working environment of the period make this dangerous and speculative. Above all we are conscious of Abbé Leroquais' gentle reminder of how the long dead painters would smile at modern historians' attempts to analyse their work.[26]

One notable English artist flourishing at the beginning of the fifteenth century was John Siferwas, a Dominican friar, whose portrait and name appeared in the great missal illuminated under his supervision for Sherborne Abbey *circa* 1400–1407. He was also involved in the production of the lectionary made for Salisbury Cathedral at the order of John, Lord Lovel of Titchmarsh (died 1408). He took ideas from everyone and adapted them with great talent, combining native traditions with the new international gothic style, and has been praised for his fine portraiture.[27] This theme of portraiture is manifest in several English manuscripts of the early fifteenth century, such as the Bedford Hours and Psalter and, in a minor key, the Hours of Richard III.

One of the greatest products of the international gothic style, probably of the first decade of the fifteenth century, was the missal made for the Carmelites of London. It was a complicated, co-operative piece of work by several groups of artists in London under the supervision of a continental Master, variously described as Dutch or Flemish – it seems likely that whichever of these two nationalities was the Master's, the other was a dominant influence over him. The missal also shows the influence of the older English schools of illumination at Westminster and in East Anglia.[28] Apart from the particular hand of the unknown Master in this manuscript, the hand of Herman Scheerre has been detected.[29]

The workshop of Herman Scheerre was identified in the 1920s, and documentary evidence was found later to suggest that he originated in Cologne. His art, however, had strong Flemish connections. He lived in England in the first two decades of the fifteenth century and it is possible he leased property in Paternoster Row near St. Paul's Cathedral, the heart of the London book trade.[30] Herman occasionally signed his work: he did so in a small book of prayers and offices probably made about 1405–10 and extensively decorated with small, intense renderings of religious subjects (BL. Add. 16998), a large breviary probably made for the future Archbishop Chichele between 1408 and 1414 (Lambeth 69), and the Hours and Psalter made for John Duke of Bedford *circa* 1420 (BL. Add. 42131).[31] Mottoes associated with his workshop have been found in other manuscripts. His work has been extensively identified and discussed, perhaps more because his name is known than for any other reason, and his personal achievement has had its detractors, but for the moment at least, his reputation appears to stand high.[32] His was a spiritual art: his figures have soft draperies, flat bodies and long, pale faces set against formal backdrops of colour patterned with gold. He worked on both large and small commissions, often doing one or a few miniatures himself in each. He was extensively copied.

A named contemporary of Herman Scheerre was Johannes, who put his name on his famous picture of Venice illustrating a copy of Marco Polo's *Li Livre du Graunt Cam, circa,* 1410 (Bodley 264). Johannes had a more lively and robust style than Scheerre – like him he was extensively copied. The 'Johannes group' of artists delighted in bright, clear colours, often with a lot of yellow, and pictures full of characters; their people had heavily featured faces, protruding eyes and exotic clothes.[33]

The most remarkable manuscript produced by the Johannes group is the Hours of Elizabeth the Queen, named for Elizabeth of York, a later owner (BL. Add. 50001). It was made in the late 1420s and its first known owner was Cecily Nevill, daughter of Richard Nevill, Earl of Salisbury, who married first Henry Beauchamp, Duke of Warwick (died 1446) and then John Tiptoft, Earl of Worcester, whom she predeceased in 1450.[34]

There was considerable communication and cross-fertilisation between Scheerre and Johannes and their associates, and several manuscripts show collaboration of artists belonging to each group.[35]

The Historiation of the Hours of Richard III: Annunciation, Christ in Judgement and Funeral

An Annunciation is an extremely simple scene: a dialogue between the Virgin Mary and the angel. There is little action or variety of gesture available to the painter. God could be added to the scene and the Holy Ghost, as a dove; a scroll with the angel's words of greeting was a very early addition; other decorative features such as Mary's lilies, her book of hours, pieces of furniture and details of background were emphasised or forgotten by different groups of artists.[36] With such a limited range of possibilities in the iconography, the smallest detail has to be highlighted to place each version in its context, while remembering that entirely separate artists might invent the same new variation independently since they were manoeuvring in such a small field. The most important and unusual features of the Annunciation on folio 15 of Richard III's Hours are the peaceful position of the Virgin's hands, crossed at the wrists, and her jewelled coronal.

The main influences behind this particular Annunciation, so far discovered, are English and Flemish. The most striking English parallel occurs in a psalter and hours made *circa* 1395 for Eleanor de Bohun, wife of Thomas of Woodstock, Duke of Gloucester (National Library of Scotland, Advocates Ms. 18.6.5., f.9v, fig.1). The Annunciation is a simple one: a kneeling angel with scroll; Mary standing, her head draped in her mantle, and with her arms crossed over her bosom; her book of hours is forgotten behind her on a barely visible lectern; neither God nor the dove is present, and no attempt has been made at a realistic background. The artist of this manuscript is thought to have collaborated earlier on the Litlyngton Missal, made at Westminster *circa*

Figure 1. Psalter and Hours made for Eleanor de Bohun, wife of Thomas of Woodstock, Duke of Gloucester, *circa* 1395. National Library of Scotland, Advocates Ms.18.6.5., f.9v. Annunciation, with an early English representation of the Virgin with her arms crossed.

1384–5, which contained a similar Annunciation (f.235v), but with the Virgin resting one hand on her prayer book and the other raised, palm outward towards the angel. Later this artist worked on the Carmelite Missal throughout its production, painting another Annunciation (BL. Add. Ms. 29704–5, f.99) with similar iconographical details including a Mary with crossed arms.[37] It seems likely, therefore, that the immediate origin of this gesture, as used in English fifteenth century manuscripts, was English, and from Westminster in particular.[38] A far more magnificent and influential use of the same gesture of acceptance was to appear in Flanders on the reverse of Jan van Eyck's Ghent altarpiece in 1432.[39]

It has been suggested that the overall prototype was created by Melchior Broederlam for a Dijon altarpiece made *circa* 1391–4. This

Annunciation is set in an architectural background and is supremely elegant and rich in ornament. The kneeling angel on the left lightly restrains a scroll from floating upwards between himself and the Virgin who kneels at an altar or *prie-dieu* on the right. The soft and demure Virgin has her own book of hours open before her; half turning to the messenger she raises one hand in modest deprecation of the honour done her. At the top left there is a representation of God the Father (often reduced to a red or blue cloud on which God is sketched in a darker shade of the same colour), and from him a dove descends in a ray of light to the Virgin (sometimes a child *follows* the dove). Whether Broederlam's altarpiece can be called the prototype or not, his elegant model was extensively copied, with endless variations, on the continent, by such as the so-called Rouen Master as early as 1400 in Bruges, and the Boucicaut Master who practised in Paris around 1405–1430. It was taken to England by such painters as Herman Scheerre.[40]

Two of the earliest and finest renderings in England were one by John Siferwas in the Sherborne Missal,[41] and another by Herman Scheerre for a psalter made for John Beaufort the elder (died 1410) and his wife Margaret Holand (died 1439) about 1404–7.[42] In both versions one hand of the Virgin lies on her book and the other rises towards her breast — they are not yet in repose. More significant for the present study are two other very simple Annunciations, one by Scheerre and the other by an associate. Scheerre's was made about 1405–10 for the small book of prayers and offices which contains his name (BL. Add. 16998, f.17, fig. 2). This shows the Virgin kneeling with both her hands in repose, although not yet crossed — the rest of the composition is already very close to that of Richard III's Hours. To the elegance of the continental model Scheerre has added the restful, accepting hands, a detail which it has been suggested was English. He and his associates were to make the motif their own.[43] The other example, probably around 1415–20, occurs in the Bodleian Library manuscript Lat. liturg. f.2, a Flemish book of hours to which English additions were made by Scheerre and his associates.[44] The small Annunciation (f. 13, fig.3) is undoubtedly by an untalented associate: it is poorly proportioned and ugly, but it has the striking feature of the crossed hands, large and ungainly though they are. Like Scheerre's small version, it has all the component elements of an Annunciation scene.

Figure 2. Book of prayers and offices, bearing the name of the painter Herman Scherre, *circa* 1405–10. British Library, Additional Ms. 16998, f.17. Annunciaton.

Figure 3. Book of hours, Bodleian Library, Ms. Lat. liturg. f.2, f.13. Annunciation. This manuscript is in poor condition.

To Scheerre is also attributed another fine Annunciation in the Hours and Psalter of John Duke of Bedford, *circa* 1420, a manuscript of which he is now generally considered to have been the overall Master.[45] This version (fig.4), however, again shows the Virgin with one upraised hand.[46]

The model reoccurs in three other manuscripts painted by artists from both the Scheerre and the Johannes groups: the Nevill Hours, the Hours of the Duchess of Clarence, and a less pretentious hours, now Hart 21018, of which no early owner is known. The first known owner of the Nevill Hours was George Nevill, Baron Abergavenny (died 1492); it is an elaborately decorated manuscript and contains a motto associated with the Scheerre group of artists. It has two Annunciations: a full miniature (f.100) with a seated Virgin, and an historiated initial (f.15, fig.5) with a design close to the Richard III version except in its

Figure 4. Bedford Hours and Psalter, made for John, Duke of Bedford *circa* 1420. British Library, Additional Ms. 42131, f.7. Annunciation.

Figure 5.　An Annunciation in unusual colouring: the angel is in blue with green wings, the Virgin in pink at a table draped in green, and the background is red. Berkeley Castle, Nevill Hours, f.15. Annunciation.

unusual colouring. In both versions, however, the Virgin has one hand upraised and one on her book.[47] This gesture also separates the version in the Hours of the Duchess of Clarence from that of Richard III's Hours, although otherwise the details are strikingly similar (f.15, fig.6). The angel in particular can be noted as identical in both colouring and drawing, but the Virgin is more poorly proportioned. These Hours were first owned by the same Margaret Holand mentioned above as the wife of John Beaufort (died 1410), who married secondly Thomas Duke of Clarence, brother of Henry V and John Duke of Bedford.[48] In the third example (Hart 21018, f.7, fig.7) the Virgin's book is replaced with a scroll bearing her answer to the angel, and the Virgin's hands are one above the other in front of her, not quite in repose but also not in any active display of emotion.[49]

Closest to the Annunciation in the Hours of Richard III is the one in the Hours owned by the Benedictines of Altenburg (f.9, pl.4). Differences are that the Virgin has her blue mantle over her head in the latter and that her hands, although in repose, are not crossed at the wrists. (In the Altenburg manuscript her hands are in fact closest to the

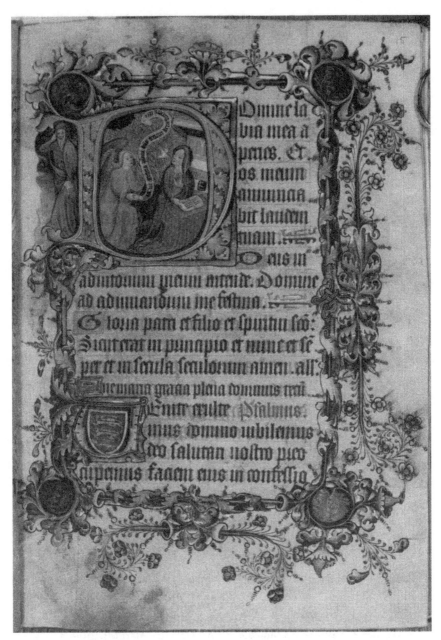

Figure 6. Hours of Margaret Holand, wife of Thomas, Duke of Clarence, brother of Henry V and John, Duke of Bedford. Executors of Major Abbey Ms. JA.7398, f.15. Annunciation.

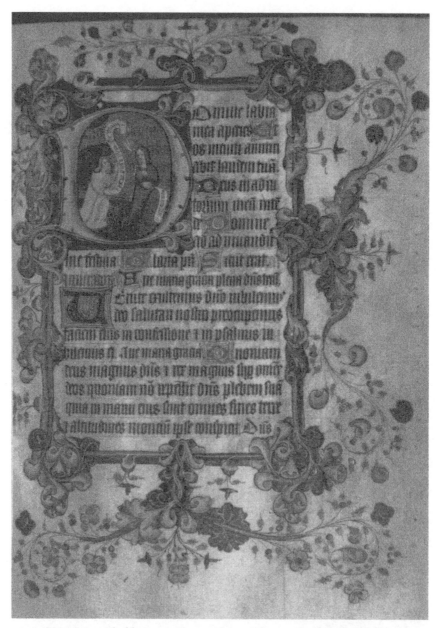

Figure 7. Blackburn Museum and Art Galleries, Hart Ms. 21018, f.7.
Annunciation.

pose used by Scheerre in the small prayer book Annunciation, fig.2). The Altenburg Hours have been dated to *circa* 1410–12, but in light of recent opinion a date 1415–20 may now have to be preferred. The Annunciation has also been attributed to Herman Scheerre – perhaps too boldly.[50] The Annunciation in Richard III's Hours certainly cannot be so attributed: the proportions of the Virgin are a little ungainly, the head and long neck are graceful but her whole person seems slightly too large for the arrangement of the picture and for the framework of the initial. Herman's figures are always slim and well proportioned, both in themselves and within their frame. She bears more resemblance to the round faced, chinless damsels to whom David displays the head of Goliath in the Bedford Hours and Psalter (f.122, fig.8), than to Scheerre's refined,

Figure 8. David bringing home the head of Goliath. Bedford Hours and Psalter, British Library, Additional Ms. 42131, f.122. This shows a female type very close to that used for Mary in the Hours of Richard III.

long faced ladies.[51] All these ladies are relatives, however – they were all produced under the supervision or influence of Herman Scheerre.

No precise parallel has been found in any of these manuscripts – nor in the later versions of the Annunciation which will be discussed next – for the unusual jewelled coronal worn by the Virgin in Richard III's Hours. It is similar to but much less rich than that worn by the Virgin on the front of the Ghent altarpiece (1432). The closest parallel is on the head of a man in an initial of the Hours of Elizabeth the Queen (f.7).[52] It is in fact more usual to find the Virgin either with her mantle covering her head or bareheaded and nimbated in these English manuscripts.[53]

This model of the Annunciation continued in use in London in the following decades. Three striking examples can be given. The first in date is the charming, small hours made for Queen Katherine de Valois around 1425–30 in London to the use of Paris. The manuscript as a whole suggests her French taste influenced the decoration as well as the use, but in general terms it falls within the 'Johannes' group of manuscripts.[54] The figures of its Annunciation (BL. Add. 65100, f.27v, fig.9) are remarkably similar to those already discussed, although their positions are rearranged: most importantly, the Virgin is uncovered and has her arms crossed.

The 'dismal' Annunciation in the Hours and Psalter of Henry Beauchamp, Duke of Warwick also uses this model.[55] The figures of both angel and Virgin lack proportion, their faces are vacuous and ugly, and the flat background is almost aggressively unrelated to the figures (Pierpont Morgan M. 893, f.12, fig.10). For all its intense colour the miniature as a whole comes a poor second to the lavish border surrounding it, although the same artist may have been responsible for both. These Hours are datable to the 1430s and must predate the Duke's death in 1446.[56]

The model continued in use into the 1470s. There is a version, poorer in quality than that in Richard III's Hours but close in its details, in a book of hours and offices of that date (BL. Harleian 2887, f.29, fig.11). The Virgin is bareheaded with a large rayed nimbus, her hands are at her breast, a scroll is unrolled on the prayer-table before her. The angel is kneeling on both knees instead of on one, and his cloak has become a plain gown. Backdrop, tiled floor and the blue cloud of God are all in place.[57]

Figure 9. Hours of Queens Katherine de Valois, made *circa* 1425–30, during her widowhood. Use of Paris, but made in London. British Library, Additional Ms. 65100, f.27v. Annunciation.

The later London artists of Richard III's own lifetime do not match Herman Scheerre and his associates for talent but they are the descendants of their workshops and their traditions, and they have inherited their models.[58]

Strictly speaking the illumination of the second historiated initial opening the Penitential Psalms (f.55) of Richard III's Hours should be treated at this point, but as it no longer survives, having been cut out, the identification of its picture must depend on the establishment of a group of books of hours closest in style and iconography to Richard's Hours. The third historiated initial, for the Vigil of the Dead, which does survive has therefore to be studied first, before any conclusions can be ventured about the missing picture.

Figure 10. Hours and Psalter of Henry, Duke of Warwick (died 1446). Pierpont Morgan Library, New York, M.893, f.12. Annunciation.

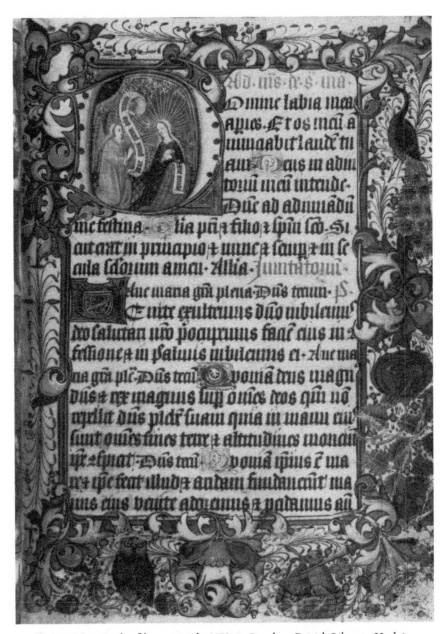

Figure 11. Book of hours, made 1470s in London. British Library, Harleian
Ms. 2887, f.29. Annunciation

Like the Annunciation, the Funeral that introduces the Office or Vigil of the Dead was taken from a standard model. Monks chanting the actual office of the dead was the most common image used to illustrate this section of a book of hours; others included the requiem mass, the burial of the corpse or the raising of Lazarus.[59] In Richard's Hours the chosen motif is an extremely simple composition (f.72, pl.2): a draped coffin dominates the scene, behind it four clerics sing with their service book open on its top, two mourners droop on a bench in the foreground (they are now very smudged) and a single tall candelabra stands to their left. The floor is green tiles and the backdrop is red painted with a gold pattern as in the Annunciation. It is all carefully depicted and the faces have some individuality and animation. There seems to be no reason to suppose that the artist of the Annunciation did not also paint the Funeral.

The earliest and simplest version of this scene had been produced *circa* 1400 on the continent, by followers of the Rouen Master in Bruges, to illustrate books of hours for the English market. For example, Bodleian manuscript Lat. liturg. f.2 (f.79v, fig. 12) shows an enormously tall, grey draped coffin standing on a beige and black tiled floor with three lumpish clerics behind it in mauve, red and blue.[60]

Brighter and better examples were produced in England,[61] such as Richard III's Hours, and such as a Bodleian book of hours, Rawlinson liturg. d.1, which has an almost identical funeral to Richard III's Hours in both details and colours (f.59, fig.13). The mourners are missing and two of the clerics are differently dressed but the characterisation of the latter is remarkably similar in both manuscripts.[62] The figures of the Rawlinson manuscript are slightly too large for the initial: the grouping is the same but the Richard III Hours is more refined and successful in its facial details and in the placing of the figures within the initial. Another trio of clerics behind a coffin illustrates Hart 21018 (f.49, fig.14).

This group of singing clerics was too useful a device not to be used in other contexts: very similar groups appear behind lecterns to illustrate two psalters (BL. Royal 2 B viii, f.88v and Gonville and Caius College, Cambridge, 148/198, f.206), both of which are closely related in their style of decoration to the Hours of Richard III and produced by the same circles of artists.[63]

Figure 12. Book of hours, made *circa* 1400 by followers of the Rouen Master in Bruges, for the English market. Bodleian Library, Ms. Lat. liturg. f.2, f.79v. Funeral.

An extremely simple funeral scene can also be found in the Bedford Hours and Psalter (f.46, fig. 15). Though it is a luxury manuscript, its iconography is always plain and to the point. The Funeral has been attributed to Herman Scheerre himself.[64] Only a few additional details differentiate it from Richard's Hours: the seated mourners or poor men are on stools, not a single bench, and they face to the right holding cierges rather than show their backs to the reader; other mourners, probably family, stand at the end of the coffin.

The grander manuscripts already mentioned in the context of the Annunciation, with the very important exception of the Bedford manuscript, indulge in the more elaborate scene of the requiem mass: the Clarence Hours (f.75, fig. 16), the Hours of Elizabeth the Queen (f.55) and the Warwick Hours and Psalter (f.60, fig. 17). Many of the same

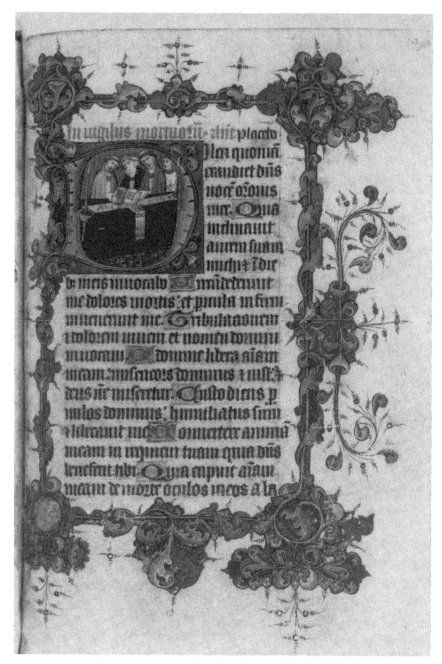

Figure 13. Book of hours, Bodleian Library, Ms. Rawlinson liturg. d.1, f.59. The Funeral most closely resembling that in the Hours of Richard III.

Figure 14. Blackburn Museum and Art Galleries, Hart Ms. 21018, f.49. Funeral.

elements are present such as the centrally placed coffin, the mourners with or without their bench, candles, tiled floor; almsmen or congregation are added along with the coped priest before the altar for the mass.[65]

The small and less pretentious Hours of Katherine de Valois has a funeral service with some additional details (f.193v, fig. 18) and an architectural background. Finally, the Harley Hours of the 1470s has a version close to that of Richard III's Hours (Harleian 2887, f.80, fig.19): green tiles, draped coffin, three clerics with a book and two mourners behind, a pink backdrop patterned with gold.[66]

The iconography of both the Annunciation and the Funeral used in the Richard III Hours has been found to be close to that used in several other London manuscripts. Unfortunately the other historiated initial, introducing the Penitential Psalms, is now lost, but the information accumulated on the other images enables it to be described precisely.

The usual image to introduce the Penitential Psalms in England and the Low Countries from the thirteenth to the fifteenth centuries was Christ in Judgement; in France an image from the life of David became more popular in the fifteenth century. In England Christ in Judgement

Figure 15.   Bedford Hours and Psalter. British Library, Additional Ms. 42131, f.46.
Funeral

meant Christ at the Second Coming: between two swords, wrapped in
his mantle or in a loincloth alone, he displayed his wounds seated on a
rainbow above the earth's surface from which the dead are beginning
to rise up; he was flanked by the Virgin and the Baptist, as intercessors,
and angels with trumpets.[67] This is the subject illustrating the Penitential
Psalms in all the manuscripts so far searched for Annunciations and
Funerals, with the one exception of the Hours of Katherine de Valois
which unsurprisingly adopts the preferred French image of David at
prayer (f.133v). The Bedford Hours and Psalter, whose simple iconography has been found to be so close in spirit to that of Richard III's Hours,
has Christ in his mantle, displaying his wounds, seated on a rainbow

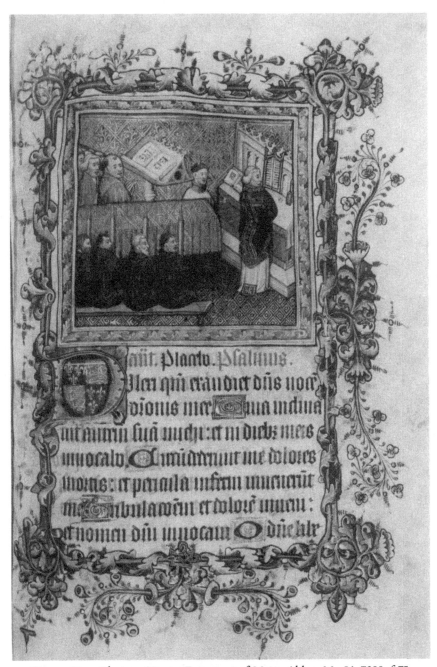

Figure 16. Clarence Hours, Executors of Major Abbey Ms. JA.7398, f.75. Requiem mass.

Figure 17. Hours and Psalter of Henry, Duke of Warwick. Pierpont Morgan Library, New York, M.893, f.60. Requiem mass.

Figure 18. Hours of Queen Katherine de Valois. British Library, Additional Ms. 65100, f.193v. Requiem mass.

which ends abruptly in two dish-like clouds; souls emerge from their tombs below him; there is a red, gold patterned backdrop (f.37). The Christ in Judgement which is undoubtedly closest to the lost initial of Richard III's Hours is that in the Bodleian manuscript, Rawlinson liturg. d.1 (f.40, fig.20) whose simple representation shows only Christ on the rainbow, the two swords, grassy earth beneath, and nothing else but a patterned background. The same picture in Hart 21018 (f.35v, fig.21) is close: the grass on the earth's surface is depicted in the same way but the background is a louring grey and Christ is surrounded by rays.

In the Nevill Hours the image is equally simple (f.62) with no additional figures, but the Duchess of Clarence Hours (f.57, fig.22) has a more complicated iconography close to that in the Hours of Elizabeth the Queen (f.27). The latter has an elaborate, even idiosyncratic,

Figure 19. Book of hours, 1470s. British Library, Harleian Ms. 2887, f.80. Funeral.

image in keeping with the rest of its decoration: Christ in a loincloth looking as though he is about to slide down his rainbow, attended by two angels with trumpets, two with emblems of the Passion, as well as the Virgin in crown and ermine mantle and St. John the Baptist, while souls emerge from their tombs below. The Warwick Hours and Psalter (f.44v, fig.23) also adopts this elaborate picture, and it is extended into the corner motifs of the border where more angels and souls are depicted.

Harley 2887, of the 1470s, the final example in this survey, chooses, as it has before for the Annunciation and Funeral, the simplest design: Christ alone on the rainbow against a pink background (f.68, fig.24).[68]

The study of the iconography of the two surviving historiated initials of Richard III's Hours has shown that their artist used models that were extremely popular throughout the fifteenth century. He chose from among the simpler versions and these are closely related to others produced in London in the first three decades of the century. Most

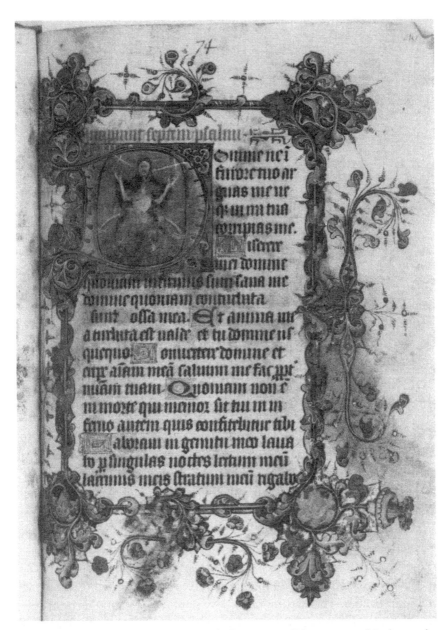

Figure 20. The missing miniature at the beginning of the Penitential Psalms in the Hours of Richard III probably looked very like this example of Christ in Judgement from the book of hours, Bodleian Library, Ms. Rawlinson liturg. d.1, f.40. The complete border of trumpet flowers and foliage also gives some idea of what has been lost from the Annunciation border of Richard III's Hours.

Figure 21.   Blackburn Museum and Art Galleries, Hart Ms. 21018, f.35v. Christ in Judgement.

important of all, close parallels can be found in a manuscript that can be dated to *circa* 1420, the Bedford Hours and Psalter.

The Portrait Heads

The native English portrait tradition of the first decade of the fifteenth century observed in the Sherborne Missal and Lovel Lectionary had several brilliant exponents. Later it was to degenerate via the work of such as William Abell, and only the remnant of good teaching lightened the heavy hands of talentless pupils.[69] The interest in the human face among early fifteenth century artists in England is relevant to the decoration of the Annunciation page of Richard III's Hours: two finely done 'portraits' of Saints Peter and Paul and three round-faced angels, all in one colour, are set in the border. The features of the two saints are instantly recognisable, St. Peter with his square beard, St. Paul with his long beard, etc. The sensitive rendering of the saints in Richard III's Hours (in monochrome) is very close to that of the same saints in the Bedford Hours and Psalter (in natural colours).[70] Their types are, however, in such common use that it is not possible to make a definite conclusion of association on that fact alone.[71]

Figure 22.   Clarence Hours, Executors of Major Abbey Ms. JA.7398, f.57. Christ in Judgement.

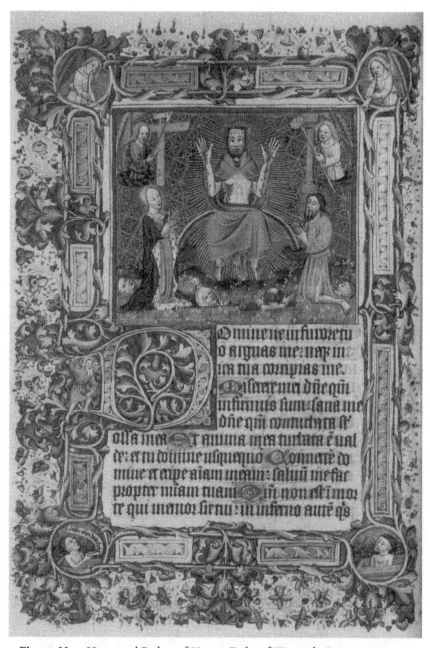

Figure 23. Hours and Psalter of Henry, Duke of Warwick. Pierpont Morgan
Library, New York, M.893, f.44v. Christ in Judgement.

Figure 24.   Book of hours, 1470s. British Library, Harleian Ms. 2887, f.68. Christ
in Judgement.

Far more important is the use of monochrome and of the portrait
or human face as decorative devices, employed together to such good
effect in the Richard III Hours. A striking parallel can be immediately instanced from the Hours of the Duchess of Clarence, where the
Penitential Psalms has a border with corner bosses containing two profile
and two full-face angels in pink and blue monochrome (f.57, fig.22),[72]
the middle one on the right of Richard's Hours being very close to the
angel on the bottom right of the Clarence Hours. Further examples of
the use of monochrome faces can be found in several of the other manuscripts already cited as close to Richard's Hours in their iconography.
The Bedford Hours and Psalter uses monochrome faces in its borders
(e.g. ff.7, 73); and so does the Hours of Elizabeth the Queen (f.98v),
some of the latter being formed out of foliage (f.7) like strange green
men. The Hours and Psalter owned by the Duke of Warwick and made
in the 1430s similarly makes a striking use of monochrome faces set into
its borders (e.g. ff.12, 44v).

Many of these examples, however, lack the quality of the Peter and
Paul of Richard III's Hours. To find this, comparison must be made with
the portraits in natural colours in the Bedford Hours and Psalter, the
Rawlinson Hours (fig.25) and the Hours of Elizabeth the Queen.[73] Of
these the most relevant for the study of Richard's Hours are the elaborate and remarkable set of over 280 portrait-head initials in the Bedford

Figure 25. Portrait initials (the Virgin and St. John the Evangelist) illustrating the last two stanzas of the prayer *Omnibus consideratis* (see ff.132-134 of the description of the contents of the Hours of Richard III). These full colour portraits are comparable in quality to the monochrome portraits of Saints Peter and Paul in Richard III's Hours. Bodleian Library, Ms. Rawlinson liturg. d.1., f.110v.

manuscript, some the work of Herman Scheerre,[74] and the less elaborate series of portraits in Rawlinson liturg. d.1,[75] obviously by an artist very much aware of the Scheerre style. Among the second series the portrait of the Virgin is close in type to the Virgin of the Annunciation in Richard III's Hours: a child with a high forehead and her hair tucked behind her ears; the Rawlinson St. John the Evangelist is the same type as the angel of Richard's Hours (fig.25).

The portraits in its Annunciation border again place Richard III's Hours within a small group of manuscripts surrounding the great Bedford Hours and Psalter of which Herman Scheerre was the Master, *circa* 1420, and on which artists of the Johannes group collaborated. Associates of Scheerre worked on the Rawlinson Hours, collaborating once more with artists of the Johannes group who contributed the Passion scenes both in this manuscript and in the Clarence Hours. Some of these artists went on to work on the Hours of Elizabeth the Queen.[76] The tangled web of influences and collaboration in early fifteenth century London illumination cannot be over-emphasised.

Cleverly executed faces, in natural colours or in monochrome, were clearly a hallmark of manuscripts produced in London by both the Scheerre and Johannes groups of artists.

Borders, Initials and Colour

The Annunciation page border is incomparably the finest in the Hours of Richard III. It seems reasonable to suppose that much of it is by the artist responsible for the historiation, in particular the three-dimensional effects and faces. The wide border is composed of monochrome bands sculpted like masonry boxes containing three different patterns: a plain scroll wrapped round a rod; acanthus leaves wrapped round a rod; a long acanthus leaf forming a continuous undulating scroll. The initial itself on this page is also composed of acanthus scrolled round rods. Set in the centre of three of the borders, like jewels, are three faces of angels, each in one colour; at the top a flower and an acanthus leaf and at the bottom fine monochrome portraits of Saints Peter and Paul form the three-dimensional centres of the corner clusters. The surrounding foliage of these clusters is composed mostly of scrolled acanthus with some trefoil leaves, all highlighted with delicate white shading and a fine white crust of beading along the spines and veins of the leaf and flower shapes. The sprays of foliage that have not been cropped by the binder have terminals of bell-flowers, simple lobe-shaped leaves as well as five-petalled flowers, some with sepals. Small sprays end in gold dots and squiggles smudged over with green.

The 'portraits' have been discussed above. Otherwise the most notable feature of the border is the use of three-dimensional acanthus. It is not used to such effect in the rest of the book although similar enclosed bands of acanthus occur in some demi-vinets (ff.25, 124). The device of three-dimensional acanthus is a common feature of the manuscripts already compared with the Hours of Richard III, in the decoration of initials, single leaves in the centre of clusters or scrolled borders.[77] Three-dimensional flowers are also employed as centres. The use, in two of the manuscripts consulted, of precisely the same flower which appears as the centre of the top left cluster of the Annunciation page of Richard III's Hours – Rawlinson liturg. d.1, f.40 (fig.20) and Gonville and Caius 148/198, f.1 – again shows how close these manuscripts are in their manufacture and date.[78] The three-dimensional effect in mono-chrome challenged the virtuosity of the artist and seems to have become a trademark of skill for London artists of this date.

The rest of the illumination of the Hours of Richard III is unlikely all to have been painted by the artist of the Annunciation page and the two historiated initials, although it is possible he did some of the scrolled acanthus (e.g. f.25). It was probably left to assistants who specialised in border decoration, and who were probably responsible for the similar decoration of the Altenburg Hours. The handling is heavier but the work is finished and agreeable. The two full vinets of the Vigil of the Dead and the Penitential Psalms each have two-bar borders, one in colour and one in gold, from which erupt clusters of formal foliage and flowers at each corner, at the centre of the three free sides and in the terminals of the initial on the fourth side. The leaf motifs are repetitive and trumpet flowers with dotted fruit centres occur. Sprays emerge from the clusters with a variety of terminals: four- or five-petalled flowers with or without sepals, small trumpet flowers, trefoil, kidney or lobe-shaped leaves. Smaller pen sprays ter-minate in gold dots with squiggles smudged with green paint. All these terminals may be found in the manuscripts already searched for comparable historiation.[79]

The fourteen demi-vinets accompanying the seven-, eight- and nine-line initials usually have band borders extending down the left-hand margin in a variety of forms and patterns. Some adopt the three-dimensional scrolled acanthus of the Annunciation page (ff.25, 124), others (e.g. ff.37v, 41, 43, 90v, 101) have undulating patterns of trefoil-leaves, lobe-shaped leaves or three-petalled flowers, curling back on themselves and creating a figure of eight in a design comparable to those of the borders of the Annunciation page of the Altenburg Hours and those used frequently in the Nevill Hours to frame the miniatures. Exactly the same pattern with trefoil-leaves is used on folio 50v of the Nevill Hours and on folio 101 of the Hours of Richard III. Done with incomparably more skill and discipline is the variant used on folio 7 of the Bedford Hours and Psalter. A third type of demi-vinet border in Richard III's Hours is composed of unconfined acanthus leaves twisted over themselves in such a riot of blue and pinky orange that the bar about which they are supposed to twine is forgotten, as in the example on folio 152. Acanthus leaves looped over themselves like the tongues of garters or belts can be found in several of the related manuscripts.[80] From these demi-vinets erupt sprays similar to those described above for the vinets. Additional terminals include trumpet-shaped flowers, sometimes collared, sometimes with serrated petals, or with yellow dotted fruit centres.[81]

These strawberry-like fruits, often dotted with yellow and protruding from funnel flowers and leaves, have been noticed as a motif used with increasing frequency in fifteenth century English illumination.[82] They are conspicuous in Richard III's Hours and the Altenburg Hours, there are some in the Bedford manuscript, in the Clarence Hours and Rawlinson liturg. d.1,[83] some splendid ones in the Gonville and Caius Psalter, and they are in the later Hours of Elizabeth the Queen as well as the Warwick Hours and the Psalter.[84] They become endlessly repetitive and boring in such manuscripts as Lambeth 459 in the 1470s–90s.[85]

All the large and small initials in the Hours apart from the historiated ones are decorated, according to their size, with a simple interlaced pattern of clusters of four, three or two lobe-shaped leaves twisted to fill the spaces created by their stems. The leaves are regularly patterned and high-lighted with white. Sometimes the leaves are replaced by trumpet or open flowers with spotted fruit centres, and occasionally a minor variation is introduced, such as an unsuccessful attempt at three-dimensional leaves in a three-line initial (ff.163, 163v) or unusual leafy trumpet sprays coming off another three-line initial (f.279v). The initials themselves are mostly one colour, shaded with white in a button-hole pattern and beaded with white dots; others are patterned with simple scrolls wrapped round a rod. Their stiff, jutting sprays and terminals are as those described for the vinets and demi-vinets. If two or more four-line initials occur on one page, the artist allows their individual leaf clusters to run into each other or links them by a bar running up the margin. Except for its lack of variety of borders, the Altenburg manuscript bears the closest resemblance to the Hours of Richard III in its subsidiary illumination: its four-, three-, two- and one-line initials are all comparable, as are its line fillers.[86]

The development of border decoration in the last twenty years of the fourteenth century and early fifteenth century in England is not easy to trace; the standard designs and patterns were used very widely and in endless variations and combinations. The new devices introduced have been noticed and studied: new feathery sprays of foliage, bell-shaped flowers, spoon-shaped leaves, borders composed of rigid bars or decorated bands with clusters and bosses at the corners and other points, an increasing use of green dots of paint on terminals, and the attenuation of marginal branches into slender hair-like sprays. Most conspicuous of all developments at this time were the brilliantly coloured scrolls of acanthus in borders and initials, in all the variants noted above – these became characteristic of all English work up to *circa* 1450.[87]

The luxuriant borders of the associated manuscripts of the Hours of Elizabeth the Queen and the Warwick Hours and Psalter need to be briefly mentioned. The border of the latter's Annunciation (f.12, fig.10) is similar in type to that surrounding the Last Supper of the first manuscript (f.7).[88] Both of the borders are against a solid backing of gold, the Warwick manuscript's gold precisely finished off to a line on either side, the other allowing its gold to follow the more erratic line of the sprays and foliage. The Warwick manuscript then goes one better and has a subsidiary border extending out to the furthest point of the corner decorations and consisting of a riot of foliage, flowers and birds on a smaller scale than its main border (see figs. 10, 23). The designers of this have a different concept of a border from that held by the designers of the Bedford Hours and Psalter, the Clarence Hours, Rawlinson liturg. d.1

or the Hours of Richard III: they want to fill up the margin and are no longer content with an uneven decoration of sprays.[89] This regularisation of outline becomes a feature of later fifteenth century English borders.[90]

The colour scheme of the Hours of Richard III is pink and blue with an extensive use of orange, a little green, with gold. A striking and unusual use of green in this manuscript is the line defining the inner border of the Annunciation page and completely encircling the text.[91] The other manuscripts used so far to place the book in its context use the same colours in different balances: the Bedford Hours and Psalter uses pink and blue, some orange, and a lot of olive green (the pink is often brown toned[92] and the green can be an 'emerald') with a wide range of vivid colours in its historiation, including yellow; the Clarence Hours, the Nevill Hours, the Gonville and Caius Psalter and Rawlinson liturg. d.1 all use pink and blue predominantly, with green and orange, and brightly coloured historiation, the Clarence Hours making a great use of olive green upon occasion (e.g. f.44);[93] the Altenburg manuscript uses pink and blue with some orange and green, its use of orange being less marked than in the Richard III Hours. Yellow and green are conspicuous in the Hours of Elizabeth the Queen, while the Warwick Hours veers to concentrate on red, pink, blue and green. The technical study of the use and availability of pigments and colours is in its infancy, but comments on colours in use in England in the early fifteenth century argue that Scheerre's workshop, for example, went in for bright colours and a striking use of orange. Such usage has been attributed (probably fairly) to the foreign influences at work on and through Scheerre and on English illumination in general at this date, but such warmth and richness of colours were certainly not without native precedents.[94]

Conclusion

The Annunciation page is by the hand of the artist who must be called the Master of the Hours of Richard III. It shows us the artist's character as clearly as is possible. Its main elements – the colour scheme of blue and pink brilliantly warmed by the orange so frequently found in Scheerre manuscripts, the portrait heads, the saints set in clusters of leaves, the angels set like intaglio gems[95] in circles of gold on the bands of three-dimensional, entwined acanthus leaves, and the contrasting, darker toned, bright blue and pink historiated initial – are all convincing evidence that this page is by an accomplished painter. Its restraint in comparison with the flamboyance of the later 'Johannes' type manuscripts, and its accomplished design, are close in spirit to the Bedford Hours and Psalter overseen by Herman Scheerre about 1420. Many of its component elements and iconography can be found in this and other manuscripts of the same group. The monochrome faces show traits visible earlier in the Big Bible, in the more closely contemporary Bedford manuscript, and more prominent and idiosyncratic in the later Hours of Elizabeth the Queen, the *tour de force* of the Johannes group.

Other manuscripts show the complicated interplay of work and influences of the two identifiable painters and their associates: the Gonville and Caius Psalter, the Hours of the Duchess of Clarence, and the Rawlinson Hours which has no ducal or royal title. These were certainly worked on by artists of both groups and they, in particular, clarify and suggest the chronology of the manuscripts. They fit neatly into the few years that separate the Bedford Hours and Psalter and the Hours of Richard III (and its closest companion, the Altenburg Hours) from the Hours of Elizabeth the Queen.

M. R. James first noticed the similarity of the Hours of Richard III to the British Museum's newly acquired Bedford Hours and Psalter in 1932.[96] His eye was unerring. It can be safely concluded that a painter who was primarily under the influence of Herman Scheerre and collaborated with him on the Bedford Hours and Psalter, *circa* 1420, and who also collaborated on the Sarum Hours now called Rawlinson liturg. d.1 with artists of the Johannes group, was the Master of the Hours of Richard III.[97]

FOUR

Ownership

Although the Hours of Richard III was written and illuminated *circa* 1420, he is the first known owner. There is no doubt that he owned it as king: his date of birth was added to the Calendar as *Ricardus Rex* and the long prayer – 'the prayer of Richard III' – inserted for his use refers to him as king. There is no sign that he owned the manuscript as duke. The collect of St. Ninian, the saint of the Western March, could have been added while he was duke or king as regards subject and text but its hand and illumination is of a piece with 'his' prayer. The other additional devotion at the very end of the book is also in this style and was probably added at the same time, but this cannot be proved beyond doubt.

No evidence exists to suggest where Richard got the book and there is nothing to connect it with anyone before Richard or with Richard as duke.[98]

The inclusion of the collects of the male saints Christopher and George in a prominent position, plus the fact that wherever the supplicant can insert his own name in a prayer the text has the masculine Latin forms, makes it virtually certain that the first owner was a man. The liturgical contents of the original book suggest that it was made for a cleric or someone with a clerical training.[99] One of the personal devotions at the end of the book may throw some light on his identity: a prayer 'on the blessed Joseph' (not the husband of Mary but the Old Testament patriarch) was included for him. Prayers with Old Testament

49

'saints' as their subject are very rare[100] and this inclusion may mean that the manuscript was made for someone called Joseph. It is, however, more likely that it was the very successful career of the son of Jacob which was interesting, rather than his name.

Richard must have put on one side the Hours he used as duke and acquired a new one with no signs of ownership or from which all fly-leaves with such signs could be easily removed – a clean manuscript may have been particularly appropriate as a gift or acquisition for the King. New leaves were then added, the book rebound fittingly and the additional prayers and collect commissioned by the King; he added his birthday and place of birth himself.[101] If this is what happened and if the new prayers had any particular significance and relationship to his personal needs, the Hours could have been acquired as late as 1484 or 1485.

There is not much doubt that the Hours must have been part of the booty of Richard III's tent after his death at Bosworth. It is a tradition that this went to the Stanleys and that Richard's tent hangings were still to be seen at Knowsley, the main family's seat, as late as the seventeenth century.[102] The next owner to inscribe the book was Margaret Beaufort, Countess of Richmond, mother of Henry VII and wife of Thomas Stanley, Lord Stanley and Earl of Derby. It has been suggested that it was she who expunged Richard III's name from 'his' prayer in a spirit of hatred.[103] This is not tenable: a revengeful person would scarcely have missed the entry for his birth in the Calendar – which includes his title – and it is more likely that the erasures were made by a pious later user of the prayer who did not want the name *Ricardum* to interfere with his or her devotions. This person was not sufficiently interested in Richard III to erase *regem* as well, as Margaret Beaufort would probably have done.[104]

Margaret gave the book away to an unknown person whom she asked to pray for her 'in the honour of God and Sainte Edmonde'.[105] The idea that the recipient was Elisabeth, Lady Scrope and Upsall, daughter of John Nevill, Marquis Montagu, who recorded in her will of 1514 a gift of a primer and psalter from Margaret, is attractive, but the lack of a psalter and of any hard evidence argue against it.[106]

Later signs of ownership are notes in the Calendar that Thomas Harward 'happened' to die 28 March 1542 and that AF died 26 August 1548. A 'Henry Lynghe gent.' of an unnamed city is referred to in the first person,[107] and someone made notes referring to an Ysabel Bradfort and seven years, the usual term of apprenticeship.[108] None of these people has been identified.

The book was in the library of the see of Canterbury early in the seventeenth century, most probably part of the gift of his large personal library to the see from Archbishop Bancroft (died 1610), which created the Lambeth Palace library, but possibly part of the smaller number of manuscripts collected and bequeathed by his successor, George Abbot (died 1633). It was among the manuscripts transferred to Cambridge University Library 1647–1664, and there catalogued and given the press mark, G θ 23, in the top left hand corner of the inside front cover. Later in the seventeenth century at Lambeth, it received the additional shelf mark 8vo 40 (according to its size) in the same place. The book escaped the rebinding programme of Archbishop Sancroft (deprived 1690).[109] In view of the long period it has been at Lambeth Palace, it cannot be assumed that all the erasures in the text and the mutilation of folio 55 occurred in the sixteenth century.

FIVE

Analysis of Contents

In this description of the contents of the Hours of Richard III the more usual items of a book of hours are not discussed in great detail and not all texts or beginnings of texts are given – these can be found in the main reference books. The more unusual additional devotions, however, some of which are rare or very rare, are treated individually. Their *incipit* (first line) is given, together with some information about their purpose and contents; their origins where possible have been traced and other copies, printed editions and comparable material referred to. Completeness has been attempted but not necessarily achieved.

In the Latin quotations the spelling and capitalisation have been left as they are in the manuscript. The original punctuation has been indicated by either commas or full stops. Abbreviations have been silently extended. Translation is given in round brackets, editorial additions and comments on the Latin text and the translation are in square brackets. An attempt has been made to make the translation both accurate and comprehensible – criticism from Latin scholars and from those who expect Cranmer's translation is thus inevitable. The problem of where and when to use capitals for divine names and biblical formulas has not been satisfactorily solved, but it is hoped this will not distract the reader.

Psalm numbers are given according to the Vulgate. When the word 'rubric' is used, an introductory heading or title written in red ink is meant.

f.1. Collect of St. Ninian.

Written in a later hand than the main text, this prayer is likely to have been included at Richard III's request. The original book had a gathering of two ruled leaves (four pages) at the beginning. These remained blank until the collect of Ninian was added on the third page. It is a short prayer asking for the saint's intercession:

> O God who has converted the peoples of the Britons and the Picts by the teaching of St. Ninian your confessor to knowledge of your faith, grant of your grace that by the intercession of him by whose learning we are steeped in the light of your truth, we may gain the joys of heavenly life. Through Christ our lord. Amen.

St. Ninian, according to the anonymous chronicle possibly owned and certainly consulted by Richard, was a Briton educated in Rome who returned to his native country to convert the Southern Picts to Christianity. He was buried at 'White House' (Whithorn) in Galloway, named after a church he had built there of white stone, a custom not usual among the Britons.[110] Both this shrine and Ripon became centres of his cult; dedications to him were mainly in the north of England and Scotland. He was the patron saint of the Western March towards Scotland, of which Richard was warden as Duke of Gloucester. Richard seems to have deliberately taken up and extended his cult for he included his worship at each of his religious foundations at York, Middleham and Barnard Castle, and also at Queens' College, Cambridge, where he endowed four priests.[111] In the statutes of his college at Middleham Richard instructed the collect to be said daily after matins and St. Ninian's day (16 September) was to be a principal feast, together with St. George's, St. Cuthbert's and St. Anthony's. The stall dedicated to him was to be the fourth of six in the church, after those of the Virgin, St. George and St. Katherine.

In general the inclusion of a collect or memorial to St. Ninian suggests a Scots owner of a book of hours, but there is clearly sufficient evidence in this case that Richard III had a special devotion to this saint.

ff.2–2v. Memorials to St. Christopher and St. George.

These are short prayers for the relevant saint's intercession, preceded by antiphon, versicle and response.[112] The placing of these saints' memorials

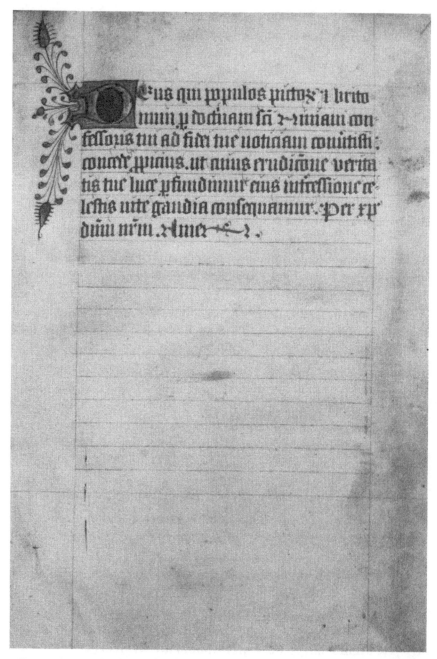

Figure 26. Richard III's Hours, Lambeth Ms. 474, f.1. The collect of St. Ninian added for the King.

Figure 27. St. Ninian shown with a supplicant and angel. The saint depicted as a bishop, with fetters and a Bibe, symbols of his releasing prisoners and his evangelism. Edinburgh University Library Ms. 42, f.72v.

in this prominent position probably reflects the preferences of the first owner, just as the placing of the collect of St. Ninian is an example of Richard III's. The memorial of St. Christopher is the longer; it is a request for protection from 'sudden death, illness, hunger, fear and poverty'. Both saints may be supposed to have been chosen by a man.

ff.3–8v. Calendar.

The Calendar, usually the first item in a book of hours, occupies the remainder of the second gathering of eight leaves. Its use and purpose can best be explained with the help of the page illustrated, the month of October.

The days of the month are indicated by the small Arabic numerals in brown ink in the last column. They were evidently added later, after the insertion of the birth of Richard III on 2 October, for they were all written one line too low.[113] Originally this numbering would have been unnecessary as early owners could have used the red Roman numerals in the third column and the abbreviations N (for Nones), Id (for Ides) and Kl' for (Kalends) in the fourth, which give the date according to Roman practice.[114]

The first column, an apparently random series of Roman numerals, gives the so-called Golden Number of the year and indicates the day of the new moon, while the second has the Dominical or Sunday letter. Both were essential to calculate the date of Easter, the first Sunday following the first full moon on or after 21 March.[115]

The Latin rhymes at the top of the page differ for each month and tell the reader which are the two evil or 'Egyptian' days (*dies Egyptiaci*). Two numbers are worked into each cryptic verse: the first indicates one ill-omened day counting from the beginning of the month, the second gives the other, counting backward from the end. Each day is marked in the Calendar by a capital D in red. The rhyme of October reads: 'The third and the tenth are like unfriendly death'. The Latin of these lines is corrupt, probably because they are very old – similar lines pointing to the same days have been found in fourth-century manuscripts. Their origin is not clear; they may go back to Chaldean astrologers. Christian writers suggested that they were the anniversaries of the plagues of Egypt, or that they were discovered by the Egyptians, who were famous as astrologers. Such rhymes occur in many books of hours and it is impossible to know how much attention owners paid to them. It was considered inadvisable to do certain things on these days, for example being bled, building a house, buying or selling, or cutting one's hair, beard and nails.[116]

The last line at the foot of the page indicates the relative length of day and night in the various months. In October 'the night has fourteen hours, the day ten'. For the clergy the intervals between the offices were longer in summer, and the times at which they were said, as well as the hours of eating and sleeping, varied with the season.

The list of saints' days and feast days is the main part of the Calendar. Most are written in black or red ink, and a few in blue, according to their importance. Blue is used here for the great festivals connected with Christ and the Virgin (e.g. Epiphany, Annunciation), the Apostles and the Evangelists, and, for instance, All Saints and the Invention of the Cross; red is used for the other important feasts to be celebrated by everyone, not only the clergy (red letter days). To be noted is the presence in red of St. Erconwald or Erkenwald, bishop of London; 30 April (principal feast) and 14 November (translation).[117] The Calendar is not graded in the sense of giving more specific liturgical instructions.

Later hands have made some additions and changes. On 5 January the deposition of St. Edward, king and confessor (the commemoration of his burial), was completely erased.[118] In every instance the abbreviation for 'pope' (*ppe*) was deleted – see for example 14 (here 13) October (fig.28) which date should have *Sancti Kalixti pape et martiris* ([the feast] of St. Calixtus pope and martyr). These erasures, like similar ones in the rest of the manuscript, were made after Henry VIII's break with Rome.

On 28 March a neat hand has written: *Isto die obiit Thomas Harward contingenter Anno domini 1542* (on this day died T.H. through an accident [?], unexpectedly [?]). On 25 August is written: *1548 Isto die obiit AF.* The persons referred to are unknown. The hands of these notes are similar to each other and to the one that added the Arabic numerals in the last column of each month.

At an unknown date the feast of St. Michael was inserted at 29 September, a fact one is tempted to associate with the apparently unique inclusion of St. Michael in the text of the prayer added for Richard III on folio 182 of this manuscript,[119] though the original omission of this popular feast is perhaps more remarkable than its later insertion.

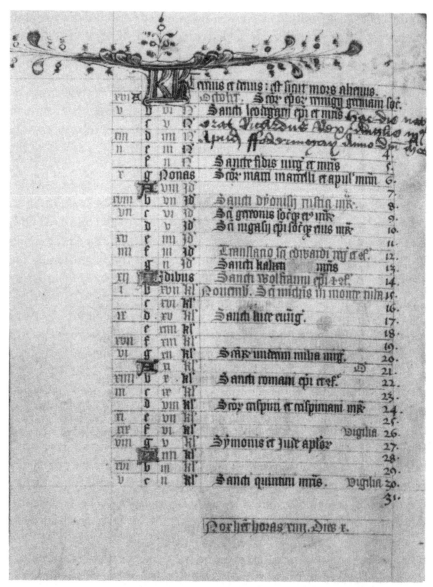

Figure 28. Richard III's Hours, Lambeth Ms. 474, f.7v. The Calendar page for October showing the entry for the King's birthday, made probably by himself, which now partly disappears into the spine.

By far the most interesting note is the one at 2 October (f.7v): *hac die natus erat Ricardus Rex Anglie tertius Apud Foderingay Anno domini mlccccliio* (on this day was born Richard III King of England AD 1452), written in a large, sprawling script that, unlike the other additions, makes no attempt to imitate the neatness of the original scribe, spills into the right margin and fills the lines reserved for the next two days as well. It must have been added after 6 July 1483 and probably by the King himself.[120] The note was left untouched by later owners.

The Calendar contains no other special features.

In many books of hours the Calendar is followed by the gospel fragments and intercessory prayers to St. Mary and St. John (*Obsecro te* and *O intemerata*). The gospel fragments do not occur in this manuscript and the prayers are on folios 156v–159, below.

ff.9–14. Instructions for the seasonal variations of the Hours of the Virgin.

On folios 9–12 detailed instructions are given on which texts of the hours are to be changed during Advent, followed on folios 12v–14 by similar instructions for the period from Christmas to Candlemas (2 February). During the rest of the year the hours were recited as they are given in the main text. Although in some liturgical books the three variant forms of the hours are given in full, it is usual to have only the text needed for the period between Candlemas (or Purification) and Advent. It must have taken some training to interpret and use these abbreviated and highly condensed instructions correctly and easily, and their presence suggests that the first owner of the book was a cleric or someone with a clerical background.

f.14v. *ihesus. [I]hesu christe fili dei qui natus es* ... (Jesus Christ, son of God, you who are born ...) fills only the first eight lines of the page leaving the remainder blank. The illuminator forgot to fill in the three-line capital I of this, the last text of this section and of the third quire.

ff. 15–54. Hours of the Virgin

Matins, the first of the hours, prefaced by *Hic incipiunt matutine de sancta maria* (Here begin ...) and beginning *Domine labia mea aperies Et os meum annunciabit laudem tuam* (O Lord open my lips and my mouth shall announce your praise, Ps.50,17) is on folios 15–25, followed by Lauds on folios 25–31.[121] Lauds and the other hours except Compline begin with the words *Deus in adiutorium meum intende Domine ad adiuvandum me festina* (O God come to my aid. O Lord make haste to help me, Ps.69,2). As is usual in books of hours of Sarum use, Lauds has at its end a series of memorials to various saints and others. In Richard III's manuscript these are to the Holy Spirit, the Trinity, the Cross, All Angels, John the Baptist, Peter, Andrew, Thomas of Canterbury (untouched), Stephen, Laurence, Nicholas, Mary Magdalen, Margaret, Sitha, the Relics of the Saints, All Saints, Peace; this series contains only one unusual item.[122] Compline, on folios 49–54, can be recognised by its opening words *Converte nos deus salutaris noster Et averte iram tuam a nobis* (Convert us, o God, our saviour, and turn your anger away from us, Ps. 84,5).

The very brief Hours of the Cross (or Passion) *and* the Hours of the Compassion of the Virgin have been added together at the end of the main devotion of each hour (starting with Lauds), in each instance written as one composite text headed by the rubric *De passione*. The Hours of the Cross have the seven quatrains of the famous poem *Patris sapientia* as their variable text. It begins *Patris sapientia, veritas divina, Deus homo captus est hora matutina* (The wisdom of the father, the divine truth, God-and-man was taken in the morning hour) and each of its quatrains describes what happened to Christ at each of the seven hours on the day of his death.[123] This variable text is followed by the same prayer in every instance, *Domine ihesu christe fili dei vivi pone passionem ...* (Lord Jesus Christ, son of the living God, put your passion ...).[124] The Hours of the Compassion also consist of a variable text and an invariable prayer. The former is a poem of seven quatrains beginning *Matris cor virgineum trena totum trivit, quando suum filium nocte captum scivit* (The virgin heart of the mother was devastated by grief when she knew that her son had been captured in the night).[125] Each quatrain is followed by the prayer *Domine sancte ihesu christe dulcis fili virginis qui pro nobis mortem crucis tollerasti ...* (Holy Lord Jesus Christ, son of the sweet virgin, who for us suffered death on the cross ...).

The hours end with a series of prayers to St. Mary (ff.52–54).[126]

ff.54v–71v. Penitential and Gradual Psalms and Litany.

The Penitential Psalms (*psalmi penitentiales*)[127] are a group of seven, expressing the grief of the faithful for their sins. They are recited in order to engender a spirit of penitence and to obtain God's pardon. These psalms were named by Cassiodorus (died *c*.580) and have remained the same ever since. They are accompanied by the antiphon *Ne reminiscaris delicta mea vel parentum meorum* (Do not remember my sins and those of my parents, Tob.3,3) and are here introduced by the prayer *Suscipe sancta trinitas unus deus hos psalmos consecratos …* (Accept, Holy trinity, One God, these consecrated psalms … , f.54v). Part of psalm 6 is lost because the six-line initial that depicted the Last Judgement was cut out and folios 55 and 55v were damaged.

The Litany of Saints is closely connected with the Penitential Psalms and often follows immediately after, but here, as in most hours of Sarum use, the Gradual Psalms were put in between, beginning with only a two-line initial and ending with the same antiphon *Ne reminiscaris*.

The Fifteen (or) Gradual Psalms, like the Penitential Psalms, were added to the existing Divine Office in the eleventh century. Originally they were recited by the monks before Matins and divided into three groups: one for all the faithful living, one for all the dead, one for the recently deceased. As is usual, only the first few words of the first thirteen are given (psalms 119–130), and the last three in full (psalms 131–133), because the latter do not occur in a preceding part of the hours.[128]

The Litany (ff.62v–71v) follows. It is one of the oldest liturgical prayers. Its main feature is its repetitive request (Greek *litaneia*) for the intercession of all apostles and saints, and for salvation and the mercy of God. 'The prayer of Richard III' (see chapter 6, below) recalls part of the repetitive 'Lord deliver us' (By your nativity, by your baptism … Lord deliver us), and also the list of evils from which the supplicant begs to be saved (From all evil, from the snares of the devil… , deliver us). The list of saints invoked contains no names that call for special attention. Curious but not unusual is the inclusion of Martial (30 June) among the apostles. This high status is the result of legend and forgery and was widely accepted.[129]

The Litany ends with a number of collects for various purposes. They have no rubric allotted to them here, but they are known from other sources as prayers 'for devoted friends', 'for peace', 'for continence', 'for acting justly', 'of the saints whose relics remain in the holy church', 'against evil thoughts', 'for all the faithful deceased', 'for all Christian souls' and one to be said 'after the Sacrament'. Several of these are still in use today.[130] The final text *Pietate tua quesumus domine solve vincula omnium delictorum* ... (We beseech you, Lord, loosen the bonds of all our sins by your mercy ...) asks for the intercession of Mary and all the saints for those 'related to us by blood, friendship, confession or prayer'.

Nearly a line and a half in this last prayer were deleted and filled with line-fillers in the ink of the original hand. Comparison with other copies shows that there are no 'offending' words to erase here and that the scribe himself had made the error. On folio 67v, in the prayers asking for the preservation of the church, the prelates, the king and all the faithful, some offending references – to the pope and the abbots – were deleted completely.

ff.72–90. Office of the Dead.

The Office or Vigil of the Dead (*Vigilie mortuorum*) found in books of hours is a long text, its contents the same as those in the clergy's breviary. They are the prayers and devotional texts that were said by those who kept vigil around the coffin in the night before burial, and could be used privately in memory of the dead and as a reminder of the need for repentance. It consisted only of Vespers and Matins plus Lauds, the first called *Placebo* after the first antiphon *Placebo domino in regione vivorum* (I shall please the lord in the land of the living), the second *Dirige* after the antiphon *Dirige domine deus meus in conspectu tuo viam meam* (O Lord, my God, direct my way in your sight). *Placebo* was said after Vespers of the day, *Dirige* after Lauds of the next day. Each office consists of psalms and lessons.

ff.90v–100v. Commendations

The Commendation of Souls (*Commendationes animarum*) in books of hours differs from the *Commendatio animae* still in use in the Catholic church, said by the priest over the dying. In Richard III's Hours it consists of all twenty-two parts of psalm 118 (*Beati immaculati*), preceded and followed by the antiphon *Requiem eternam dona eis domine* (Give them eternal rest, o Lord), psalm 138 (*Domine probasti me*), a dialogue of versicles and responses and the prayers *Deus cui proprium est misereri* ... (O God who is always full of pity ...), *Tibi domine commendamus animas famulorum* ... (Lord, we recommend to you the souls of your servants ...) and *Misericordiam tuam domine sancte pater* ... (O Lord and Holy Father, your mercy ...). These devotions were meant to help the dying in their passage to the next world, commending their souls to God, as Jesus had commended his on the cross.

ff.101–112. Psalms of the Passion.

They are introduced in the last line of folio 100v by the rubric *Psalmi de passione christi* (Pss.21–30). Because of their contents they were considered appropriate as a devotion on the crucifixion. A primer in English and Latin of 1537 has 'in these psalms ... diverse prophecies concerning the passion, death and resurrection ... are contained'.[131] The last psalm *In te domine speravi* (In you, Lord, I put my trust) breaks off after verse 6: 'Into your hands I commend my spirit for you have redeemed me, O Lord, God of truth ...', because there was a tradition that Jesus recited these psalms while he hung on the cross and died after speaking those words.[132]

The psalms are followed by two short prayers,[133] and three *Miserere* psalms 50, 55 and 56, of which the first has a full seven-line initial. They are followed by a rubric: 'This prayer is to be said after three *Miserere*', and the prayer *Omnipotens sempiterne deus qui humano corpori animam ad similitudinem tuam inspirare dignatus es* ... (O almighty everlasting God, who deigned to breathe a spirit in your likeness into a human body ...).[134]

ff.112–122v. Psalter of St. Jerome.

In the middle of folio 112, marked by a two-line initial, begins the page-long explanatory rubric of a selection of lines from the psalms traditionally ascribed to St. Jerome (died 420), the maker of the Latin Bible translation, the Vulgate. On f.112v there is a seven-line capital of the first word of the text *Verba mea auribus percipe* ... (Give ear to my words ..., Ps.5, 2). In a book with a richer scheme of illumination the initial, or the preceding full page, would have had a picture of Jerome writing, dressed in red as a cardinal, with his lion beside him.

In Richard III's Hours the rubric reads: 'The blessed Jerome composed this psalter in this world [the scribe wrote *mundo* instead of *modo*, 'in this way'] when an angel of the lord taught it to him through the Holy Spirit. This psalter was abridged for those who are happy [should be 'anxious'; the scribe wrote *felicitudinem* instead of *solicitudinem*] or who lie sick or are working hard or are ship-wrecked [should be 'at sea'] or constantly fighting hard against the enemies of Christendom or one who has vowed to sing the whole psalter every day but is quite unable to do so, for him who is weak from a severe fast and for those observing festivals and solemn feast days and unable to sing the psalter. Whoever wants to save his soul and gain eternal life should sing this psalter assiduously'.[135] The earliest known copy of the text that follows dates from the end of the tenth century and is possibly of English origin. In the present manuscript it consists of 183 single and double lines taken from a great number of psalms, each starting with a decorated capital.

Three short prayers follow, all containing the phrase *famulus tuus .N.* (your servant N) enabling the supplicant to insert his own name (ff.122–122v).[136]

ff.122v–123v. Verses of St. Bernard.

The rubric reads: 'One finds in the book of St. Bernard that the devil said to him that he knew eight verses and that he who said them every day would be saved. When the blessed Bernard asked which they were he said he would not make them known. The blessed Bernard answered that he would say the whole psalter every day. When the devil heard this he made them known at once. And they are these.' The Verses themselves consist of eight lines from various psalms and they are followed by the prayer *Libera nos domine de morte ad vitam, de tenebris ad lucem* … (Save us, o Lord, from death to life, from darkness to light …).[137]

ff. 124–145. Prayers to God and Christ.

The relative importance of these devotions is shown by the size of their opening letters: most have three-line initials, some have four-line ones, as indicated. The long capital Is, written in the margin, elude such precise classification.

ff. 124–126. The *Confiteor,* introduced by an eight-line decorated initial and a demi-vinet. It is an extended formula of the well known text, which was believed to give absolution for daily sins. Before God, Christ, St. Mary and all the saints – none are mentioned by name – acknowledgement is made of errors of pride and vainglory, of anger, envy, desire for money and honour, idle talk, and every conceivable mental and physical shortcoming, and forgiveness is prayed for.

The *Confiteor* is followed by four rhyming, metrical invocations to the Father, the Son, the Holy Spirit and the Trinity, each headed by a rubric beginning *Invocacio ad* … [138]

ff.126–127. *O pater clementissime, mundane factor machine* … (O most merciful Father, creator of the earthly world …).

ff.127–127v. *O patris unigenite, fili lumen de lumine* … (O only-begotten Son of the father, light from the light …).

ff.127v–128. *O spiritus paraclite, o amborum almiflue* … (O intercessory Spirit, o beneficent [love] of both [the father and the son] …).

ff.128–129. *O adoranda trinitas, et predicanda unitas* … (O Trinity to be worshipped, and unity to be proclaimed …).

These and the next two prayers:[139]

ff.129–129v. *Iudex meus clementissime noli me secundum peccata mea iudicare* … (My most merciful judge, do not judge me according to my sins …) and

ff.129v–130. *Ihesu, ihesu miserere mei. Ihesu, ihesu obliviscere superbum provocantem* … (Jesus have mercy on me, Jesus forget him who provokes out of pride …) are closely related to the *Confiteor* in spirit and were seen as one devotion.

ff. 130–131. The rubric *Qui hanc prosam in honorem fili dei quotidie dixerit dum tamen in peccato mortali scienter non fuerit eternaliter certissime dampnari non poterit.* (He who says this sequence[140] daily in honour of the son of God, as long as he is not knowingly in mortal sin, can certainly not go to hell for ever) introduces the text *Ihesus ex deo genitus, Ihesus [pre]figuratus* … (Jesus born of God, Jesus who was prefigured …). It consists almost entirely of rhyming epithets, describing Christ's life and passion, and was probably composed by St. Bonaventure (died 1274), who used the lines as separate chapter headings in his *Lignum Vitae* (The Tree of Life).[141]

ff.131-132. *Iuste iudex ihesu christe rex regum et domine* … (Righteous judge, Jesus Christ, king of kings and lord …) was written by the polemical theologian Berengar of Tours (died 1088). Whether he hoped to protect himself against spiritual enemies or his opponents is not perfectly clear. The text occurs in the *Ancrene Riwle*, where it is called one of the *Cruces*, prayers to the Holy Cross.[142]

ff.132-134. [rubric] *Ad ymaginem crucifixi dicatur. oracio.* (To the image of the crucifix should be said [this prayer]. A prayer). [text] *Omnibus consideratis, paradisus voluptatis, es ihesu piissime.* (When all things have been considered, you, most merciful Jesus, are the paradise of delight). A sequence on the wounds of Christ, it is divided into ten stanzas of twelve lines: to the crucifix, the cross, the head, each of the five wounds, to St. Mary and to St. John.[143] The text occurs in many books of hours. It recalls the symmetrical scene depicted in miniatures and paintings of the crucifixion, with the Virgin in blue on the left, St. John in red on the right. The prayer compares the wounds of Christ's hands and feet to the rivers Phison, Gihon, Tigris and Euphrates that irrigated the garden of Eden; they wash away misery and sin and are gates that lead to salvation. From the wound in the side flow sweet springs, breaking the power of evil.

The author is thought to have been Jean de Limoges, monk at Clairvaux at the end of the thirteenth century. In more luxurious books of hours each stanza-initial is decorated with a tiny miniature of each wound, the cross, and of St. Mary and St. John; the last two can be very attractive when small and yet perfectly executed (see fig.25).

f.134v. *Omnipotens sempiterne deus qui unigenitum filium* ... (Almighty everlasting God, [you were willing to let] your only-begotten son [suffer] ...): this prayer frequently follows *Omnibus consideratis,* as it does here.[144]

ff.134v–135. *O bone ihesu duo in me agnosco* ... (O good Jesus, I acknowledge there are two things in me ...), is sometimes ascribed to St. Bernard; in it the supplicant asks Christ to take away the evil part of man created by man himself, and leave him the good part that Christ created.

ff.135–136. *Domine ihesu christe fili dei vivi te deprecor per sacratissimam carnem* ... (Lord Jesus Christ, son of the living God, I pray you by the most sacred flesh ...) names many events of the life and suffering of Christ and for the sake of these the speaker prays to be delivered of his sins of the past, present and future. The name of the supplicant can be inserted in the text. The last two prayers often go together.[145]

ff.136–136v. *Concede michi domine spacium vite et graciam bene vivendi* ... (Grant me, Lord, time to live and the grace to live well ...); this prayer requests help in the hour of death, the blessing of the last sacrament and deliverance 'from the horrible face and the power of the devil'.[146]

ff.136v–138. *Domine ihesu christe qui septem verba die ultimo vite tue in cruce pendens dixisti* ... (Lord Jesus Christ, who spoke the seven words on the last day of your life hanging on the cross ...). This text has a four-line initial and the rubric reads: 'A prayer of the Venerable Bede, the priest, on the seven words of Christ hanging on the cross. Who says this prayer devoutly every day on bended knees cannot be harmed by devil or evil man and will not die unconfessed, and for thirty days preceding his death he will see the glorious Virgin Mary prepared to help'. The text is usually ascribed to Bede and is very common in books of hours. It tries to relate each of the seven words of Christ to the seven cardinal sins, but does not succeed in making a specific connection. It may be compared to the devotions to the wounds, the sacred face, and the Hours of the Cross, all meant to arouse the pity of the faithful and make them meditate on the suffering of Christ. The 'Seven Words' are a frequent theme: they also occur in 'Richard III's prayer' (see chapter 6, below) and in the Fifteen Oes (see ff.145v–151v).[147]

ff.138–138v. *Precor te piissime domine ihesu christe propter illam caritatem ...* (I pray you, very merciful Lord Jesus Christ, because of that charity ...) is sometimes supposed to have been written by Pope Gregory III (died 741) at the request of a queen of England – or he may have conferred indulgences on its users. It is a 'levation prayer'[148] on the Passion, describing Christ's suffering in its physical details: 'with outstretched hands, with deadly hue, with tearful eyes ...'[149] In some manuscripts its rubric promises as many days of indulgence as Christ had wounds.[150] It could be said during or after the elevation of the host or anywhere before an image of the Crucifix.

ff.138v–139. *Domine ihesu christe qui hanc sacratissimam carnem tuam et preciosissimum sanguinem tuum ...* (Lord Jesus Christ, who [assumed] this your most sacred flesh and your most precious blood ...) is another levation prayer, here opened by a four-line initial. The rubric was erased completely, but the text's popularity allows it to be reconstructed from other sources: 'To whoever says the following prayer between the elevation of the host and the third *Agnus Dei* 2,000 years of indulgence are granted by Pope Boniface VI at the request of Philip, King of France'.[151]

ff.139–139v. *Deus qui voluisti pro redempcione mundi a iudeis reprobari et a iuda traditore osculo tradi ...* (God, you were willing for the redemption of the world to be condemned by the Jews and to be betrayed with a kiss by the traitor Judas ...) is here simply headed *oracio devota* (a devout prayer), but in some books of hours is has a more impressive rubric, ascribing it to various popes or even to St. Augustine himself, and promising indulgences between thirty days and 80,000 years. In the short text all the events and instruments of the passion are remembered and deliverance from the 'punishments of hell' is asked for.[152]

ff.139v–140v. *Deus propicius esto michi peccatori et sis custos mei omnibus diebus vite mee* ... (Lord, be merciful to me a sinner and be my guardian all the days of my life ...), here merely called 'a devout prayer', in other copies has a long rubric explaining how effective it was against many kinds of evil and danger. It is frequently ascribed to St. Augustine and also closely connected with St. Michael. In the text he and the other archangels and angels are asked for their protection. Towards the end it reads like an incantation and the sign of the cross is made ten times by the supplicant with the words: 'Holy, holy, holy, Cross of Christ save me, Cross of Christ protect me, Cross of Christ defend me'.[153]

ff.140v–141. *Salve sancta facies nostri redemptoris, In qua nitet species divini splendoris* ... (Hail, holy face of our Saviour, in which the beauty of divine splendour shines ...) opens with a four-line initial and the rubric 'a prayer of St. Veronica'. It is immediately followed by psalm 66 (*Deus misereatur*), versicles and responses. The prayer itself was sometimes said to have been composed by Pope John XXII, who granted 5,000 or 10,000 days of indulgence to those who said it 'while beholding the glorious ... visage of our lord'. One could also say five *Pater Nosters* instead. The text honours Veronica and the veil, or vernicle, on which the image of Christ's features was left when she wiped the sweat from his face. It is often accompanied by a miniature showing the vernicle with Christ's face.[154]

ff.141–141v. *Deus qui nobis signasti lumine vultus tui* ... (O God who marked for us with the light of your face ...) is in many devotions to the vernicle and often found with the preceding text.[155]

ff.141v–142. *Te sancta crux adoro ut pectus meum munias* ... (I adore you, Holy Cross, that you may strengthen my heart ...) is addressed to the cross itself, asking for its assistance and beneficial influence.[156]

ff.142–142v. *Obsecro te ihesu christe fili dei vivi, per sanctam crucem tuam* ... (I beseech you, Jesus Christ, son of the living God, by your holy cross ...) calls for Christ's help and protection for all the parts of the supplicant's body in the name of the cross: 'for the sake of the blessed cross protect my eyes, for the venerable cross protect my tongue...'. This text is undoubtedly of Celtic origin and is found in a collection of prayers dating from the eighth century.[157]

This series of devotions to God and Christ ends with prayers on the sacrament:

ff.142v–143v. *Ad mensam dulcissimam convivii tui* ... (To the very sweet table of your feast ...) is to be said before communion and is usually ascribed to St. Ambrose.[158]

ff.143v–144v. *Omnipotens et misericors deus ecce ad sacramentum corporis et sanguinis* ... (Almighty and merciful God, here [I come] to the sacrament of the body and the blood ...) is also to be said before communion and is sometimes attributed to St. Thomas Aquinas.[159]

ff.144v–145. *Sancte spiritus qui uterum castissime semper virginis marie tua virtute fecundasti* ... (Holy Spirit, who by your virtue made fruitful the womb of the very chaste Mary who was always a virgin ...) followed by versicles, responses and the prayer *Deus qui sacratissimam cenam cum discipulis tuis celebrasti* ... (O God, who celebrated the most holy supper with your disciples ...) form the final devotion on the sacrament and of this section.[160]

ff.145v–151v. The Fifteen Oes.

The next important item in the book, introduced by an eight-line capital O and a demi-vinet, but without rubric, is the famous Fifteen Oes or Fifteen Prayers, a series of invocations to Jesus all beginning *O ihesu*. The theme is the passion and each section cleverly contrasts an aspect of Christ's divine powers with one of his human sufferings and relates them to the supplicant's needs and requests. The Fifteen Oes are very common in English books of hours from the early fifteenth century on. Though probably not composed by St. Bridget of Sweden herself – to whom they are often ascribed in rubrics – they may well have originated with the Bridgettine order. The text also has links with the north of England. The prayers are often prefaced by a long rubric containing a variety of promises, but in most cases it is 'merely' claimed that by saying them one will save fifteen souls from purgatory, convert fifteen sinners, comfort fifteen of the faithful and obtain great blessings for oneself. This rubric scandalised later readers and was often erased.[161]

1. *O ihesu christe eterna dulcedo te amantium* ... (... eternal sweetness of those that love you ...) remembers all that Christ suffered in mind and body before the actual crucifixion, during the last supper, the trial and flagellation. True contrition and absolution before death are prayed for.

2. *O ihesu mundi fabricator quem nulla divisio* [should probably read *dimensio*] *vero in termino metitur* ... (... maker of the world, of whom no one can calculate the true limit ...) asks to receive fear and love of Christ for the sake of the accumulated pain that he suffered when he was nailed to the cross and his limbs stretched to fit it.

3. *O ihesu celestis medice, recordare langoris livoris et doloris* ... (... heavenly healer, remember the weakness, the pallor and the grief ...) remembers how Christ did not heed his own pain and said: Father, forgive them.

4. *O ihesu vera libertas angelorum paradisus deliciarum* ... (... true angelic freedom, paradise of delights ...) recalling how Christ was despised and maltreated, it asks for protection against enemies.

5. *O ihesu speculum claritatis eterne* ... (... mirror of eternal brightness ...) remembers Christ's prophetic vision of how the elect shall be saved by his passion. It includes his words to the robber crucified beside him.

6. *O ihesu rex amabilis amice totus et desiderabilis*... (... king to be loved, entire and desirable friend ...) describes how Christ, forsaken by all, commended St. John and St. Mary to each other, and asks for comfort in time of trouble.

7. *O ihesu fons inhauste pietatis* ... (... inexhaustible well of mercy ...), how Christ's love of mankind made him 'thirst' for its salvation even on the cross. The supplicant prays that his own evil desires may be quenched.

8. *O ihesu dulcedo cordium, ingensque suavitas mencium* ... (... sweetness of the heart and immense delight of the mind ...) contrasts Christ's sweetness and love with the bitterness of the gall he drank and hopes to be healed and comforted for its sake.

9. *O ihesu regalis virtus iubilusque mentalis* ... (... royal power and joy of the mind ...) recalls Christ's cry of anguish: Why have you forsaken me?! The supplicant hopes Christ will not forget him in *his* despair.

10. *O ihesu alpha et oo* ... (... beginning and end ...) remembers how Christ suffered from head to foot and asks to be taught true charity.

11. *O ihesu abyssus profundissime misericordie* ... (... deepest abyss of pity ...), the supplicant asks to be hidden safely from God's anger in the deep wounds of Christ.

12. *O ihesu veritatis speculum* ... (... mirror of truth ...) asks for all wounds to be 'written' with Christ's blood on the supplicant's heart so that they can always be 'read' there.

13. *O ihesu leo fortissime rex immortalis* ... (... strongest lion, immortal king ...): when Christ's strength failed him he said: It is finished. He is prayed, for the sake of this anguish, to remember the faithful in their final hour.

14. *O ihesu unigenite altissimi patris* ... (... only son of the highest father ...): for the sake of his own recommendation of his soul to God, may Christ help the supplicant to resist evil and receive his soul, 'for I am but an exile and a pilgrim'.

15. *O ihesu vitis vera et fecunda* ... (... true and fruitful vine ...) describes in detail how blood and water flowed from Christ's wounds. The person praying begs to be 'wounded' by the passion and wishes to shed tears of penitence and love, day and night.

The Fifteen Oes are followed by two short prayers:[162]
f.151v. *Ihesu nazarene respice ad meas miserias* ... (Jesus of Nazareth, regard my misery ...) and *Domine ihesu christe pater omnium credencium* ... (Lord Jesus Christ, father of all who believe ...) asking for deliverance from anxiety and danger generally.

ff.152–156. *Salve virgo virginum* ... (Hail, virgin of virgins ...). A rubric beginning *Has videas laudes* ... (See these praises ...), a nine-line decorated initial and a demi-vinet introduce a 'farced' version of the *Salve regina.* This is a long devotion of thirty four-line stanzas, each headed by and beginning with one or more words from the *Salve regina* itself. These headings, written in red, thus form the original text. The first lines of the first two stanzas read: *Salve virgo virginum, Regina regnancium.*[163] This metrical and rhyming salutation of the Virgin, with its verse rubric, occurs in many books of hours, often, as here, followed by the prayer beginning:
ff.156–156v. *Deus qui de beate marie virginis utero* ... (God, who from the womb of the blessed virgin Mary ...).[164]
ff.156v–158. *O intemerata et in eternum benedicta* ... (O immaculate and blessed forever ...) and
ff.158–160. *Obsecro te domina sancta maria* ... (I beseech you, holy lady Mary ...). These two long prayers will be found in most books of hours, frequently in a more prominent position than they have here. In Richard III's Hours the four-line initials, however, indicate their relative importance. Both prayers address the Virgin directly, the first St. John the

Evangelist as well, who is often found connected with her.[165] The *O intemerata* was probably written in the sphere of Cîteaux in the middle of the twelfth century and survives in several redactions. St. Edmund of Canterbury is said to have recited it every day. In it the help and intercession are requested of Mary and John, 'jewels of heaven', 'divine lamps' and virgins both.[166] The *Obsecro te* is directed to Mary alone and after saluting her by various titles, enumerates many events of her life, her joys and sorrows. The supplicant asks exhaustively for all kinds of help and blessings and concludes: 'at the end of my days show me your face and tell me the day and the hour of my death'. In one manuscript the text is said to have been composed by St. Augustine on the day he died. Many powers were attributed to it, which accounts for its popularity.[167]

ff.160–161. *Precor te piissima dei genitrix* ... (I beseech you, most merciful mother of God ...), a long series of names and salutations.[168]

ff.161v–162. *O sanctissima et certissima spes omnium* ... (O holiest and surest hope of all ...)[169] followed by versicle and response and the collect *Deus qui beatissimam virginem mariam* ... (O God, who [gave joy] to the most blessed virgin Mary ...).[170]

f.162. *Ave et gaude virgo et mater* ... (I salute you and wish you joy, Mary, virgin and mother ...) a very short text with a two-line initial closes this section of the book.[171]

ff.162v–180. Devotions to the Virgin and Miscellaneous Prayers.

ff.162v–164v. *Virgo templum trinitatis* ... (Virgin, temple of the Trinity ...). A six-line decorated initial introduces this metrical and rhyming devotion on the Seven Joys of Mary, one of the innumerable meditations on the joys (and sorrows) of the Virgin, written in Latin and the vernacular languages, that celebrate events of her life, numbered from five to twenty-five. The present meditation was made by Philippe de Grève, chancellor of Paris (died 1236), and survives in many manuscripts. In Richard III's *Horae* its five-line rubric was erased, but apart from the word 'pope' it is perfectly legible. It claims that 'whoever pronounces the Seven Joys once every day will obtain a hundred days of indulgence from Pope Clement who wrote it with his own pen'. Each stanza has a three-line initial and remembers a joyful event of Mary's life: the Annunciation, the Nativity, Adoration, Resurrection and Ascension of Christ, the Descent of the Holy Spirit and the Assumption of Mary

herself. Each ends with a few lines of verse written in red, containing the words *per hoc gaudium* (through this joy) and asking the Virgin's help.[172]
ff.164v–165. *Te deprecor sanctissima maria mater grade* ... (I pray you, most holy Mary, mother of grace ...), a series of names of Mary that frequently goes together with *Virgo templum trinitatis*. It contains the formula *Intercedas pro me peccatore .N. famulo tuo* (intercede for me your servant N a sinner) enabling the supplicant to insert his own name.[173]
ff.165v–166. *Digna virgo flos nubes regina theotecos theoteca imperatrix pacifica* ... (Worthy, virgin, flower, cloud, queen, mother of God, divine one [?], empress, bringer of peace, ...) contains titles that go back to salutations of the eleventh and twelfth centuries and shows that the Virgin was correctly called 'rich in names'. The first title varies in copies of the text and minor differences are legion, but the series as a whole is easily recognisable. It contains such names as 'turtle dove', 'tuba', 'rose' and 'lily'. The rubric here promises the visible presence of the Virgin in one's final hour; in another copy the names are said to have been revealed to a certain bishop by an angel and it is claimed that who says them for seven years will be cured of leprosy. A brief dialogue of versicle and response run this text and the next prayer together in a single devotion.[174]
f.166. *Fiat michi queso domine ... firma fides* ... (I ask you, Lord, let me have strong faith ...). Even a short prayer like this can have an extremely complicated and confusing history of composition and it is a good example of the process: it closely resembles the middle part of another prayer on folios 180–180v of the present manuscript and both texts also occur separately or in other contexts in other devotional books. In the present text the supplicant asks for virtues of body and mind, in this case through the intercession of the Virgin. It uses the phrase 'a helmet of grace on my head', which suggests that the text is related to the old Celtic *loricae,* prayers that are literally called 'cuirasses'. These are often long and ask for the protection of the Trinity, angels and saints against spiritual and especially temporal dangers. These dangers and the parts of the body for which protection is asked are enumerated in great detail. Such devotions were often ascribed to important saints and they were very popular in Celtic regions.[175]
ff.166v–167. *Melliflua mater maria* ... (Honey-sweet mother Mary ...) The first five lines of this prayer have not been identified, but the remainder, beginning [*Gaude*] *dei genitrix virgo immaculata. Gaude que gaudium ab*

angelo suscepisti … (Rejoice mother of God, immaculate virgin. Rejoice you who received joy from the angel …), is a slightly corrupt version of a prayer based on the Antiphon of the Five Joys, written by Peter Damian (died 1072). Legend has it that a certain monk used to say these five salutations to Mary frequently and devoutly. When he fell ill and was in great distress the Virgin appeared to him and said: Do not fear, you will find joy as you have always wished it to me. The sick man thought he would recover but when he rose in hope from his bed, his soul left his body and he received the joys of paradise.[176]

ff.167–168. *Ave cuius concepcio solemni plena gaudio* … (I salute you who conceived in solemn joy …) specifies the Five Joys: the Conception, Nativity, Annunciation, Purification and Assumption.[177] This text occurs in many books of hours, followed, as here, by versicle, response and the collect *Deus qui nos concepcionis, nativitatis … letificas …* (O God, who makes us happy [when we remember Mary's joys] of the conception, the nativity …).[178]

The Five Joys of Mary are followed by the Five Sorrows:

ff.168–169. [rubric] 'Whoever says the Five Sorrows of the Blessed Virgin Mary every Saturday with one *Pater noster* and one *Ave Maria*, devoutly and properly and with a pure heart will be safely delivered from all troubles'. *Maria dulcis miseros nos audi loquentes* … (Sweet Mary, listen to us wretches when we plead …). This metrical and rhyming devotion on the 'great sorrows' – Simeon's prophecy concerning Jesus, Jesus in the temple, Jesus' arrest, the Crucifixion and the Deposition – has a four-line initial.[179] It is followed by versicle, response and another text referring to the Sorrows: *Maria virgo virginum consolatrix miserorum* … (Mary, virgin of virgins, comfortress of the wretched …).[180]

ff.169–169v. *O Domina gloriosa virgo maria dignare meis peticionibus indignissimis annuere* … (O glorious lady, virgin Mary, deign to listen to my most unworthy pleas …) enables the supplicant to pray 'for all the living and dead Christians, of every sex, age or order, for my father and mother and all my relations, benefactors and enemies'.[181]

ff.169v–170. *O regina poli, peccantem linquere noli. Da michi tua dona, dulcissima virgo maria* … (O queen of heaven, do not desert a sinner. Give me your gifts, sweetest virgin Mary …) is followed by versicle, response and the prose prayer *Precamur te piissima dei genitrix virgo maria per amorem filii tui* … (We pray you, most merciful mother of God, virgin Mary, by the love of your son ...) and constitutes a single devotion to the Virgin, beseeching her not to abandon the sinful supplicant.[182]

f.170v. *Ave maria mitis et pia gracia plena conserva me a pena* ... (Hail Mary, gentle and merciful, full of grace, preserve me from punishment ...), a farced version of the *Ave Maria,* incorporating the words of the well known prayer on the angel's salutation (compare ff.176v–177, below).[183] It is here followed by versicle, response and the collect *Deus qui beatam virginem mariam super choros angelorum exaltasti* ... (O God, who raised the blessed virgin Mary above the choirs of angels ...).[184]

ff.170v–172. *Suscipere digneris domine deus omnipotens laudes et oraciones* ... (Deign to accept, lord God almighty, the praises and the prayers ...). This devotion falls into two parts though it is written as one. The first section serves as an introduction to a series of twenty-six salutations to the Virgin, which has been called 'a charming prayer' and is said to have been composed in the twelfth century.[185] It begins *Ave maria gracia plena dei genitrix super solem et lunam pulcherrimam* ... (Hail Mary, full of grace, mother of God, fairer by far than the sun and the moon ...) and is very rare. Other salutations are 'Hail lady of angels and archangels', 'Hail hope of the wretched', but most refer to events in Mary's life.

ff.172–172v. *Sancta maria mater domini nostri ihesu christi in manus eiusdem filii tui et in tuas, commendo* ... (Holy Mary, mother of our lord Jesus Christ, into the hands of your son and into yours I commend ...), a general plea to the Virgin for protection of the various parts of the body and against both physical and mental dangers.[186]

ff.172v–173. *O cunctis excelsior angelorum choris* ... (O you that are more exalted than all the choirs of angels ...) is a metrical and rhyming devotion to Mary, full of epithets and descriptive detail. The present manuscript contains only five of the ten known stanzas of this text.[187]

ff.173–174. *Stabat mater.* This is one of the best known poems on the suffering of Mary. Though it has no rubric in Richard's book of hours, its importance is acknowledged by the four-line opening S. There is still no unanimity on the poem's authorship, but there is an extensive literature on the subject. The text has frequently been translated and set to music. In other books of hours its rubric promises indulgences and it is often accompanied by a miniature of the *Pietà,* Mary with the body of Christ. It begins *Stabat mater dolorosa iuxta crucem lacrimosa* ... (The sorrowing mother stood weeping beside the cross ...) and contains the famous passage *Quis est homo qui non fleret matrem christi si videret in tanto supplicio* ... (Who is the man who would not weep if he were to see Christ's mother in such torment?).[188]

ff.174–176v. *Gloriosissima et precellentissima dei genitrix virgo maria* ... (Most glorious and most exalted mother of God, virgin Mary ...): these words introduce a long and moving prayer inspired by the popular legend of Theophilus. He was a cleric who repudiated the Virgin and Christ, signed and sealed a document to that effect, giving it into the keeping of the devil. Later he became deeply penitent and prayed to Mary, who rebuked him in a vision and returned the paper to him, thus delivering him from the devil's power. The enormity of Theophilus' crime and the depth of his despair and penitence are well expressed in the prayer and it must have appealed to many medieval supplicants: 'For which of my crimes shall I ask pardon first? ... To whom shall I turn? ... What shall I answer on the day of Judgment, when all shall be revealed? ... Who will have pity on me? ... To what haven can I flee ... except to you, most merciful Mary, and to him that was born to you?'.[189]

ff.176v–177. *Ave mater grade virgoque perpura. Maria tu diceris adiutrix secura* ... (Hail mother of grace, purest virgin. Mary, you are called the secure help ...), another metrical and rhyming prayer that incorporates the words of the Ave Maria, at the beginning of each line. This is the last devotion to the Virgin in the present manuscript.[190]

ff.177–177v [rubric] *Oracio de archangelis* [text] *Obsecro vos o sancte michael, sancte gabriel, sancte raphael, cum sociis vestris qui astatis ante claritatem dei clamantes quotidie ac dicentes, sanctus, sanctus, sanctus, dominus deus sabaoth* ... (I beseech you, O St. Michael ... and your companions who stand before the splendour of God and daily cry: Holy, holy, holy, Lord God of Hosts ...). This prayer to the archangels is the first of the miscellaneous devotions of the last section of the original part of this book. It is a rare copy of a text dating from the twelfth century.[191]

ff.177v–178. [rubric] *Oracio. De sancto iohanne evangelista.* [text] *Sancte et beate iohannes apostole et evangelista* ... (Holy and blessed John, apostle and evangelist ...) is said to have been a favourite of St. Edmund of Canterbury (died 1240), who had a special devotion to the apostle and said the prayer every day.[192]

ff.178–178v. [rubric] *De beata anna* [text] *Salve parens matris christi Anna ferens mundo tristi pacem cum letitia* ... (Hail, Anne, mother of Christ's mother, bringing peace with joy to the sorrowful world ...). After this hymn that serves as antiphon this suffrage to St. Anne is completed by versicle, response and the collect *Deus qui universum mundum beatissime anne puerperio letificasti* ... (O God who brought joy to the whole world by the lying-in of the most blessed Anne ...).[193]

ff.178v–179. [rubric] *De ioachim et anna* [text] *Salve sancte ioachim virginis* [sic] *dans esse* ... (I salute you, St. Joachim, who gave life to the Virgin ...): this antiphon introduces another suffrage, to Saints Anne and Joachim jointly. It is completed by versicle, response and the collect *Deus qui beatos ioachim et annam pene sterilitatis afflictos* ... (O God who [was willing to make fruitful] Joachim and Anne who were afflicted with barrenness ...).[194]

f.179. [rubric] *Eundo ad cubitum. oracio.* (On going to bed. A prayer) [text] *Dominator domine omnium* ...; the full text in translation reads: 'O lord, ruler and protector of all, who separated light from darkness, we pray you as supplicants that your right hand may protect us through the darkness of the coming night and that we may rise joyfully at the light of dawn'. The text also alludes to the deliverance of the elect from purgatory and the return of light after Christ's death.[195]

ff.179–179v. [rubric] *Oracio. Ad bonum angelum.* (To the good angel) [text] *O mi angele qui es sanctus esto michi propicius* ... (O my angel, you who are holy, have mercy on me ...); the guardian angel is asked to make the supplicant perform God's will and he is prayed to be helper, companion, 'true physician' and protector against all visible and invisible enemies.[196]

f.179v. [rubric] *De beato ioseph. Oracio* [text] *Deus qui prudenciam beato ioseph in domo domini sui et coram pharaone dedisti* ... (O God who gave wisdom to the blessed Joseph in the house of his lord and in the presence of pharaoh ...). It is surprising to find a devotion that has Joseph, the son of Jacob, as its subject. The text recalls how Joseph was saved from the envy of his brothers and raised to high honours. The supplicant asks to be similarly saved from the plots of his enemies and to be allowed to find favour in the eyes of his 'adversaries and all Christians'. Why the original owner of the book chose this devotion is a mystery. It is possible that his Christian name was Joseph – though in that case he could have chosen a prayer on Joseph the husband of Mary – but a special interest in the successful career of the son of Jacob may also explain his preference. The text is comparable to the enumeration of biblical deliverances in

'Richard III's prayer' (see chapter 6, below). The supplicant hopes to be heard as many others were heard, and it has to be remembered that in the case of Joseph and, for example, Daniel and Job as well, not only were their problems solved, they were also 'over-compensated' and brought to higher honours and better fortune than they had had before.

In the Middle Ages Joseph's life was often seen as a prefiguration of the life of Christ, but there is no suggestion of such a comparison in this short simple prayer.[197]

ff.179v–180. *Pax christi que exsuperat omnem sensum* ... (Peace of Christ that surpasses all understanding ...), a prayer that asks for peace and reconciliation, not only generally but also very specifically. Three times the name of the person with whom good relations are sought can be inserted in the text. Christ is asked to make peace between the supplicant and 'N' for the sake of the 'peace' – in the sense of love and concord – that he made between angels and men, between St. Mary and St. John the Evangelist, and between the apostles (John. 14:27).[198]

ff.180–180v. *Salvator mundi salvum me fac domine ihesu christe qui solus salvare potes* ... (Saviour of the world, lord Jesus Christ, who alone can bring salvation, save me ...): this last complete devotion of the original book, as it was made for the first owner, is also a text with a specific purpose. Christ's assistance is asked to help the faithful live according to *his* will, and it continues, 'Grant that I will be able to do, know, wish, perform, and accomplish what pleases you and is good for me', and 'counsel in trouble', 'help in persecution', 'moderation in anger' are prayed for. The second half of the text is reminiscent of the prayer on folio 166 of the present manuscript, though the wording is not the same.[199]

f.180v. The rubric of a prayer to St. Julian the Hospitaller [incomplete]. The last surviving line of the original text of the book as it was commissioned by the first owner, that is the last line of folio 180v, has caused considerable confusion among modern commentators. The next folio is missing, that is, the one which contained both the greater part of a devotion written in the 1420s *and* the beginning of the long prayer added for Richard III, 1483–5. Of the first, a prayer to St. Julian, only a few words of the rubric remain: the whole of the text itself has gone; and of the prayer added for Richard III, the rubric is lacking although most of the text survives. The position and incompleteness of these two devotions have led to several curious hypotheses.[200]

Plate 1. Richard III's Hours, Lambeth Ms.474, f.15. Annunciation and the beginning of the Hours of the Virgin. The page has suffered severely at the hand of a sixteenth-century binder.

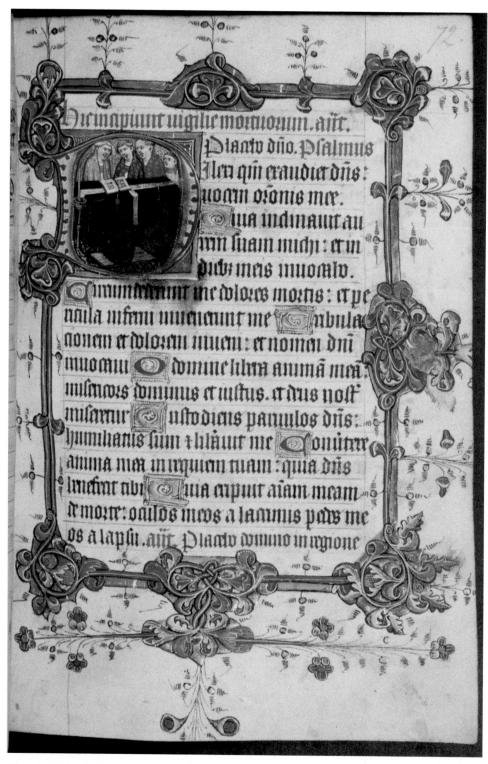

Plate 2. Richard III's Hours, Lambeth Ms.474, f.72. Funeral and the beginning of the Vigil of the Dead.

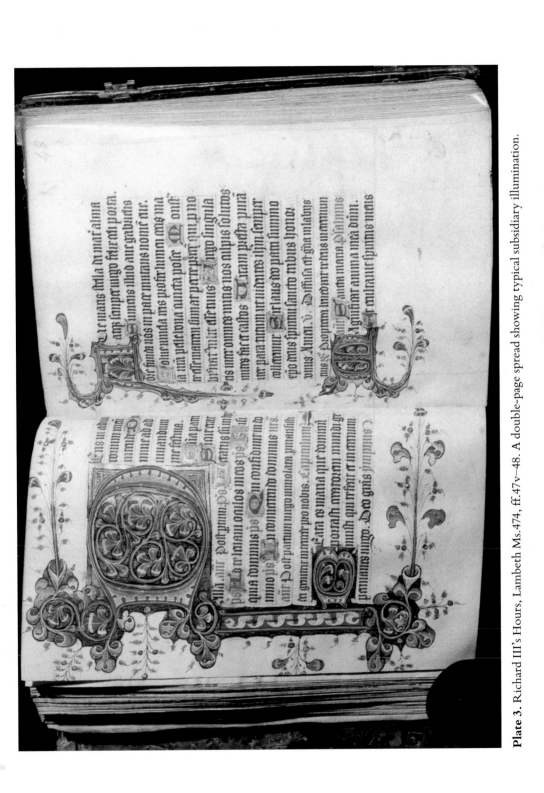

Plate 3. Richard III's Hours, Lambeth Ms.474, ff.47v–48. A double-page spread showing typical subsidiary illumination.

Plate 4. Altenburg Hours, Altenburg Ms.AB6C4, f.9. Annunciation and the beginning of the Hours of the Virgin. This manuscript, though simpler, is the closest in type and status to that of Richard III.

The facts are these: the prayers in this last section of the book all have, as has been seen, a specific purpose or object. The suffrages to St. John, Saints Anne and Joachim, the prayer to be said when going to bed, the prayer on the Old Testament figure of Joseph, are all meant to be used by a particular person or in a particular situation, more so than the more general devotions on the preceding pages. The occurrence of such 'additional' devotional texts at the end of a book of hours is quite common.

The surviving bit of rubric at the end of folio 180v suggests that the prayer originally included here was a similar one. It reads, in red ink: *De beato iuliano. Cum volueris pere-* ... (On the blessed Julian. Whenever you have decided [to?] ...). It must be emphasised that none of these words is part of the actual prayer, they merely explain the subject and purpose of the following text, which is now lost. The text on the next surviving folio was added sixty years later, during the reign of Richard III, and has no connection whatsoever with the fragmentary rubric.

There are two clues in the remaining words of the rubric and they need each other's support to make any conclusion possible: *iuliano* and *pere-*. The Julian referred to is most likely to be St. Julian the Hospitaller, who was the most popular of the saints of that name and the one most frequently the subject of prayers.[201] The choice of Latin words that begin with *pere-* is limited, and almost the only possibility is *peregrinari* (to travel, to wander).[202] Since Julian was the patron of innkeepers, ferrymen and travellers and many prayers survive asking for his protection in that capacity, it is highly probable that the lost prayer had analogous contents, and that the rubric explained when it should be said. On the evidence of other texts it may be concluded that the prayer was meant to be spoken 'whenever you have decided to travel', probably in the morning when setting out, and that a safe journey, shelter for the night, a good and pleasant host and a safe return were asked for, through the intercession of St. Julian. It was the original owner who had this useful devotion included towards the end, or at the very end, of his book of hours. Its actual text, though not identified, was probably far from unique.

ff.181–184v. Devotions added for Richard III.

The exact contents of the missing leaf between folio 180v and folio 181 have also to be guessed at. The recto side was no doubt filled partly by the rest of the rubric and the prayer to St. Julian, the length of both of which is uncertain. The lower part of the verso side must have contained the first four or five lines of the next surviving devotion, 'the prayer of Richard III', which now lacks its beginning. It is possible that St. Julian's suffrage was the last text of the original book and that the lower part of the page it ended on was blank, and that the other side of the leaf was also blank. The scribe who added 'Richard III's prayer' in 1483–5 then used this blank side for the new prayer's rubric – which may have been fairly long – a three- or four-line initial, some decorative sprays in the margin similar to those of the other additions of the book (e.g. on folio 1, fig.26) and for the first few lines of the text itself. As at the beginning of the manuscript, a gathering of two unused leaves, four pages, was available at the end, and together with the leaf now missing and the present folios 181 and 181v they sufficed for the complete text of the King's prayer.

ff.181–183v. 'The prayer of Richard III'. The rubric and the first four or five lines of this text are missing because the leaf that preceded folio 181 is lost (see above), but an almost accurate rendering of the beginning was added in a sixteenth-century hand in the upper margin (fig.29). The script of the prayer is the same as that of the other text added for Richard III, the Collect of St. Ninian (f.1; fig.26), and it is likely that the decoration of the initials of the missing rubric and first line were also similar, possibly more elaborate. There is no decoration of any kind on folios 181–183, on 183v the capitals are touched in red. On folio 182 the word *Ricardum* was erased in the phrase *me famulum tuum Regem Ricardum* (me, your servant King Richard), and on folio 183, in the same formula, *Ricardum* was partly obliterated, but the final -*m* is still visible. In both instances M.R. James was able to read the erased words: '[it] is legible in the second, and I have revived it in the first'.[203] The inclusion of the King's name and title makes it certain that the text was added for him after 6 July 1483.

More details and the history and contents of the prayer are given in the next chapter, followed by a full text and translation.

ff.184–184v. 'The "litany" of Richard III'. After 'the prayer of Richard III', which ends on folio 183v, the quality of the parchment changes. Three stubs are visible between folios 183v and 184 and it is clear that three leaves were cut out. Folio 184 and the two blank end-leaves are made of slightly rougher parchment. Script and decoration (two-line initials) on both sides of folio 184 are very similar to those of the other texts added for Richard III, that is the Collect of St. Ninian and the King's prayer. It cannot be established with absolute certainty that this final addition was made for him, because the rubric and much of the text itself are missing and the supplicant is not referred to by name as in the long prayer, but it is more than likely. For reasons given below it has been tentatively called 'the "litany" of Richard III'.

Because the devotion appears to be unique the text is here given in full, followed by a translation and a discussion of its contents and their possible implications. In the text printed below punctuation and capitalisation follow the manuscript. Abbreviations have been silently extended; rubrics are in italics; foliation and editorial additions are in square brackets.

[f.184] ... optimum nos serves a languore, ihesu pro tuo nomine sublimi glorioso, expurga nos a crimine omnique delicto. *Versus.* Ne memineris iniquitatum nostrarum antiquarum. *Responsorium.* Cito anticipent nos misericordie tue quia pauperes facti sumus nimis. *Versus.* Adiuva nos deus salutaris noster. *Responsorium.* Et propter gloriam nominis tui domine libera nos et propicius esto peccatis nostris propter nomen tuum. *Versus.* Laudate dominum ihesum omnes ang[e]li eius. *Responsorium.* Laudate eum omnes virtutes eius. *Versus.* Domine salvum fac regem. *Responsorium.* Et exaudi nos in die qua invocaverimus te. *Versus.* Domine exaudi oracionem nostram. *Responsorium.* Et cl[amor meus ad te veniat].

Oremus. Exaudi nos domine ihesu, omnipotens sempiterne deus et mittere digneris sanctos tuos de celis qui custodiant foveant protegant visitent et defendant omnes habitantes in hoc habitaculo. Per christum dominum [nostrum].

Oremus. [f.184v] Omnipotens sempiterne deus in cuius manu sunt omnes potestates ac omnia iura regnorum respice in auxilium christianorum ut gentes paganorum qui de sua feritate confidunt dextera [sic] tue potencia conterantur. Per christum dominum nostrum Amen. Kyrieleison. Kyrieleison. Kyrieleison. Domine ihesu miserere. Domine ihesu miserere. Domine ihesu miserere. Christus dominus factus est pro nobis obediens usque ad mortem autem crucis. Pater noster.

Oracio. Respice domine super hanc familiam tuam pro qua dominus noster ihesus christus non dubitavit manibus tradi nocencium et crucis subire tormentum. Recordare domine testamenti tui et dic angelo percucienti: cesset iam manus tua ut non desoletur terra et ne perdas omnem animam vivam. *Versus.* Quiescat domine iam ira tua a populo tuo. *Responsorium.* Et a civitate sancta tua ut non desoletur. Pater noster. (... best [?] ... keep us from weakness, Jesus, for the sake of your sublime name, cleanse us of offence and all crime.

Verse. Do not remember our former sins.

Response. Have mercy on us because we have been brought very low.

Verse. Help us, O God of our salvation.

Response. And for the glory of your name rescue us and forgive our sins for the sake of your name.

Verse. Let all the angels praise the lord Jesus.

Response. Let all his heavenly armies praise him.

Verse. Lord, save the king.

Response. And hear us when we call.

Verse. Lord, hear our prayer.

Response. And may my cry reach you.

Let us pray. Hear us, Lord Jesus, almighty, ever-living God, and deign to send your saints from the heavens to keep, support, protect, visit and defend all who live in this house. Through Christ our lord.

Let us pray. Almighty, ever-living God, in whose hand are all the powers and all the rights of kingdoms, come to the help of the Christians and let the peoples of the heathen who trust in their fierceness be destroyed by the power of your right hand. Amen. *Kyrie eleison. Kyrie eleison. Kyrie eleison.* Lord Jesus have mercy. Lord Jesus have mercy. Lord Jesus have mercy. The lord Christ was obedient for our sake, even to accepting death, death on the cross. Our Father ...

A prayer. Look down, Lord, upon this your people for whom our lord Jesus Christ did not hesitate to deliver himself to those that would harm him and to suffer the agony of the cross. Remember, Lord, your covenant and say to the destroying angel: Now stay your hand! And let not the earth be made desolate and do not destroy every living soul.

Verse. May your anger, Lord, now be lifted from your people.

Response. And from your holy city, and let it not be made desolate. Our Father ...)

The composition of this fragment suggests that the complete text possibly was a 'private litany', similar to those that were composed in great numbers in the fifteenth and sixteenth centuries.[204] Whatever its exact format, it was probably written at the request of Richard III and for his needs. Most of its elements – as far as can now be seen – are taken from the Bible and texts existing in his time, but the devotion as a whole has not been found elsewhere. The greater part is capable of a more general application, but some of its texts suggest a royal choice. It should be emphasised, *ad nauseam,* that the excessively penitent tone, the pleas for pardon, the requests to God not to visit past sins on the supplicants, do not allow of 'personal' conclusions. A great number of prayers in many devotional books give expression to such intense feelings of guilt and humility and they are an essential feature of a litany.

Instead of drawing ominous or gratuitous *ad hominem* conclusions it is more interesting to try and discover in what context the same phrases are used elsewhere and what their purpose may have been in this instance.

... optimum nos serves ...: this incomplete sentence (a response? an antiphon?) can unfortunately not be identified as the other verses and responses can. The line may have begun *Per verbum tuum bonum et optimum* ... (Through your good and very good word ...), but no parallel texts have been found.[205] The word *languore* could be the key-word. In Biblical and medieval Latin *languor* means either bodily illness (that can perhaps be cured), or a reprehensible state of mental weakness that makes the faithful fall short of proper Christian activity and hope, and should be shaken off. In the Bible the word more often means the former. Either may have been intended here.

V. Ne memineris ... R. Cito ... V. Adiuva ... R. Et propter ...: these versicles and responses (psalm 78, verses 8 and 9) are used especially in times of trouble and penitence: in the post-Tridentine missal as tract on the mass in Lent and in the votive masses 'to avert death' and 'against the heathen'. In the ninth-century St. Emmeran prayer book they form a prayer *pro peccatis et neglegentibus nostris* (for our sins and neglects) following a litany.[206]

V. Laudate ... R. Laudate ...: these exhortations to praise God are taken from psalm 148, verse 2. In the 1570 missal they occur after the *Alleluia* on the second Sunday after Epiphany; in the Sarum missal, in the same position on the next Sunday.

V. Domine ... R. Et exaudi ...: this phrase specifically asks God to protect the King. It is the last verse of psalm 19 (verse 10) and frequently used. In other contexts it usually goes together with similar entreaties for the protection of other authorities, temporal as well as spiritual, but here it stands alone. In the St. Emmeran prayer book it occurs after the litany as a separate short prayer *pro rege nostro* (for our King).[207] The text could obviously have been chosen by Richard III or with him in mind.

V. Domine ... R. Et cl[amor] ...: the opening lines of psalm 101, one of the Penitential Psalms, used in the post-Tridentine missal as *Alleluia* verse on the seventeenth Sunday after Whitsun and in the votive mass 'for the sick'. The sentence often precedes the versicle *Dominus vobiscum* (followed by the response *Et cum spiritu tuo*) at the end of a section of a composite devotional text.[208]

Oremus. Exaudi nos ...: this brief prayer asks for the protection of all who live in the supplicant's house. Elsewhere it is called 'for a family'.[209] Here it may refer to the King and his wife and son, or to his household in a wider sense. Perhaps, in the context of this book of hours and of this devotion, it refers to all the King's subjects.

Oremus. Omnipotens sempiterne deus in cuius manu ...: these first lines form the main prayer of the votive mass 'against the heathen', said to have been composed in the fifteenth century when the threat to western Europe from the Turks was at its height.[210] It is tempting to conclude from the central position of this text and from the fact that it is followed by three *Kyrie eleison* and three *Domine ihesu miserere* (that emphasise the litany-like character of the entire devotion) that this is the distinctive element. The section is completed by a text also used as gradual and antiphon in Holy Week, taken from St. Paul's letter to the Philippians (2:8) remembering the greatness of Christ's sacrifice, and finally the *Pater noster*.

Oracio. Respice domine ...: the first part of this prayer again remembers Christ's sacrifice and his willingness to die for man. It is a prayer 'over the people' used on several occasions in Holy Week, in the missal as well as in the breviary, for example as collect on Good Friday.

Recordare ...: the second half of this prayer was also used as introit to the mass 'to avert death'; it is especially connected with pestilence and sudden death. In a late fifteenth-century French prayer, for instance, these words form the first line of a prayer 'against death, illness, tempest, famine, war and all enemies'.[211]

V. Quiescat ... R. Et a civitate ...: the final versicle and response are based on Exodus 32:12-3, where Moses asks God to repent of his anger against the Israelites.

It is an inevitable conclusion that these are the remnants of a highly personal devotion, though compiled from existing formulas. They may have been actually chosen by the King, perhaps with the help of a priest, and reflect his preoccupations. If this is true, it is very unfortunate that so much of the text is missing. If it *was* a litany it could have told us what saints Richard III venerated and from whose intercession he expected help. The missing pages may have held all, or many, of the saints that he 'had devotion unto', listed in the statutes of his college at Middleham, but they may have contained a narrower and more revealing selection, or could have shown that the King expected special benefits from reciting the names and titles of Mary or Christ. If the list was short the pages obviously may have held yet another devotion. It is also possible that the folios that were cut out contained a long rubric, explaining the purpose of the prayer and promising an inordinate number of indulgences, which scandalised later owners and led to their destruction.

The text as a whole leaves the reader with a first impression that its user needed support against death and illness for himself and his companions and dependents, but this feeling is lessened and contradicted by the prayer 'against the heathen', which is so central in (the remnants of) this devotion and given greater intensity by the repeated *Kyrie* and 'Jesus have mercy'. If, as is possible, the threat from the East was seen as an imminent 'pestilence', it may have been the safety of Christendom as a whole that was foremost in the supplicant's mind, and the *languor* from which God is begged to preserve 'us' may refer to the slackness of the princes of the Christian West in supporting a new crusade with deeds as well as with words, and their endless excuses and prevarications.

During the few years of Richard's reign – the period in which this prayer must have been added – the immediacy of the danger from the East was brought to his attention on at least one occasion: on 21 November 1484 Pope Innocent VIII, who had been elected at the end of August, sent an encyclical to almost all kings and princes of Europe, warning them of the increase of the Turkish threat to the Western church and culture. He asked for speedy assistance: ambassadors with sufficient powers should be sent and delay was no longer possible. This was, of course, not the first attempt of its kind by the fifteenth-century popes, and like the others it proved completely unsuccessful. Princes always found an excuse for not tackling the problem in the inimical behaviour and untrustworthiness of their neighbours. Though he was willing to talk enthusiastically about crusading, Richard's response, if there was one, may have been in the same vein. It is possible, however, that he was sufficiently moved to have a special prayer made.[212]

We can only interpret the scraps of evidence given by this fragmentary text in the light of others equally incomplete. Whoever cut out the first three pages of 'the "litany" of Richard III' has left us with enough to make us painfully aware of how much is missing and how much fuller our picture of Richard and his piety could have been.

SIX

The 'Prayer of Richard III'

Father most true, this day my cause defend!
Thou that to Jonah Thy succour didst extend
In the whale's belly, and safely draw him thence, ...
Thou that didst save thy servant Daniel
From torments dire within the lions' den,
And the Three Children amid the fire protect,
Lord, be Thy love this day my present help; ...
[Charlemagne's prayer in *The Song of Roland*][213]

Charlemagne made this appeal to God for aid, remembering others who had been aided in the past, on the day he fought the Saracens and revenged Roland's death. Roland himself, in the very hour of his death, had turned his face towards Spain, recalled his victories and prayed in almost the same words: he had asked God to save his soul as he had delivered Lazarus from death and Daniel from the lions' den.[214]

The section of 'Richard III's prayer' that closely resembles the lines quoted here is very old. Such invocations which called to mind past examples of God's goodness go back to the very beginning of the church, probably to pre-Christian times, and originated in the East. Early Christian wall-paintings in the catacombs of Rome depict scenes of biblical deliverances, and there survive prayers in various languages, in both literary and liturgical contexts, that contain 'lists' of such events, ranging from Adam and Noah, Joseph and Isaac to Peter and Paul and John the Evangelist. These texts have been called typical 'lay' prayers that any Christian could use in great distress or danger, before battle and especially when close to death.[215] Some are very short and could be said in the moment of crisis itself; some, probably composed under clerical influence, are very long and narrate the biblical stories at some length and also bear witness to the suppliant's faith in the events he enumerates. These series of Old and New Testament deliverances and names even now read like powerful incantations. We can still appreciate their emotional appeal and that they were genuinely held to be effective, even without the evidence of their early origins and wide-spread use, and their occurrence in literary works.[216]

The entire text of Richard III's prayer as it was copied into his book of hours is probably no older than the middle of the fourteenth century, despite the antiquity of some of its component parts. The earliest copies so far traced date from the end of the fourteenth century.[217] Two of them form part of two books of hours *cum* missals, one of Franciscan and one of Roman use, preserved in the Bibliothèque Nationale in Paris.[218] These manuscripts have been dated to the last two decades of the fourteenth century and the text of the prayer in the older of the two is still comparatively free of the curious inconsistencies and scribal errors that disfigure many later copies. It is impossible, however, to say how far even this copy is removed from the original. The provenance of these, and other later manuscripts in which the prayer occurs, may point to an Italian and Franciscan origin of the text.[219] The devotions composed by Franciscans and often ascribed to great members of the order, St. Francis himself or St. Bonaventure, have a special and deep concern with Christ himself, with love of Christ and contemplation of his life and especially his passion.[220]

A third early copy that seems more or less to link the southern copies mentioned above and the northern one described below, is a book of hours made in Bruges in the 1380s for a client from Catalonia in Spain. The text of the prayer itself is in Latin without any special features, the rubric is in the owner's native language. It is impossible to tell whether the text was known in Bruges at the time or merely copied from a Catalan exemplar for the occasion.[221]

Another possibly fourteenth-century copy of the prayer survives in an interesting context but is impossible to date with any certainty. It occurs in a composite manuscript known as the *Grandes Heures* of Philip the Bold, Duke of Burgundy (died 1404). The manuscript was written in many hands over a period of at least seventy-five years and is famous for its illumination rather than its contents. Ordered by Philip the Bold in 1376 it passed to his son, John the Fearless, and his grandson, Philip the Good, during whose lifetime additions were still being made. The text of the prayer was probably added about 1400 and must have been familiar to all the Valois dukes of Burgundy and their wives. The book shows signs of intensive use.

In the Burgundy hours as well as in most other copies the prayer was credited with a famous author: 'Saint Augustine made this prayer which follows …'.[223] This is partly due to an understandable wish to ascribe every devotional text to an author whose fame and holiness will guarantee its effectiveness. It is also because the opening lines closely resemble that of a far older prayer which was traditionally made by St. Augustine. The latter text is found as early as the ninth century and its very similar beginning, *Domine Ihesu Christe qui in hunc mundum propter nos peccatores de sinu patris advenisti* (Lord Jesus Christ, who came to this world from the bosom of the Father for us sinners …), has led even modern scholars to confuse the two texts.[224] Medieval copyists or their patrons were probably only too willing to exploit any resemblance and associate the name of the great father of the church with the fourteenth-century prayer.

The rubric of Richard III's prayer is lacking in his hours[225] because the leaf that contained it is missing from the manuscript, but it is likely that it held at least a reference to St. Augustine's authorship and probably a longer introduction, similar to the one found for example in a prayer book made for Alexander, Prince of Poland, in 1491:[226]

Whoever is in any distress, anxiety or infirmity, or has incurred the wrath of God, or is held in prison, or has experienced any kind of calamity, let him say this prayer on thirty successive days, and he must be without mortal sin. It is certain that the Lord God will hear him completely, that all his trouble will turn to joy and comfort, whether he says it for himself or for another. And this has been proved by many trustworthy persons.[227]

The wording of this rubric is typical of most introductions to Richard III's prayer, especially those written during his lifetime. Most of them specify the necessity of saying it on thirty (or thirty-three) consecutive days on bended knees. If one is unable to read one can have it read out by someone else and its value will be the same. The supplicant must be contrite, without mortal sin and without hate, but provided he is, it will wash away his own sins and save the souls of others from purgatory. In one case reciting the prayer is said to be equivalent to singing the complete psalter a hundred times. Many rubrics end by attesting that the prayer's effectiveness has been proved again and again – an addition that is reminiscent of similar assurances at the end of medieval medical recipes.

One of the more impressive rubrics – and perhaps one that appeals more to the modern mind – is the one in Philip the Bold's Hours.[228] Though most other versions promise that God will turn one's trouble to comfort, this particular text appears to suggest that saying the prayer in itself will bring relief:

> … let him say it … on thirty consecutive days in honour of God and Our Lady and he shall be uplifted in such a way (*exauchies tellement*) that his sadness will turn to joy.

The text of the devotion itself and the effect of repeating will, it implies, bring comfort and relief. A text which encourages the reader to remember so many hope-giving events from the Old Testament and reiterates in such detail Christ's deeds and his suffering for mankind was probably well suited to have a therapeutic effect.

One of the greatest attractions of certain prayers in the later middle ages was the number of indulgences attached to them. One text in Richard III's hours, ascribed sometimes to Innocent VI, sometimes to Boniface VIII and composed, according to its rubric, at the request of King Philip (IV) of France, was said to give as many as 20,000 days, or in other versions 2000 years, of remission from the pains of purgatory.[229] Rubrics with promises of this nature scandalised later owners during and after the reformation and they were often erased, as was done with the six-line introduction to this same prayer in the present manuscript (f.138v). In one instance, in a late fifteenth-century or early sixteenth-century volume the rubric to 'Richard III's prayer' was also scrubbed out, but its simple two-line text cannot have contained much offending material,[230] for generally such a short rubric would merely have mentioned St. Augustine's authorship. Many copies are simply headed 'a prayer in affliction', a title which became usual for the prayer in the sixteenth century and later, when the text also became standardised.

Since the rubric of this prayer nowhere, in none of the copies found, contains mention either of popes – a frequent reason for erasure – or of the incredible indulgences they were supposed to have granted, it is unlikely that the page plus rubric in Richard III's hours disappeared *because* it offended a later owner. Whatever the cause of its loss, however, it is a pity that we cannot know with any certainty what value and hopes the prayer held for Richard III. It is clear that he valued it enough to have it specially added to his devotions, with his name as king in the text. In other copies of the prayer high-born owners did not have their names inserted (Alexander of Poland and Maximilian I[231]), or they had it written in without their title (Frederick of Aragon[232]). It is possible, of course, that someone else had the prayer, including the royal title, copied into the volume before it was given to the King; in that case the nature, quality and execution of the book suggests a friend or relation: it is hardly a formal presentation copy. Obviously Richard III's piety was, or was thought to be by someone who knew him, no different in depth or direction from that of the many contemporaries who had this prayer included among, or even especially added to, their personal devotions. Certainly to modern eyes the Hours of Richard III in its original condition had enough long items to satisfy any owner's religious needs in any situation.

The missing page (between folios 180v and 181) of Lambeth Ms.474 on which the rubric must have been written also contained the initial and first four or five lines of the prayer, which now begins abruptly with the last syllable of a word: *-res*. A later reader, probably sixteenth-century, knew – or thought he knew – what was lacking and he wrote some opening lines in the upper margin of folio 181:

Clementissime domine jesu christe vere deus qui a summi patris omnipotentis sede missus es in mundum peccata relaxare, peccatores ... (Most merciful lord

Jesus Christ, very God, who was sent from the seat of the highest
almighty Father to forgive sins, ... sinners ...).

He added a caret mark after the last word, another in the left margin
opposite the first line of the text of the page and crossed out the -*res*
of the original script. He apparently had an accurate mind and having
omitted to break off his own last word, he deleted the now superfluous
syllable from the original text.[233]

The added lines, however, cannot be correct and cannot have been the
ones that Richard III knew: none of the other copies of the prayer has
this beginning; virtually all start with *Dulcissime* or *O dulcissime* (most
sweet or most gentle) instead of *Clementissime* (most merciful) and none
have *a summi ... patris ... sede* (from the seat of the highest ... Father).
This is corroborated by all the accessible French, Dutch and German
versions.[234] It is also more usual to use *dulcis* (sweet) of Jesus and *clemens* (merciful) of God himself[235] and there are other instances of prayers
beginning *Dulcissime Domine Jesu Christe*. Perhaps the sixteenth-century
corrector was quoting from memory, or he used a faulty copy in which
sinu and abbreviated *summi* (*sumi*) had become confused and the resulting
incomprehensible sentence had been put right by adding *sede*.[236] The
text of the prayer as a whole does not leave any room for doubt that
Richard's copy should begin and did begin like the other surviving ones
and that it is the same prayer and not merely a similar one.

There is also evidence that the scribe of these pages of Ms.474 was
either a scholar himself or had a good exemplar to work from. Whoever
brought the prayer to King Richard's attention and copied out the original, certainly knew his Latin. Apart from one instance its wording and
grammar are correct, the text makes sense at every point and there are
no scribal errors, in contrast to many other copies of the text.

It is necessary to take the text of the prayer step by step to see if
Richard III's copy has any unique aspects.

The first lines were probably inspired by the prayer mentioned earlier
as ascribed to St. Augustine. The words 'from the bosom of the Father'
echo John 1:18: 'the Son *qui est in sinu Patris*', now translated as 'he who
is nearest to the Father's heart' or 'who is the same as God and is at his
Father's side'.

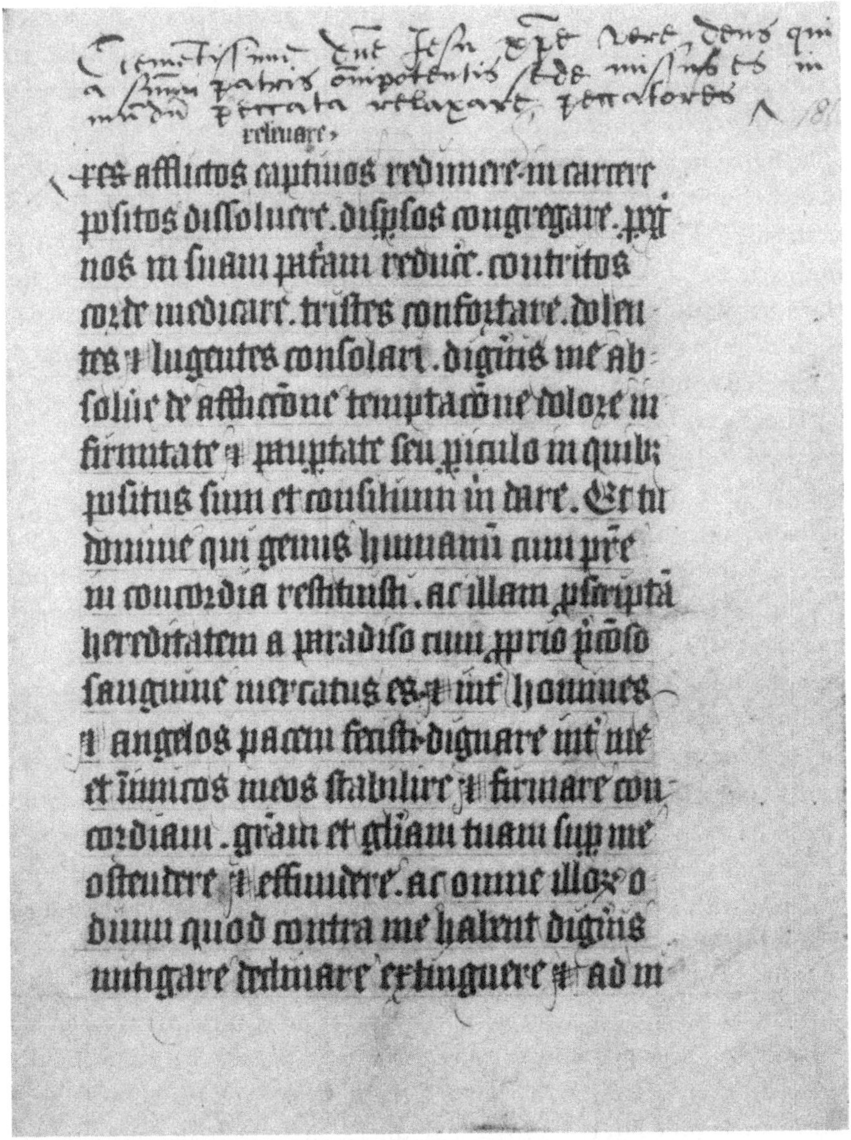

Figure 29. Richard III's Hours, Lambeth Ms. 474, f.181. The first remaining page of the long prayer added for the King. The lines in the upper margin were added in the sixteenth century in an attempt to supply the missing beginning. They differ only slightly from the first lines known to Richard III.

The series of Christ's works – the first of several litany-like series in this prayer – resembles the Works of Mercy in a general way. In many copies of the prayer there is unnecessary repetition; for example, Richard's text should probably read *peccatores salvare* instead of *peccatores afflictos relevare* (*relevare* was inserted later by the scribe, see fig.29), but the general hopeful meaning of the long sentence is clear and shared by all versions.[237] The sonorous *dolentes et lugentes* (the sorrowful and mourning), whom Christ will console, recall Matthew 5:4: 'How blessed are the sorrowful (*lugentes*); they shall find consolation'. Richard's text is slightly longer here than the other copies but there is nothing to suggest a personal contribution or application.

There may be proof of some personal involvement, however, in the description of the situation in which the person praying finds himself (or herself[238]). In Lambeth Ms.474 the list of afflictions includes *dolor* (grief), *infirmitas* (infirmity) and *paupertas* (want), which are found nowhere else. Though some of these extras may originate from scribal confusion, *dolor* (grief) may be unique.[239] The standardised sixteenth- and seventeenth-century texts merely have the very general terms 'affliction' and 'tribulation'.

Only a few manuscripts of books of hours resemble Richard's text as far as the next lines are concerned. There is no doubt that all versions go back to one original, but numerous successive scribal errors have in some places led to an entirely new wording and interpretation. Only Richard's Hours and a few others[240] mention the 'concord' between God and men which Christ 'restored'; the oldest text must have had *custodia* (keeping) into which Christ 'received' (*recepisti*) humanity and this is echoed by all other copies. In the next sentence the composer had probably written *omni incredulitate deposita paradisum cum sanguine mercatus es* (when all unbelief had been taken away you purchased paradise with your blood), but many copyists found this beyond them. Errors and variants of these words are legion, but the 'proscribed inheritance' (*proscriptam hereditatem, l'eritaige … prescripte*) is found in a small number of manuscripts which must therefore belong to one textual family.[241]

The series of Old – and some New – Testament examples led to minor confusion among individual scribes. The biblical knowledge of some of them cannot have been impressive. Misunderstanding of *de hur caldeorum* (out of the city of Ur of the Chaldeans) was eventually solved by putting *de manu* or *de manibus caldeorum* (from the hand(s) of …), but one scribe wrote that Noah was saved 'by Abraham from the waters of the flood'. The stories chosen hardly ever vary.[242] The writer of Richard's copy, however, left in no inconsistencies and produced a straightforward, comprehensible text. There is nothing in these lines that implies a more than usual personal involvement; no words were used that were not used in at least several other copies. It has to be stressed that though St. Brendan himself when faced with a real whale during his miraculous voyage to the Promised Land could *appropriately* pray: 'Save us, Lord, as you saved Jonah from the belly of the great sea monster',[243] none of these invocations in the prayer should be interpreted in a 'realistic' way. The stories of the biblical deliverances are general evidence of God's miraculous willingness to save men and their souls, they give promise of eternal life and are symbols of hope.[244] Few of the dozens of medieval Christians who used and liked the present prayer will have been in actual danger from lions, giants, whales or burning furnaces, or even of imprisonment or false witness, and to connect Richard III and his reputation with Susanna and the false testimony of the elders which, but for the intervention of Daniel, would have meant her death, is unjustifiable.[245]

In another context, but for the same general purpose, a series of biblical *exempla* was used to illustrate the power and effectiveness of the act of praying itself. In the *Tractatus de Regimine Principum,* a didactic work on the conduct of princes written for Henry VI in the late 1430s, probably by a clerical author, most of the biblical stories found in 'Richard III's prayer' are repeated in similar words to show that the protagonists prayed and were thereby saved: Peter prayed in prison and the chains fell from his hands, Christ prayed on the cross and he was saved.[246] The actual nature of the Christian's trouble is irrelevant, his confidence in God's goodness – of which the precedents bear witness – is what counts.

Only the later copies of the prayer allow for the insertion of the reader's name in the next sentence. The words *famulum tuum .N.* (*N* for *nomen* (name)) are very common in such texts. *Famulus tuus* (your servant) or *servus tuus* (your slave) with descriptive additions like *indignus* (unworthy) or *peccator* (sinner) are followed by *.N.* or by the owner's name. This helps to identify the owner and establish the fact that the book was made to order, or that it was produced for an individual woman (if it has the feminine Latin forms plus a name) or for a convent (if it merely has the feminine endings).[247] In Richard III's hours the phrase *famulus tuus* occurs several times, all in the non-committal masculine form.[248] The presence of the King's name in the hand of the scribe suggests a wish to give the prayer a personal application; the inclusion of the royal title as well is unique. The re-occurrence of *dolor* in this sentence is also unique to the present manuscript; 'tribulation', 'anxiety' and 'snares of enemies' are shared by almost all other versions.

Special significance may perhaps also be attached to the request for the intervention of St. Michael, which occurs only in Richard III's text of the prayer. St. Michael is the commander of the heavenly hosts, soldier, protector and fighter against evil *par excellence*. He represents the angel sent to deliver the three children from the fire, Daniel from the lions and St. Peter from his chains, and his name is often connected with these miraculous deliverances. He is the receiver of the souls of the dead and is mentioned to this day in the Offertory chant in the mass for the dead: 'may the standard bearer Michael introduce (the souls of all the faithful departed) to the holy light'.[249] In the *Song of Roland* the hero's soul is taken to Paradise by God's angels, 'Cherubim and Saint Michael of Perils'.[250] The saint's feast day, 29 September, was specially added to the Calendar of the present manuscript in a neat late fifteenth- or early sixteenth-century hand. This insertion suggests that some owner had a particular devotion for the archangel – or at least regretted the omission. His inclusion in the prayer may also be the result of St. Michael's frequent association with the biblical stories of deliverance, in liturgical texts as well as in other contexts.

After a brief reference to the rebellion of Absalom and Achitophel's evil counsel – to which again no other meaning should be attributed than that of another instance of God's intervention[251] – there follows a long enumeration of events in the life and passion of Christ, which resembles the one towards the end of the Litany: *Per misterium sancte incarnationis, libera. Per sanctam nativitatem tuam, libera …*, and was probably inspired by it. In the prayer the text goes on to include all the events and instruments of the passion and ends with the Seven Words spoken by Christ on the cross.[252]

The Seven Words had been the subject of special devotion and study since the twelfth century. Early writers called them the Five or the Six Words and the order in which they were quoted varied, but seven became the usual number. They were described as 'the seven leaves of the mysterious vine', 'the seven flames of Christ's love' or 'the seven notes that the nightingale sang so high that his noble heart broke'.[253] Elaborate treatises were written on the meaning of each and there survive at least two devotional texts based on them which were especially popular in English books of hours: the 'prayer on the Seven Words' attributed to Bede, and the 'Fifteen Oes', often said to have been composed by St. Bridget of Sweden. Both are included in Richard III's Hours.[254]

The Seven Words are followed by a renewed request for protection and deliverance in words which occur in many prayers: *ab omni malo atque ab hoste maligno et ab omni periculo presenti preterito et futuro* (from all evil and from the devil and from all danger, present, past and future). Again the name *Ricardum* was erased in these lines, though *regem* was not, and again *doloribus* (grief) is unique to this manuscript. The prayer is here given intensity by naming Christ's deeds after his crucifixion: his legendary descent into hell, his resurrection, his appearance to his apostles, his ascension, as well as the descent of the Holy Ghost and Christ's return on the day of Judgement. This series is common to all copies, though words vary and some, for instance, read *per diem tremendum iudicii* (by the *fearful* day of judgement).

The next passage gives thanks to God for all his gifts and remembers the unworthiness of the suppliant: 'because you made me out of nothing'. It is similar in spirit to the preamble of the foundation charter of Richard's college at Middleham (1478):

Know ye that where it haith pleasid Almighty God, Creatour and Redemer of all mankynd, of His most bounteuouse and manyfold graces to enhabile, enhaunce and exalte me His most simple creature, nakidly borne into this wretched world, destitute of possessions, goods and enheretaments, to the grete astate, honor and dignite that He haith called me now unto, to be named, knowed, reputed and called Richard Duc of Gloucestre, and of His infynyte goodnesse not oonly to endewe me with grete possessions and of giftys of His divyne grace, bot also to preserve, kep and deliver me of many grete jeoperd', parells and hurts, for the which and other manyfold benyfits of His bounteuouse grace and godnesse to me, without any desert or cause in sundry behalves shewed and geven, I, daily and ourly according to my deuty remembring the premisses, and in regognicion that all such goodnes cometh of Hyme ... [255]

In the prayer the words of gratitude are common to all copies, but the sincerity of Richard's feelings may perhaps be gleaned from the Middleham text.

The Old Testament words describing the hidden ways in which God's wisdom works, quoted by St. Paul in his first letter to the Corinthians, form the last section that occurs in virtually all copies of the prayer. About half the manuscripts traced have an ending more or less identical with that of the present book, the others have a shorter one. Instead of *Rogo te dulcissime* ... they read *Te adoro et laudo et glorifico nomen tuum quia to es benedictus et laudabilis et gloriosus in secula seculorum. Amen* (I worship and praise you and I glorify your name, because you are blessed and praise-worthy and glorious for ever and ever), or words that are very similar and equally brief. There seems to be no connection between the place of origin of the manuscript and the version of the prayer's ending, and both occur in books of hours as well as prayerbooks, though the later and the printed texts tend to have the longer version as in Richard III's hours.

In a few instances [256] the prayer is only part of a more complicated devotional text which also includes psalm 135 *Confitemini domino* (Give thanks to the Lord) with the antiphon *O clavis David et sceptrum domus Israel* (O key of David and sceptre of the house of Israel) and sometimes a prayer beginning *Domine Ihesu Christe preliator fortissime princeps exercitus celestis domine qui dyabolum vincisti* (Lord Jesus Christ, strong champion, prince of the heavenly army, lord who defeated the devil). There is no trace of these other texts in Lambeth Ms. 474.[257]

Richard III's preference for the prayer called after him was not unique. We have seen that Maximilian I and Frederick of Aragon, princes whose lives were as troubled and uncertain as that of the English King, owned the text and must have used it. In Eastern Europe the King of Poland had it in his personal prayerbook made for him in his youth, and a certain Wenceslas Magirus filled in his name in the place where the former owner's had been erased.[258] In Spain a Thomas inserted his name in the text of the prayer about 1460[260] as did, in Italy, an unknown Elisabetta,[261] a Nicholas,[262] Iohannes d'Ascoli[263] and others. French,

German and Dutch owners of books of hours or prayers must have put in their Christian names when they spoke the words in their language. In the Burgundian lands the Dukes or their wives said the prayer for themselves or others, and a Flemish contemporary of Richard III, Paul Deschamps of Bruges (died 1483), servant of the Dukes in several capacities, owned a text that was decorated with a full-page miniature of the Trinity of an unusually high quality, probably a copy of a panel painting and made about 1475.[264]

In England the prayer was not unknown: John Talbot, first Earl of Shrewsbury, and Margaret Beauchamp, his wife, both had the Latin text in their French-made books of hours – hers was probably made for her on the occasion of her marriage in 1425.[265] The prayer also occurs in two manuscripts made in London in the 1460s. No owners of the first are known. The prayer is decorated with a six-line initial D depicting Christ as Salvator Mundi, dressed in a grey robe, blessing and holding an orb. The text of this copy is not closely related to Richard's and the origin of the King's copy cannot be sought here.[266] Unfortunately the wording of the prayer in the other London manuscript also precludes any close connection with his text. This book of hours probably belonged to his sister Anne, Duchess of Exeter, but the fact that the series of biblical deliverances in her book is far longer than in her brother's and that there are many other basic differences make it unlikely that the one derives from the other.

No other English manuscripts containing the prayer have been found. Most of those now in British libraries appear to be of French, Italian or Spanish provenance. Only in the sixteenth century did the text, in Latin and English, and printed in Antwerp for English Catholics, become better known in this country.[268]

The question remains: how did Richard III learn of the prayer's existence? Though few English copies now survive it may have been fairly well known at the time and if so, any intimate could have brought the comfort-promising text to the King's attention at a particularly distressful period of his reign. It may, of course, have been the King's confessor, the Franciscan friar and doctor of theology John Roby, who copied it or had it copied, together with other devotions, into his master's personal book of hours, but it must be emphasised that his intervention is as conjectural as the prayer's Franciscan origins.

Text and Translation[269]

[f.181]O dulcissime Domine Iesu Christe verus deus qui de sinu patris omnipotentis missus es in mundum peccata relaxare, peccato-res[270] afflictos relevare, captivos redimere, in carcere positos dissolvere, dispersos congregare, peregrinos in suam patriam reducere, contritos corde medicare, tristes confortare, dolentes et lugentes consolari, digneris me absolvere de affliccione temptacione dolore infirmitate et paupertate seu periculo in quibus positus sum et consilium michi dare, Et tu domine qui genus humanum cum patre in concordia restituisti, ac illam proscriptam hereditatem a paradiso cum proprio precioso sanguine mercatus es, et inter homines et angelos pacem fecisti, dignare inter me et inimicos meos stabilire et firmare concordiam, graciam et gloriam tuam super me ostendere et effundere, ac omne illorum odium quod contra me habent digneris mitigare declinare extinguere et ad ni[f.181v]chilare, sicut extinxisti odium et iram quod habuit esau adversus iacob fratrem suum, brachium tuum extentum et graciam super me ostende, et me liberare digneris ab omnibus angustiis et doloribus in quibus positus sum, sicut liberasti abraham de manibus caldeorum et Isaac de immolacione per arietem, Iacob de manibus fratris sui esau, Ioseph de manibus fratrum suorum, Noe per archam ab aquis diluvii, Loth de civitate sodomorum, et famulos tuos moysen et aaron et populum israel de manu pharaonis et de servitute egipti, et similiter saul de monte gelboe, David regem de manu saul et golie gigantis, Et sicut liberasti susannam de falso crimine et testimonio, et Iudith de manu olofernis, danielem de lacu leonum, et [f. 182] tres pueros de camino ignis ardentis, Ionam de ventre ceti, filiam mulieris chananee a diabolica vexacione et adam de profundo inferni cum tuo proprio precioso sanguine, ac petrum de mari, paulum de vinculis, Ita domine iesu christe fili dei vivi liberare digneris me famulum tuum regem [Ricardum] ab omni tribulacione dolore et angustia in quibus positus sum et ab omnibus insidiis inimicorum meorum et mittere digneris in adiutorium meum michaelem archangelum contra eos, et eorum mala consilia que contra me faciunt vel facere volunt digneris domine iesu christe evacuare, sicut evacuasti consilium achitofel qui consolatus est absalon contra david regem, ita me liberare digneris per sancta beneficia tua, per incarnacionem tuam, per [f.182v] nativitatem tuam, per baptismum tuum, per ieiunium tuum, per famem et sitim, per frigus et calorem, per laborem et affliccionem, per sputa et calophia, per alapas et clavos, per coronam spineam, per lanceam, per potacionem aceti et fellis, per sevissimam et turp[i]issimam mortem tuam crucis et per verba que cum pendisti in cruce dixisti primo patrem deprecans domine pater ignosce illis, quia nesciunt quid faciunt dixisti domine latroni pendenti in cruce, hodie mecum eris in paradiso, dixisti domine matri tue, Mulier ecce filius tuus et discipulo, Ecce mater tua, dixisti domine heloy heloy lamazabathani, quod interpretatur deus meus deus meus ut quid dereliquisti me dixisti domine, sicio, scilicet salutem animarum sanctarum dixisti domine, Pater [f. 183] in manus tuas commendo spiritum meum, dixisti domine consummatum est, Significans labores et dolores quos pro nobis miseris suscepisti, iam finisti, Propter hec omnia rogo te dulcissime domine iesu christe ut custodias me famulum tuum Regem [Ricardu] m et defendas ab omni malo atque ab hoste maligno et ab omni periculo presenti preterito et futuro et liberes me ab omnibus tribulacionibus doloribus et angustiis in quibus positus sum, et me consolari digneris, per descensionem tuam ad inferos, per resurreccionem tuam, per frequentem discipulorum tuorum consolacionem et visitacionem per admirabilem ascencionem tuam, per graciam sancti spiritus paracliti, per adventum tuum in die iudicii, domine exaudi me per cuncta beneficia tua pro quibus [f.183v] tibi gracias ago et refero et pro cunctis beneficiis seu bonis michi collatis quia tu me fecisti ex nichilo et redemisti me ex tua benignissima pietate et misericordia ab eterna dampnacione perpetua[271] vitam eternam promittendo, Propter ista et alia que oculus non vidit nec auris audivit, nec in cor hominis ascendit, Rogo te dulcissime domine iesu christe ut ab omnibus periculis corporis et anime pro tua pietate me adiuves, et me semper deliberare digneris et succurrere, et post huius vite cursum ad te deum vivum et verum me perducere digneris, Qui vivis et regnas deus, Per christum dominum nostrum Amen.

O most sweet lord Jesus Christ, true God, who was sent from the bosom of the almighty Father into the world to forgive sins, to comfort afflicted sinners, ransom captives, set free those in prison, bring together those who are scattered, lead travellers back to their native land, minister to the contrite in heart, comfort the sad, and to console those in grief and distress, deign to release me from the affliction, temptation, grief, sickness, need and danger in which I stand, and give me counsel. And you, Lord, who reconciled the race of man and the Father, who purchased with your own precious blood this proscribed inheritance of paradise and who made peace between men and angels, deign to make and keep concord between me and my enemies, to show me and pour over me your grace and glory, and deign to assuage, turn aside, destroy, and bring to nothing the hatred they bear towards me, even as you extinguished the hatred and anger that Esau had for his brother Jacob. And stretch out your arm over me and spread your grace over me and deign to deliver me from all perplexities and sorrows in which I find myself, even as you delivered Abraham from the hand of the Chaldeans, Isaac from sacrifice by means of the ram, Jacob from the hands of his brother Esau, Joseph from the hands of his brothers, Noah from the waters of the flood by means of the ark, Lot from the city of the Sodomites, your servants Moses and Aaron and the people of Israel from the hand of Pharaoh and the bondage of Egypt, and likewise Saul from Mount Gilboa, and King David from the hand of Saul and of Goliath the giant. And even as you delivered Susanna from false accusation and testimony and Judith from the hand of Holofernes, Daniel from the den of lions, and the three young men from the burning fiery furnace, Jonah from the belly of the whale, the daughter of the woman of Cana from the torment of devils, and Adam from the depths of hell, with your own precious blood, and Peter from the sea and Paul from chains.

Even so, lord Jesus Christ, son of the living God, deign to free me, your servant King Richard, from every tribulation, sorrow and trouble in which I am placed and from the plots of my enemies, and deign to send Michael the Archangel to my aid against them, and deign, lord Jesus Christ, to bring to nothing their evil plans that they are making or wish to make against me, even as you brought to nothing the counsel of Achitofel who incited Absalom against King David, even so deign to deliver me by your holy goodness, your incarnation, your nativity, your baptism, and your fasting, by the hunger and thirst, the cold and heat, by the labour and suffering, by the spit and buffets, by the blows and the nails, by the crown of thorns, the lance, the drink of vinegar and gall, by your most cruel and shameful death on the cross and the words which you spoke while on the cross. First, praying to your Father, you said: 'Lord Father forgive them, for they know not what they do'. You said, Lord, to the thief hanging on the cross: 'Today you shall be with me in paradise'. You said, Lord, to your mother: 'Mother, behold your son', and to the disciple: 'Behold your mother'. Lord, you said: 'Heloy, heloy, lamazabathani', which being interpreted means: 'God, my God, why have you forsaken me?' You said, Lord: 'I thirst', that is to say for the salvation of the blessed souls. Lord, you said: 'Father, into your hands I commend my spirit'. You said, Lord: 'It is finished', signifying that you had come to the end of the labours and sorrows which you bore for us wretches.

By all these things, I ask you, most sweet lord Jesus Christ, to keep me, your servant King Richard, and defend me from all evil, from the devil and from all peril present, past and to come, and deliver me from all tribulations, sorrows and troubles in which I am placed, and deign to console me, by your descent into hell, your resurrection, by your frequent visits of consolation to your disciples, your wonderful ascension, by the grace of the Holy Spirit the Paraclete, and by your coming on the Day of Judgement. Lord, hear me, in the name of all your goodness for which I give and return thanks, and for all those gifts and goods granted to me, because you made me from nothing and redeemed me out of your most bounteous love and pity from eternal damnation by promising eternal life.

Because of these things and others which the eye has not seen nor the ear heard, and which the heart of man has not understood, I ask you, most sweet lord Jesus Christ, to save me from all perils of body and soul by your love, and to deign always to deliver and help me, and after the journey of this life to deign to bring me before you, the living and true God, who lives and reigns, O God. Through Christ our lord. Amen.[272]

SEVEN

Richard III's Piety

The study of the piety of the past, whether of individuals or communities, is a difficult one.[273] Individual piety is a particularly controversial subject and the attitude to religion of men like Richard III and Henry VII has given rise to statements so divergent and conflicting that one despairs of ever coming to an acceptable conclusion.[274] In the context of Richard III's personal book of hours, however, some consideration of his piety cannot be omitted.

The very nature of the subject forces the historian to make an assessment of personality: piety can have the most intimate and private origins and is, in the last analysis, the relationship of the individual to God. Any study of the piety of a particular historical figure is, in fact, prompted by curiosity about character and motives.

The study of medieval piety, both general and particular, presents a number of problems and some of them should be borne in mind.[275] Are we, for instance, to judge the piety of a late medieval person by contemporary standards, or by ours? Can the piety of women be compared with that of men? Are we to take the examples of remarkable piety that have come down to us in biographical sources as the rule, the exception, or, at the least, as manifestations of an ideal to which most people aspired? What sources should be used, and can quantitative methods based for example on the study of many wills, ever be trusted on this 'personal' subject?[276] Finally, and most pertinently, can modern observers be sufficiently aware of their own shortcomings, scepticism and prejudice?[277]

Piety in the individual was a required characteristic in the fifteenth century – devotion to God was expected, if not always achieved. For the convenience of this study piety has here been divided into three parts. First, faith, the individual's dependence on, and relation to, God, which is ultimately unknowable and unmeasurable. Secondly, private devotion, of which only some intimates are aware (confessors, friends and prying historians), a subject which a source such as Richard III's hours should illuminate. Thirdly, there is public piety, of which the manifestation was visible to all and which was meant to be visible; it was part of the individual's social duty in a period when all were members of the Christian church, obeying its teachings, and when communal activities were carried on under the aegis and patronage of the church in its many guises, from the parish or fraternity to the prince's luxurious chapel.

The purpose of all piety was to ensure the salvation of one's own soul and those of others. The greater the consequence of the individual the more difficulty he might experience in achieving that aim, and the more responsibility he bore for those less able to care for themselves. Public piety and charity went hand in hand and were rarely distinguished as separate activities, as both benefited the soul.[278] The seven corporeal acts of mercy describe contemporary charity in both symbolic and practical terms: feeding the hungry, giving drink to the thirsty, clothing the naked, sheltering the homeless, visiting the sick, ransoming prisoners and burying the dead. Any crowd of the disadvantaged might contain the silent figure of Christ himself and it was dangerous for anyone with a soul to save to forget this – a prince had to remember it at all times.[279]

When tested on his public piety Richard III seems to have passed with flying colours in the opinion of most of his judges. His achievements in this field have been called conventional, but genuine and active.[280] His foundations were, above all, his response to the demands placed on a prince to provide prayers for the living and the dead: the college of priests at Middleham, Yorkshire, that at Barnard Castle, county Durham, St. William's College at York, which was to house a hundred chantry priests, and the endowment of four priests at Queens' College, Cambridge. These were also conscious contributions to the better education of the clergy and the improvement of services in their localities, particularly as regards the first two examples in the north of England. The vicars choral of York Minster were given a much needed endowment, and Richard can also be found paying the stipend of a chaplain at Hawes, an isolated village in Wensleydale, for one year while he was king. Richard's interest in the universities as the source of clerical education is well attested, particularly at Cambridge, where Queens' College received an endowment for four priests in 1477, further grants in 1484, and the building of King's College Chapel was generously supported.

His patronage and employment of learned and able men has also been praised. It is closely related to his founding of religious establishments and is another aspect of a prince's support of the church and awareness of the need to improve the condition of his subjects and provide himself with good counsellors and administrators. Richard only appointed two bishops while king, Thomas Langton of Salisbury and John Shirwood of Durham, but both were noted for their learning and the first was an enthusiastic educator himself. The list of other learned men in his employment is a long one.

Gifts, large and small, went to religious establishments throughout Richard's adult life, ranging from a bell to the shipmen's fraternity in Hull to contributions to widows at Great Malvern and Carlisle Cathedral Priory, but the exact scale of his everyday giving cannot be ascertained as neither his ducal nor his regal accounts survive.

The very visibility of this kind of religious activity, however, has laid it open to attack. How can a man of Richard III's political reputation be considered genuinely pious on such evidence? When confronted with a king whose personality seems to combine ruthlessness in politics with correct behaviour in religious matters[281] both medieval and modern commentators have resorted with various degrees of enthusiasm to the charge of hypocrisy.[282] Writers have not always been aware that this particular indictment derives from several ancient 'authorities'. Some discussion of these and of past characterisations and explanations of Richard III is necessary before the evidence of the Hours can be presented.

Aristotle was the first to describe the tyrant as one who, in order to maintain himself and not from any genuine virtue in him, acts with such benevolence and liberality that the difference between him and a good king is not discernible even to his subjects.[283] According to the remorseless logic of Aristotle, and of his imitators like Giles of Rome, such a ruler always remains a tyrant.[284] To this philosophical and theoretical origin of the picture of the tyrant as hypocrite was added the literary tradition of Roman historians like Suetonius and, later, Tacitus.[285] Medieval and Renaissance writers took up their methods of tendentious psychological interpretation, descriptions of revealing habitual behaviour and suggestive atmosphere, all of which matched only too well with the Aristotelian depiction of the 'ideal' tyrant and with other images embedded in the medieval mind.[286]

However authoritative and time-honoured this picture of the smiling villain may be, until Richard III's guilt of any of his crimes is proved, the charge of hypocrisy cannot legitimately be added to the other accusations.

Richard III has also been the victim of another curious prejudice, based on the slenderest of evidence. Students of his psyche have interpreted his official exhortation to his bishops to promote 'virtue' and condemn and punish 'sins and vices', and his proclamation against rebels and traitors, 'adulterers and bawds' in 1483, as both evidence of his insincerity and proof of 'an obsession with sexual morality'.[287] (The existence of two acknowledged illegitimate children seems to be the only fact used to support this theory.) It was common for rulers of Richard's time to cite moral failings against their enemies – accusations of incest, homosexuality, witchcraft and murder were as much part of late fifteenth-century propaganda as undemocratic behaviour, intolerance and racism are of twentieth-century political slander.[288] The use of such methods, however unattractive, can equally well be said to reflect a sensitivity to public opinion and an awareness of what would appeal most to their subjects in a particular situation. The promotion of public virtue was also what a prince was expected, and frequently told, to encourage – it was a central dictum of the concept of the 'good prince' and part of the church's teaching. There is no real evidence of any personal preoccupation with sexual morality on Richard's part – in his condemnation of misbehaviour he was behaving properly and 'by the book'. Insincerity is not ascertainable.

Even if some of the myths surrounding Richard's personality are disposed of (as attempted above), it has to be admitted that a study of Richard III's public piety does not contribute to an understanding of his personality. Everything depends on the interpreter's prejudice.

Sympathisers will conclude that such a pious man cannot have been capable of the crimes he has been accused of, while detractors will stick to the charge of hypocrisy and add another fault to his discredit. More neutral commentators will be left with the inconsistency.

Is inconsistency a problem? Is it possible to collect all that is known about Richard and achieve a finished picture? Not only will every gatherer of facts colour the data, make a personal collection and inevitably slip in a few uncertain but appealing facts, but it is also doubtful whether anyone is ever consistent in real life. If a historical person appears to be consistent, is he or she more human and plausible for being so? In the context of a discussion of Richard III it is perhaps worth reflecting that goodness and acknowledged piety do not always go together, efficient kings have been devout men, saints are not necessarily bad kings.

Richard's private piety must be studied next in this attempt to understand him better.

Everyone in the late middle ages who had attained a certain level of education knew what God and his church expected of the faithful – by the late fifteenth century the laity were extremely well provided with information about these expectations and how to satisfy them and save themselves from too long a term in Purgatory.[289] Ideally everyone should lead a life wholly devoted to God and spend their days in prayer and meditation – this ideal was most closely pursued by the celibate clergy. Even busy men and women of the world, however, could go about their duties in an awareness and love of Christ and devote time to religious matters as often as possible, leading the so-called 'meddled life'.[290]

It has been suggested with some credibility that late fifteenth-century princes tried to reconcile their ostentatious life-style with their religious consciences by increasing their charitable activities and by reforming their households morally as well as financially.[291] The observant or sensitive prince could have been painfully aware of how far his own way of life fell short of the ideal and how dangerously near everlasting punishment he stood. One way of salving his conscience and warding off punishment could be a meticulous correctness in his charity. Charles the Bold, for example, organised his in detail. It is said that whenever he was about to leave a town his almoner brought him a list of objects deserving his charity: old people, prisoners, women who had recently given birth, orphans, people whose possessions had been lost by fire, merchants brought low by fortune. All of them had apparently been carefully registered and checked. The Duke signed the paper and authorised the amounts to be given to each and the alms were distributed before the almoner departed. In this, as in other matters, the Duke of Burgundy liked to do his duty.[292]

The ideal set by his religion should also have made a prince aware of his own exalted position, of God's goodness to him and the fickleness of fortune. The last would not have needed expounding to Richard III: in his preamble to the statutes of the foundation of his college at Middleham[293] – a text that was made when he was still Duke of Gloucester and may bear his personal stamp – he expresses deep gratitude to God. He contrasts the 'nakedness' of his birth to the pomp of his titles using terms that were not uncommon, but the contrast cannot have been mere formula to a man who only a few years before had been in exile for the second time in his life, had had to borrow a few shillings in order to continue his journey, and now ruled most of the north of England.[294]

Apart from the Middleham statutes we do not have any personal documents of Richard III, no will or personal letters to throw light on his private piety, but we do have the book of hours he used. One fact is immediately apparent: the book is beautiful, but in such a simple and unostentatious way that it cannot have been chosen for its outward appearance. It is evident that the King did indeed choose it, or was given it, for its contents and, more specifically, its many prayers. The volume contains more of these than is usual. Both Richard and the book's first owner must have wanted this large number of devotions, and a more than conventional interest in such texts may be assumed, particularly in the first purchaser. Some of the original material in the book even suggests that it was made for a clergyman or someone with a clerical background. The most remarkable fact about the book as far as Richard himself is concerned is that he had at least ten pages of devotional text added while he was king.[295]

The central piece of this discussion must be the meaning and implications of the long prayer that was added for Richard's personal use.

Scholars have used the King's preference for this particular prayer as an argument for assuming that during his reign he was 'in a disturbed emotional condition' and felt 'under the constant threat of invasion'.[296] Some have gone so far as to state that the prayer 'reveals an attitude of mind bordering upon persecution' (sic) and that in it 'the highly charged reference to Susannah ... so prominently stands out'.[297] Richard must either 'have thought himself innocent ... or he was a very advanced schizophrenic'[298] – the one or the other of these possibilities is emphasised by implication according to the sympathies of the commentator.

All such conclusions have to be strenuously denied. After analysing the text, comparing Richard's text with other copies and relating his use of the prayer to the use some of his contemporaries made of it, it can be safely concluded that there is nothing ominously unique in his choice and that no part of it can be used to reveal evidence of his guilt or even of any sense of guilt.

This is not to deny that Richard III evidently felt the need for this particular prayer and that it may reveal to us some of his needs. The main impression is one of sorrow and grief; it is an entreaty for comfort and help against an inimical world *and it is full of hope*. In the conventional words and the well-known phrases there is trust and hope and a desire to trust and hope – others, too, after all did not hope in vain. The repetitive incantations may have strongly affected a mind brought up in the Christian beliefs of the late medieval world, steeped in its conventions, fed on its images, and led it to the intense devotional concentration that was thought desirable. On a more prosaic level, repeating the words daily for a month or more might induce a *catharsis,* a 'cleansing' of the mind, beyond our sceptical comprehension. This applies to anyone. In Richard's case it could have led the supplicant from the Castle of Care to the Tower of Truth, 'turned all his trouble and sorrow to comfort and joy'.[299]

Why was this prayer of such significance to Richard III (and to many men and women of various backgrounds from the late fourteenth to well into the seventeenth century)? Why did he find it so attractive when many devotions of a similar nature were already available in his book of hours? Its length may have appealed to him and its apparent inclusion of all possible formulas for use in extreme distress, sorrow and danger. Equally attractive may have been its intensity, expressed in a number of recitals reminiscent of the litany of saints, or its familiar language, using words taken from the daily liturgy, and its reference to well-known biblical stories. Finally there was its close association with the passion of Christ, which inspired such devotion all through the later middle ages.[300]

Comparison with other prayers, however, effectively reveals its over-all conventionality and lessens the importance of the text itself. The key to Richard III's needs and hopes lay in the rubric, and that key is lost. If only the rubric had survived – which was written for him and which he must have seen whenever he spoke the prayer and which must as often have given him hope or warning (according to the reader's prejudice) – then it would be known whether he regarded the text as merely 'a devout and useful prayer', as an authoritative relic of the hand of St. Augustine himself, or perhaps as a magical remedy that would certainly bring him comfort so long as he was 'without mortal sin'.

'Richard III's prayer' as well as all other facts known about him suggest that his private piety was no different from that of his contemporaries, although his sorrows and cares may have been greater than most people's. He directed his attention to the same things: he, too, adopted favourite saints to be his patrons and intermediaries with God[301] and had particular objects of veneration. His wealth enabled him to honour his chosen saints in a public and expensive fashion, dedicating stalls to them in his collegiate foundations and ordering the use of special devotions to them. His preference for Saints Ninian, George and Anthony stands out, they occur at both Middleham and Queens' College, Cambridge, but they are closely followed in importance by Saints Cuthbert, Barbara and Katherine.[302] The reasons for their choice are fairly obvious: Ninian and Cuthbert were the saints of the western and eastern marches towards Scotland respectively, St. George the patron of England and the order of the Garter; Anthony was a healer and associated with the boar, the animal supporting Richard's own arms; Barbara protected from sudden death and Katherine patronised scholars.[303] There are thirty-five other saints – 'that I have devotion to' – mentioned in the Middleham statutes to be honoured with double feasts. Several are obvious choices simply because of their importance, John the Baptist and John the Evangelist, Peter and Paul, Michael, Anne, Elisabeth and Christopher, and they are joined by the equally obvious choices of Wilfred of Ripon and William of York. For the rest, no conclusion can be reached about the precise reason or need behind Richard's choice.

In the matter of relics Richard is known to have expressed veneration for the holy oil of St. Thomas Becket with which he was annointed, and to have placed a 'value' on the remains of Henry VI, which he had removed to Windsor.[304] It is also known that he thought as he should on the subject of the crusade[305] and that he touched for the king's evil like other English kings.[306] Nothing is either surprising or unusual about these details: Richard's religion was that of the later middle ages, humanised, fervent and personal within the strong and controlling framework of the church.[307]

The 'library' that Richard owned as duke and king has given rise to several conclusions about his piety – some of them totally unfounded. It has been said that his books on religious subjects reflect a 'genuine religious interest'[308] and that he was 'something of a puritan'.[309] It has been stated that '*nine* of Richard's books demonstrate the type of his piety', that is 'the rather morbid piety of the late fifteenth century' (our italics).[310] In fact, of the eleven books that he probably owned only *four* can be called devotional:[311] his hours – described here – is one. Then there are an English verse paraphrase of the Old Testament, bound in with courtly tales which he owned as duke, an English translation of the New Testament and an English version of the *Book of Special Grace* of Mechtild of Hackeborn which he owned with his wife.

The Old Testament paraphrase is probably representative of his tastes as a young man; the New Testament translation is an orthodox book – he would have had episcopal permission to own it – and does not imply any Lollard or 'Puritan' tendencies.[312] The visions of Mechtild are perhaps the most interesting, but it was not an unusual book and as it bears Anne Nevill's name as well as Richard's it may reflect her taste as much as his.

There is remarkably little to go on. Richard was interested in religious literature to some extent, but the fact that only one of the books he owned was actually made for him[313] makes it difficult to be certain of his preferences. His extant library has a bias towards historical and informative books, but that was nothing unusual and only confirms an impression of conventionality.

Richard III still eludes us. Of the three elements of religious life that we have postulated, faith, the first, is not open to discussion and not subject to human judgement. Of the other two, private and public piety, the most valuable and devout acts, according to Christian doctrine, are those not noticed by others – this makes them a problematic subject of historical research.

As far as Richard's personality as a whole is concerned we get no nearer to him than his public life and the few glimpses of his private life allow. Almost every interpretation made so far can be balanced by another, and every verdict seems based on too little evidence. We will have to be satisfied with our own prejudiced explanation or live with the enigma. The enigma has best been summed up by Sir Walter Raleigh, more experienced in politics and the ways of princes, and more devout than most, in his *History of the World*:

> For the heart of Man is unsearchable: and Princes, howsoever their interests be seldom hidden from those many eyes which pry both into them, and into such as live about them; yet sometimes either by their own close temper, by some subtil mists, they conceal the truth from all reports.[314]

Notes

General Introduction

1. A good general discussion and description of books of hours, their history and usual contents is in Leroquais, *Livres d'Heures,* vol.1, pp.i–lxxxv. Other useful and recent books are Calkins, *Illuminated Books*; de Hamel, *A History,* ch.6; Wieck, *The Book of Hours.* A bibliography on all aspects of the subject is H. Koestler, 'Stundenbücher. Zur Geschichte und Bibliographie', *Philobiblon,* vol.28:2 (1984), pp.95–125.

2. Most of these devotions will be discussed in some more detail in the Contents section, ch.5 below.

3. The psalter of the laity contained all 150 psalms in their numerical order; the clergy's psalter was more complicated: the psalms and their additional texts were divided into the parts needed at the liturgical hours and the days of the week, since the clergy were expected to sing all in the course of one week. The missal contains all texts to be read and sung during the Mass. The breviary is the equivalent of the missal for the Divine Office, containing all the texts, including the psalms, to be said or sung at the eight canonical hours. The laity's book of hours was the equivalent of the clergy's breviary. Further 'specialisation' of these books led to the existence of the gradual, which has the text and the music of the sung parts of the mass, and the antiphonal, which has the same for the hours. Both were large books to ensure that they could be read by the choir.

4. Delaissé, 'The Importance', pp.203–4.

5. 'Little' because it is considerably shorter than the liturgical prayers that the clergy and religious have to say every day. It has to be emphasised that the shorter offices have the same religious 'value', but they were/are *additional* texts for the clergy and the *main* devotions for the laity. See the introduction of

The Little Office of the Blessed Virgin Mary, by A Master of Novices, Carmel of Plymouth 1983, and Stadlhuber, 'Das Laienstundengebet', p.286.

6. For a comprehensive survey of the liturgical day see K. Young, *The Drama of the Medieval Church,* 2 vols., Oxford 1933, vol.1, pp.15–75.

7. John 1, 1–14 (Christmas); Luke 1, 26–38 (Annunciation); Mat. 2, 1–12 (Epiphany); Mark 16, 14–20 (Ascension); John 18, 1–19, 42 (Passion). Nicholas Rogers has kindly informed us that the inclusion of these passages was customary in France, to a lesser extent in Flanders. When they occur in English hours (about 8 per cent according to his researches) there are indications of strong French influence.

8. See *LH,* vol.1, pp.xxxi–xl and references given there; Delaissé, 'The Importance', pp.205–8.

9. *LH,* vol.1, pp.xii–xiii.

10. *Ibid.,* p.xxix; and, for example, Gougaud, 'La prière', *passim.*

11. Barratt, 'The Prymer', *passim.*

The Manuscript, Its Scheme of Decoration and Status

12. Described and collated by M. R. James, *Lambeth,* pp.650–4. It has been the subject of an article by Joyce Melhuish which introduced it to Ricardian circles in 1968, and of an MA dissertation by Kathryn Jones, London University 1981. It appeared in the National Portrait Gallery Exhibition of 1973, *Richard III,* catalogue by Pamela Tudor-Craig, pp.26–27, item 51.

 We are indebted to Dr Mirjam Foot of the British Library for the identification of the binder.

13. M. R. James' collation: $1^2\ 2^8$ (wants 8) $3^6\ 4^8 - 24^8$ (wants 7) / 25 (two) 26 (one): 2 flyleaves.

14. Jones, 'A Study', p.4, estimates the original size as 225 x 150mm.

 Comparison has been made particularly with the Altenburg Hours, which is such a close parallel to Richard's and has large margins on two of its sides (220mm. by 150mm.), and with Bodleian Rawlinson liturg. d.1 (245mm. by 153mm.) which was cropped by a careful binder who left margins of 5–10mm. on the top and side margins of a full vinet (f.26) and a possibly over-generous 30mm. on the bottom margin.

15. For other comments on the text, its ink, the abbreviations used and the alterations made by the original scribe, see Jones, 'A Study' pp.5–6

16. 'Vinet' is the fifteenth-century term used by painters, later *vignettes.* It comes from *vigne* or vine scroll. A demi-vinet extended half or two-thirds round the text. See M. Rickert in Manly and Rickert, pp.562–3, Craigie, 'Champ and Vynet', p.171 and Diringer, p.443.

17. *Champ* = ground. This is the fifteenth century painter's term, see references in n.16.

18. Spriggs, 'Nevill Hours', p.104 n.1. The Nevill Hours is at Berkeley Castle; the Bodleian Library holds a complete set of colour transparencies which have been consulted for this study.

19. Pächt and Alexander, vol.3, no.922; James, *Lambeth*, no.459, ff.1–71 (he called the work fine). Lambeth 459, f.19v, is illustrated: Saunders, *English Illumination*, vol.2, pl.124.
20. We are most grateful to the Abbot of Altenburg for supplying us with photographs of the manuscript as well as a copy of the catalogue in which it appears: Egger, *Schatzkammer Altenburg*, item 25, where the Hours are erroneously given as North French *c.* 1400. The provenance of the manuscript is given by Schmidt, p.48.

The Illumination: Style, Workmanship and Date

21. Calkins, *Illuminated Books*, pp.243–9. De Hamel, *History*, ch.6. Delaissé, 'The Importance', pp.205–210 and *passim*. *LH*, vol.1, pp.xl–1. Wieck, *The Book of Hours, passim*.
22. Tudor-Craig, *Richard III*, pp.26–7 item 51. Melhuish, 'Hours of Richard III', pp.2–4.
23. This is a subjective statement. Compare the fact that Margaret Rickert criticises colouring that includes a lot of yellow, *Painting*, p.166.
24. Diringer, pp.21–3 for the definition of illumination. Millar, *English Illuminated Manuscripts*, pp.29–34. Alexander and Kauffmann, pp.90–1 for a useful and succinct summary of late gothic illumination 1290–1500 followed by a description of the representative manuscripts. Marks and Morgan, pp.22–31 and plates, is another helpful summary. Kuhn, 'Herman Scheerre', pp. 136–156 analyses in detail the change in style. Rickert, *Painting*, p.165 points out the limitations of our information for this period and of the analogies that can be made between manuscripts. Most recently Sandler, esp. vol.1, introduction.
25. See n.35 below. Diringer, p.443. See also Sandler, vol.1, pp.19–23 on the problems of interpreting foreign influences.
26. *LH*, vol.1, p.xli.
27. Herbert, *Sherborne Missal, passim. English Book Illustration*, vol.1, p.12. Rickert, *Painting*, pp.163–5. Millar, *English Illuminated Manuscripts*, p.33. N. Rogers on Siferwas in *Thames and Hudson Encyclopaedia of British Art*, p.244. Tolley, 'John Siferwas', *passim* and esp. pp.561–78. Siferwas' Dominican background had a very considerable effect on his iconography; whether as a friar he was ever for long a member of a London workshop is a matter of debate; he was alive in the 1420s. See Friedman for other work possibly by Siferwas.
28. Rickert, 'Reconstruction of an English Carmelite Missal', pp.99–113 and her *Reconstructed Carmelite Missal, passim*. Rickert dated the missal to before 1391 but it has since been assigned with more certainty to the first decade of the fifteenth century; her 'Dutch' Master has also been transferred to Flanders. See Kuhn, *passim*, and Panofsky, vol.1, pp.115–118. Most scholars now agree with the Flemish theory.

   The other book produced in England in this period, the Big Bible (BL. Royal I E ix), has been dated to *c.* 1412 under the patronage of Henry IV, and associated with Herman Scheerre. It is also held to be much influenced by the Flemish style, Kuhn, p.150 and Wright, 'The Big Bible', pp.17, 133–6.

29. Rickert, *Reconstructed Carmelite Missal*, p.94 and *passim*.

30. In chronological order the main works on Scheerre are:-
Millar, *English Illuminated Manuscripts*, pp.30–32; Rickert, 'Herman the Illuminator'; Kuhn, 'Herman Scheerre', preferred a Flemish rather than a Cologne origin for Scheerre, (as did Panofsky, *Early Netherlandish Painting*, vol.1, pp.115–118); Spriggs, 'Unnoticed'; Rickert, 'New Herman Attributions', notes that thirty years of research had added little to Herman's known career and adds words of caution about extending his work; she summarises the existing research in *Painting*, pp.166–174 and pls. 168–176; as do Alexander and Kauffmann, pp.104, 105–9; Spriggs developed Scheerre's *oeuvre* with more confidence in 'Nevill Hours', and was convinced of his Cologne origins; Turner, 'Wyndham Payne Crucifixion', reestablishes Scheerre's reputation but doubted the Cologne origins as well as the Broederlam influence; N. Rogers in *Thames and Hudson Encyclopaedia*, p.222, summarises. See also Tolley on Scheerre, pp.529–547 and Wright, pp. 188–209.
   The recent Paternoster Row discovery is put forward in Christianson, *Memorials*, p.50.

31. The dates of all these manuscripts are taken from Turner, 'Wyndham Payne Crucifixion'. We are grateful to Nicholas Rogers for discussing the dating of BL. Add. Ms. 16998.

32. Turner, 'Bedford Hours and Psalter', pp.267–8. Brown and others, 'Manuscripts from the Dyson Perrins Collection', p.32. Turner in 'Wyndham Payne Crucifixion' handsomely apologised to Scheerre for his previous low opinion of his talent, p.21.

33. Bodleian Library, Bodley 264, ff.218–270v. Rickert, *Painting*, pp. 164–6, 175. Kuhn, pp.154–5 (on the 'Princess Joan' group which may also be called the 'Johannes group'). Wright, p.181 and Turner, 'Wyndham Payne Crucifixion', p.11. The view that Johannes was a follower of Siferwas is not now maintained.
   We are much indebted to Michael Orr for discussing the 'Johannes' group with us and sharing his research on the Hours of Elizabeth the Queen.

34. BL. Add. Ms. 50001. This was previously in the Henry Yates Thompson Collection, see *Descriptive Catalogue, Second Series,* item 59. After Elizabeth of York it passed to her cousin Edward Stafford, Duke of Buckingham (ex. 1521).
   Brown and others, 'Manuscripts from the Dyson Perrins Collection', pp.31–32, compare the Elizabeth Hours unfavourably with the Bedford Hours and Psalter. Rickert, *Painting*, pp.174–6 also finds the Hours less delicate and restrained in their layout and less well planned. See also Turner, 'Bedford Hours and Psalter', p.270 and his 'Wyndham Payne Crucifixion', pp.11–12, *English Book Illustration*, vol.1, p.13 and Tolley, pp.570–8. It is illustrated in colour, Marks and Morgan, pl.36.

35. It has been suggested that Scheerre's workshop combined with the heirs of another major establishment, perhaps when he left England, Schmidt, 'Two Unknown English Horae', p.53. This idea was an attempt to explain in practical terms the interplay of models, traditions and influences observed by art historians in the London school of illumination at this time – it is unlikely it actually took place. It is now considered that artists had small workshops, congregated in one area, collaborated, used each other's models, etc., see esp. Farquhar, *Creation and Imitation*, pp.41–3, 50, Calkins, *Distribution of Labour*, pp. 10–11, 52–7.

36. Wieck, *the Book of Hours*, pp.60–1, *LH*, vol.1, pp.lxxix–lxxx.

37. Other mss. on which the Advocates 18.6.5 artist collaborated contain similar Annunciations: BL. Add. Ms. 16968, f.10, Cambridge University Library Add. Ms. 4086, f.9 and Cambridge Trinity College Ms. B113, f.20. We are much indebted to Dr Lynda Dennison for pointing out this early English use of the crossed arms motif and explaining the inter-relationship of these mss. Her arguments are expressed more fully in chs. 9 and 11 of her thesis.

38. On the fertility of English imagery in the second half of the fourteenth century see Sandler, vol.1, p.21 and *passim,* and on the close association of the Bohun and Litlyngton groups and the Carmelite Missal, vol.1, pp.34–37, vol.2, p.172.

It has been pointed out to us by Nicholas Rogers that an ultimately Italian origin for the crossed hands is also possible, see the altarpiece by Giovanni del Biondo (fl.*c.* 1356–1399) in the Ospedale degli Innocenti in Florence, illustrated Richard Fremantle, *Florentine Gothic Painters,* London 1975, fig.509. This Virgin also wears a thin diadem.

39. Of the same circle as van Eyck, the Limbourg brothers produced a Virgin with both the crossed hands and a thin circlet or band through her hair in the Belles Heures (f.30), 1409–12. We are indebted to Nicholas Rogers for this reference.

Several *later* continental examples from manuscripts of the crossed hands can be instanced: Wieck, *The Book of Hours,* pl.1, figs.12, 34, Panofsky, vol.2, fig.108b; or the hands in repose in Fitzwilliam Museum Ms. 49, f.28, illustrated Rogers, Thesis, pl.33.

40. Panofsky, vol.1, pp.86–89, 112–118, vol.2, figs.104, 156, 161, 165, and Rogers, Thesis, ch.4, esp. pp.79–83, and p.141. (See also Wright, pp.171–5.) For an example by the Boucicaut Master, BL. Add. Ms. 16997, f.51.

41. Herbert, *Sherborne Missal,* p.28 and pl.2. See also n.27 above on Siferwas.

42. Now in two parts, BL. Royal 2 A xviii and Rennes Bibliothèque Municipale Ms. 22. Analysed by Rickert, 'Beaufort Hours and York Psalter', pp.238–246, and her *Painting,* p.170. She is corrected in many particulars by Rogers, Thesis, pp.85–91. The original manuscript was an unusual psalter with additions made in London between 1401 and 1410, probably 1404–7. One of the additions was the very fine Annunciation with 'portraits' of the book's commissioner, John Beaufort the elder, Earl of Somerset (d.1410), and his wife Margaret Holand (d.1439), painted by Scheerre. Other additions were the imported full-page

miniatures by the Flemish artist called the Master of the Beaufort Saints, pasted in to illustrate the memorials of saints. After the death of John Beaufort the book was divided: the psalter went to his wife Margaret Holand and then to John Holand, Earl of Huntingdon (d.1443), Henry Holand, Duke of Exeter (d.1475), and to his wife Anne of York for whom were added birth dates of members of the house of York in or after 1461. (This is now Rennes Ms. 22, see Leroquais, *Les Psautiers,* vol.2, pp.176–181.) The small portion containing the Annunciation and 12 full-page saints passed to John Beaufort Earl of Somerset (d.1444) and his wife Margaret Beauchamp of Bletsoe (d.1482) who had it placed at the beginning of her book of hours commissioned in London in the early 1440s. From her it passed to her daughter Margaret, Countess of Richmond, and is now BL. Royal 2 A xviii. The hours is a much poorer piece of work and William Abell has been suggested as its painter (Alexander, 'William Abell', p.166).

For the general acceptance of Scheerre as the painter of the Annunciation, see e.g. Turner, 'Wyndham Payne Crucifixion', pp.16–22, Alexander and Kauffmann, no.74.

43. Reposeful, long-fingered hands 'cupped inwards' have been noted as characteristic of his Virgins, Turner, 'Wyndham Payne Crucifixion', pp. 13–14. (This Crucifixion shows the Virgin with hands crossed at her breast.) See also Wright, pp.191-8.

44. See especially Rogers, Thesis, pp.136–142, on Lat. liturg. f.2 which may have been owned by Henry Lord Fitzhugh (d.1427); it is a complicated (and very damaged) manuscript, part being poor quality work produced soon after 1400 for the English market in Flanders and the rest being additional, and later, work done by Scheerre and others in England. We are grateful for Nicholas Rogers for discussing the date of the manuscript with us.

45. BL. Add. 42131, f.7. Rickert, *Painting,* pp.172-4 and her 'Some new Herman Attributions', p.88. Kuhn, pp.149–50. Turner, 'The Bedford Hours and Psalter', esp. p.268 and his 'Wyndham Payne Crucifixion', p.21.

46. Other closely related Annunciations in this manner, with one hand upraised, can be found in the Chichele Breviary, one of the mss. signed by Scheerre (Lambeth Ms. 69, f.4v, illustrated Panofsky, vol.2, fig.175, and see Wright, p.312), and in BL Stowe Ms. 16, a much mutilated book of hours of before *c.* 1410, which has a delicate rendering that may be by Scheerre himself (f.9. See Rickert, *Painting,* pp.169–70.)

47. Spriggs, 'Nevill Hours', p.104–130 and pl.29a. She attributes f.15 to an associate of Scheerre and f.100 to an associate of Johannes.

48. Property of Major J. A. Abbey's executors, Ms. JA.7398. Described in Sotheby's Catalogue in December 1967, item 46. At the time this book went to press the Clarence Hours came up for sale again: it is described and illustrated in colour in Sotheby's Catalogue, 19 June 1989, item 3018. The decoration and miniatures are closely related to such manuscripts as the Bedford Hours and Psalter

and Bodleian Library Rawlinson liturg. d.1, containing both Scheerre- and Johannes-type elements.

49. Blackburn Museum and Art Galleries, Hart Ms. 21018, has no helpful indications of provenance; only the Christian names of children born at Isleham, Wicken and Granchester, Cambs., 1522–9, are mentioned. It has historiated initials of the Annunciation and the Passion. It has several demi-vinets rather than full vinets with these and with one six-line initial A decorated in a smiliar way to those in Richard III's Hours. Its rank and quality compares with the secondary decoration of Richard's Hours and the Altenburg manuscript, but its colouring is generally poorer, there is less gold and no three-dimensional effects. The whole planning of Hart 21018 in text layout and decoration is careless. Despite its more elaborate historiation, Hart 21018 is a poorer quality manuscript, its three- and two-line initials are in blue and pink with white patterning and with gold, a type that does not occur in Richard's Hours but is used for the lowest rank of illuminated initials in the Altenburg manuscript. See also Alexander, *Treasures of the North-West,* item 46.

50. Schmidt, p.51. He depended partly on the earlier opinion that BL. Add. Ms. 16998 was *c.* 1405.

51. BL. Add. Ms. 42131, f.122. Rickert, *Painting,* p.175, notes this painter's anaemic women. (Turner, 'Bedford Hours and Psalter', p.269 rather surprisingly makes *this* painter the finest of the book, but this was before he apologised to Scheerre for his low opinion of his work.) The long necked, whey-faced female type is very common, see the several Virgins in the Nevill Hours, ff.29v, 33v, 35, 78v, or the mother of Alexander, Bodley 264, f.2v (Marks and Morgan, pl.35); it can on occasion be very charming as in the Nevill Hours, f.29v or Rawlinson liturg. d.1., f.110v. And see Wright, p.195, on the female type used.

52. There are several similar variants in the Bodleian Lat. liturg. f.2 (f.19v), the Nevill Hours (eg. ff.33v, 78v) and Rawlinson liturg. d.1, as well as the crowns of the bride and groom in the Bedford Hours and Psalter, f.151v (Marks and Morgan, p.34), but these are all crowns, not coronals.

53. Nicholas Rogers has drawn our attention to the fillet worn by the Virgin in a *Legenda Aurea,* probably from Bruges *c.* 1405–10, Glasgow University Ms. Gen.1111, f.71. And see n.39 above.

54. Its series of full page miniatures and its borders immediately suggest continental taste, as do the reorganisation of the figures in the Annunciation and Funeral scenes (f.193v) and the use of David to illustrate the Penitential Psalms (f.133v). Hints of practices associated with the Caesar Master and the Owl Master are also present and K. L. Scott's forthcoming book will no doubt elucidate these links.

55. Panofsky's word, vol.1, p.404 n.2. This manuscript was in the Dyson Perrins collection until 1958. Warner, *Descriptive Catalogue of the Dyson Perrins Collection,* vol.1, pp.64–8 gives a detailed description, and plates 24–7. See also *Dyson Perrins Collection,* Sotheby's 1958, part 1, pp.45–7 and pl.D, and Adams, *Ninth*

Report... Pierpont Morgan Library, pp.27–32 and plates. It is now M.893 in this Library's collection. The Annunciation is shown in colour in Marks and Morgan, pl.38 and see p.114.

56. Illuminating the psalter in this manuscript are a series of miniatures on the life of David by the artist of its Annunciation and another. These are closely related to a similar series in Victoria and Albert Museum Reid Ms. 42, an English psalter. This relationship suggests a date in the 1430s, as does the more dubious evidence of the dress depicted in the manuscript. We are indebted to the assistance of Mr. Gregory Clark of the Pierpont Morgan Library and Dr. Rowan Watson of the Victoria and Albert Museum for details about the manuscripts in their care.

    The miniatures by the second artist of the Warwick Hours (which include the Requiem Mass and Last Judgement referred to below) have been ascribed by J. J. G. Alexander to William Abell, an English painter of modest talent who rejected the gentler forms of the International Gothic style (perhaps a natural result of his lack of talent) preferring a linear and angular style and strong, vibrant colouring (Alexander, 'William Abell', pp.167, 168–9). This ascription is, however, doubted by Gregory Clark and others.

    It has been suggested that the Richard III Annunciation is a copy of the one in the Warwick Hours (Tudor-Craig, *Richard III,* p.27. She is followed in this by Jones, 'A Study', pp.10, 28). This theory ignores the evidence of other far closer versions of this model. 'Copying' of either manuscript by the other is unlikely – all that can be said is that both Annunciations derive from the same model.

57. For discussions of this manuscript and its associations see K. L. Scott, 'A London Illuminating Shop', pp.172–182 and also Sutton and Visser-Fuchs, 'Richard III's Books IV: Vegetius' *De Re Militari,*' pp.545–9.

58. Before we leave the Annunciation, a couple of features common to this school of artists may be noticed: the figure of the angel who appears in many other compositions besides the Annunciation and who frequently doubles as St. John the Evangelist; and the floor tiles, usually green, which become ubiquitous in English historiation.

    Compare the St. John in Bodleian, Rawlinson liturg. d.1, f.110v, Gough Liturg. 6, ff.30, 32, Nevill Hours, f.26, or the Clarence Hours, f.44v. See Spriggs, 'Nevill Hours', p.129 on the tiles. Rickert, *Painting,* p.173, described the green tiles used in the Bedford Hours and Psalter's Annunciation as innovative. Tiles were an extremely common flooring in mss. originating in the Low Countries, see Rogers, Thesis, plates.

59. James, *Fitzwilliam Museum,* p.xxxvi, Leroquais, *Psautiers,* p.xlviii, and Wieck, *Book of Hours,* pp.124–6.

60. For Lat. liturg. f.2 see n.44 above. Bodleian Ms. Canon. Liturg. 116, f.92v has an almost equally poor version, by the Loredan Master (see Rogers, Thesis, p.92 and references there cited), and another early example occurs in BL. Sloane

2863, f.82b (*ibid.*, pp.67–72). All three mss. also have similar Annunciations to Richard III's and it can be assumed their Christs in Judgement would have been equally similar in type. See Spriggs, 'Unnoticed' pls.17 and 19 for illustration of Canon. Liturg. 116 and Lat. liturg. f.2.

61. Similar funerals can be found in French manuscripts as well – the model was as ubiquitous as that of the Annunciation, e.g. Boucicaut Master of which de Hamel shows two examples, *History*, p.179.

62. This manuscript has many points of similarity to Richard III's Hours, referred to below. It is a Sarum Hours and dated to *c.* 1420, Pächt and Alexander, vol.3, no.869.

63. Alexander and Kauffman, item 80, note the close affiliation between the Gonville ms. and Rawlinson liturg. d.1. It is also, perhaps more, closely affiliated to the Clarence Hours.

64. Turner, 'Bedford Hours', p.268.

65. Edinburgh University Ms. 39 is a mutilated ms. close to the Warwick Hours and Psalter in style. The initial for the Office of the Dead survives (f.70): four singing clerics and a fifth holding their book behind the coffin; mourners – one with dramatically clasped hands at the foot of the coffin may be the widow; two candlesticks, tiled floor. Illustrated in Borland, *Descriptive Catalogue ... Edinburgh University Library*, Ms. 39.

66. Comparison cannot be made with the Altenburg Hours as it has only the one picture of the Annunciation. The Nevill Hours has neither Funeral or Mass.

67. James, *Fitzwilliam Museum*, p.xxx. Wieck, *The Book of Hours*, p.97. For early Netherlandish versions for the English market see above, n.60.

68. By this date an image from David's life could also be found in English books of hours to introduce the Penitential Psalms e.g. Widener Ms. 2. Wieck, *Houghton Library*, item 46. The Annunciation and Funeral are similar to those discussed here, but with such distinctive dissimilarities that clearly other models are also at work.

69. Alexander and Kaufmann, p.91.

70. Turner, 'Bedford Hours and Psalter', p.268, fig. 2.

71. Compare for example the St. Peter in Rawl. liturg. d.1, f.11v or both the saints in the Nevill Hours, ff.23v, 27, 31, all in natural colours.

72. The Clarence Hours also has a monochrome dog (f.22v) and an unsuccessful monochrome pink lion (?) on f.28. The closely related Gonville and Caius Ms. 148/198, f.56 has a large green monochrome dog similar to that in the Clarence Hours.

73. The Hours of Elizabeth the Queen has 'portraits' in many initials.

74. Turner, 'Bedford Hours and Psalter', pp.267–70 and his later opinions in 'Wyndham Payne Crucifixion', pp.21–2. See also Rickert, *Painting*, pp.173–4.

75. Rawlinson liturg. d.1. ff.99v–111v.

76. The Passion initials of Rawlinson liturg. d.1 have been attributed to Johannes by Turner ('Bedford Hours and Psalter', p.270). These Passion scenes and those

in the Clarence Hours are remarkably similar in iconography but not always in style (Michael Orr). The small Passion scenes of the Bedford Hours and Psalter have been cautiously attributed to Johannes by Rickert (*Painting,* pp. 173–5) but Turner was inclined to give them to an associate who also worked on the Hours of Elizabeth the Queen ('Bedford Hours and Psalter', p.270 n.12). These contrary attributions and opinions all illustrate the extent of collaboration that went on during the production of these manuscripts.

It was Rickert (*Painting* p.248 n.89) who first noticed the importance of Rawlinson liturg d.1 as a 'link' manuscript displaying the influences of Scheerre *and* Johannes. The Clarence Hours and the Nevill Hours are equally important, while Richard III's Hours is a minor example of the same phenomenon.

We are most grateful to Michael Orr for his opinion.

77. Initials e.g.: Big Bible, ff.222, 234v illustrated Saunders, *English Illumination,* vol.2, pls. 120, 121; Rawlinson liturg. d.1, ff.7, 101; Gough Liturg. 6, f.22; Nevill Hours, f.8 has the same initial as the Richard III Annunciation; Clarence Hours, f.15; Gonville and Caius 148/198, ff.1, 56, 175.

   Coiled acanthus centres e.g.: Rawlinson liturg. d.1, ff.11v 59; Clarence Hours, ff.22v, 23v, 40v (very common); Gough Liturg. 6. ff.30, 41v; Nevill Hours, ff.40, 51v, 62; Rennes Ms. 22, f.32; Bedford Hours and Psalter, f.183; Hours of Elizabeth the Queen, ff.10v 100 and *passim*; Warwick Hours, f.29.

   Scrolled borders enclosed in 'masonry' e.g.: *Li Livre du Graunt Cam,* f.218; Clarence Hours, *passim*; Bedford Hours and Psalter, f.12v; Hours of Elizabeth the Queen, *passim*; Warwick Hours and Psalter, f.44v.

   A magnificent example of a blue acanthus leaf folded back on itself four times in the centre of an initial A composed of pink acanthus occurs in the Bodleian Ms. Gough Liturg. 6 (f.41v) by Herman Scheerre or his talented associate to whom the rest of the historiation in this manuscript has been attributed.

78. Very similar flowers to this one occur in pink and other colours, Rawlinson liturg. d.1, ff.57v, 103, 111, and Clarence Hours, ff.41v 60v.

   An endless comparison might be made of such three-dimensional flowers and leaves in manuscripts of this period, but this study has focused exlusively on the varieties found in Richard III's Hours.

79. Eg. 4- and 5-petalled flowers occur, Nevill Hours, f.62, Bedford Hours and Psalter, f.7, Rawlinson liturg. d.1, f.40, Clarence Hours, ff.32v, 115v, Hart Ms. 21018, f.7, 28v and *passim, Graunt Cam,* ff.218, 220, Rennes Ms. 22, ff.32, 119v and Altenburg Hours.

80. E.g. Bedford Hours and Psalter, ff.9,151v; Gonville and Caius 148/198, ff.254v, 276v; Clarence Hours, ff.22v, 53, 38, 100v (in orange and yellow). And compare Rennes Ms. 22, f.119v, illustrated by Rickert, 'Beaufort Hours and York Psalter', pl.11 (p.241). It has unfortunately only been possible to see a few photographs of this manuscript. Hart Ms. 21018 uses this device as well but there is no three-dimensional effect.

81. E.g. f.152. Compare Gough Liturg. 6, f.30 for collared trumpets, and Clarence Hours, *passim*, Rennes Ms. 22, ff.32, 94.
82. Schmidt, p.52. Rickert, 'Illumination', p.570.
83. Bedford Hours and Psalter, ff.83v, 135. Clarence Hours, ff.32v, 73v. Rawlinson liturg. d.1, ff.40, 59, 103.
84. Gonville and Caius 148/198, ff.1, 86v, 139, 206v. Elizabeth the Queen, ff.22, esp.24v. Warwick Hours, ff.12, 29.
85. Saunders, *English Illumination,* vol.2, pl.124: Lambeth Ms. 459, f.19v.
86. All these devices have fourteenth-century English precedents, see n.87 below.
    The Clarence Hours has subsidiary decoration in the same manner as Richard's, e.g. compare the initial I in Richard III's Hours, f.115v with Clarence Hours, ff.36v, 79, 113. The infill of some of the larger initials of Gonville and Caius 148/78 (e.g. ff.276v, 281) is similar to those of the Richard III ms., and the infill of the small initials in the Clarence Hours is often the same. The one-line initials and the line-fillers are the same in all three mss. Comparison may also be made with BL. Stowe 16.
87. Esp. Rickert, 'Illumination', pp.567–71 a particular study of borders and Sandler, vol.1, pp.37, 174, figs.387–418 *passim,* vol.2, p.164.
88. Illustrated Marks and Morgan, pls.36, 38. It is to be noted that other borders in these manuscripts do not have such a marked similarity to each other.
89. Rickert, *Painting,* pp. 175–6 on the changes in style visible between the Bedford Hours and Psalter and the Hours of Elizabeth the Queen.
90. This development may owe much to Netherlandish influence, see Rogers, Thesis, ch.xi on Mildmay Master and 'the Englishman', and K. L. Scott, 'A London Illuminating Shop', *passim.*
91. This is unusual; such a green border occurs round miniatures and initials in the Johannes group – Michael Orr.
92. This brownish or orange-toned pink is to be remarked in several of these manuscripts: the Great Cam, Clarence Hours, Richard III's Hours and the Bedford Hours and Psalter.
93. Gonville and Caius 148/198 uses a lot of olive green like the Clarence Hours.
94. Spriggs, 'Unnoticed', p.197. Wright, p.184. Panofsky, vol.1, p.114. Rickert, *Painting,* p.173 on the prevalent use of green in the Bedford Hours and Psalter. Rickert, 'Illumination', pp.567–71. Sandler, vol.2, pp.168–9 on the rich colours of certain late fourteenth century English manuscripts.
95. An echo of this effect can be seen in the Big Bible, BL. Royal 1 E ix, f.72v.
96. James, *Lambeth,* p.654.
97. The use of the title 'Master' does not necessarily imply a great talent in this case.

Ownership

98. It has been asserted that Richard was given the book by his wife and that it came to her from her Beauchamp mother. This is based on the idea that the illumination of Richard's Hours is a copy of the *later* Warwick Hours (see the

detailed examination of the illumination of Richard's Hours, ch.3, above). This theory was originally put forward by Dr. Tudor-Craig, *Richard III,* pp.27–8, and repeated in her 'The Hours of Edward V', pp.354–5. She was followed by Jones, 'A Study', pp.28–9.

99. See the discussion and notes of folios 9–14, 122– 122v, 139v–140v, 156v–160, 164v–165 and 179v in ch.5, Contents, below. The conclusion that the book was made for a woman, drawn by Dr. Tudor-Craig, *Richard III,* p.27, was based on its lack of 'grandness'.

100. See ch.5, Contents, below (f.179v).

101. Comparison with the handwriting of Richard III leaves little doubt that the note was actually written by him. For his royal signature see John Fenn (ed.), *Original Letters written during the Reigns of Henry VI, Edward IV and Richard III,* 2 vols., London 1787, vol.2, pl.7, no.2; J. G. Nichols, *Autographs of Royal ... Personages,* London 1829, [pl. 4], example 2 of 'The Latter Plantagenets'; Public Record Office C 81/1531/68, illustrated in Halsted, *Richard III,* vol.2, p.346. It also occurs on the first leaf of his mss. containing Guido delle Colonne's *Historia Troiae* and Geoffrey of Monmouth's *Historia Regum Britanniae* now at Leningrad, illustrated in Sutton and Visser-Fuchs, 'Richard III's Books: VII', pp.139 and 143.

102. M. K. Jones, 'Sir William Stanley', p.22.

103. Melhuish, 'The Hours of Richard III', p.3; Tudor-Craig, *Richard III,* pp.27–8, and Jones, 'A Study', p.27.

104. It is unlikely that the length or position of the note in the Calendar prevented its erasure: the obliteration of the word pope has been consistently and meticulously executed, and at least one rubric of more than five lines was scraped off completely in this ms.

105. End flyleaf. Noted by James, *Lambeth,* p.653, but since lost.

106. Jones, 'A Study', p.29; see *Testamenta Eboracensia,* ed. J. Raine and J. W. Clay, Surtees Society, 6 vols., 1836–1902, vol.5, p.51. There is no evidence in Richard's Hours that it ever included a psalter; the book is large as it is and the contents are unusually extensive.

107. Folio 1v, erased.

108. Last page: now missing, but seen by James, *Lambeth,* p.653.

109. The main analysis of the acquisition of the library is N. R. Ker's Supplement to M. R. James' Descriptive Catalogue of the Manuscripts in the Library of Lambeth Palace in *A Catalogue of the Manuscripts in Lambeth Palace Library Mss. 1222–1860,* by E. G. W. Bill, Oxford 1972, esp. pp.1–5, 27, and see also Ann Cox-Wilson, 'Lambeth Palace Library 1610–1664', *Transactions of the Cambridge Bibliographical Society,* vol.2 (1954–8), pp. 105–25. The 1612 catalogue of Bancroft's library refers to two *Maria Horaria* (Lambeth Records f.2, f.85); their size is not mentioned. The catalogue of Abbot's library contains a *horae* and an 'office of the Virgin' (Lambeth Records f.2, ff.62, 98); their sizes are said to be quarto and 16mo respectively. See also M. R. James, 'The History

of Lambeth Palace Library', *Transactions of the Cambridge Bibliographical Society,* vol.3 (1959–63), p.28. In H. J. Todd, *Catalogue of Archiepiscopal Manuscripts in the Library of Lambeth Palace,* London 1812, p.60, the manuscript's size is described as quarto, but this description appears to be used rather indiscriminately in this catalogue.

Analysis of Contents

110. For the Anonymous or Fitzhugh chronicle see Sutton and Visser-Fuchs, 'Richard III's Books: VI'. The passage on Ninian was copied from Bede's *Ecclesiastical History,* book 3, ch.4, the earliest source on the saint.

111. Dowden, pp. 156–8: at Queens' the collect of St. Ninian was to to said every day and two masses of him in every three weeks (the text of this mass is printed in *Arbuthnott Missal* … , ed. A. P. and G. H. Forbes, Burntisland 1864, pp.369–70); Dobson, pp.142, 145–6 (York); Raine, pp.161, 164–5, 169 (Middleham); *Victoria County History of Durham,* vol.2, London 1907, pp. 129–30 (Barnard Castle). See also Searle, *History of Queens,* p.89; D. H. Farmer, *Dictionary of Saints,* Oxford 1978. The same collect also occurs in the short hours of St. Ninian printed in E. S. Dewick, 'On a Ms. Book of Hours written in France for the Use of a Scottish Lady', *Transactions of the St. Paul's Ecclesiological Society,* vol.7 (1911–15), pp. 109–20.

112. An antiphon in the fifteenth century is a short devotional text introducing or ending, and more or less summarising, the contents of a longer one, e.g. a hymn, psalm or prayer; it is often short but may run to several lines (of verse). Antiphons differ with the use. – A versicle is a short line of verse sung by the priest and answered by a response. – Some memorials (or suffrages), translated into English, are printed in Wieck, *The Book of Hours,* pp. 165–6.

113. The scribe of these numerals also got confused when he added the dates for December, omitting 21 and putting in 29 twice.

114. For example, 7 October was called the Nones of that month, as was the seventh day of March, May and July, and the fifth day of the other months. 6 October was called 'the day before Nones' and numbered ii (literally *two* days before, because both days were counted), 5 October is numbered iii, etc. After the Nones the days were numbered in relation to the Ides, the fifteenth of March, May, July and October and the thirteenth of the other months, and when the Ides had passed, to the Kalends, that is, the first day of the next month. Thus on 16 October (here confusingly numbered 15) is written *xvii kl' Novembris:* seventeen days before the Kalends of November, again *including* 1 November itself.

115. The Golden Number is found by adding 1 to the year's number, dividing by 19 and taking the remainder (19 if the remainder is 0). In 1483 the Golden Number was 2 and the moon was new on 5 October. – The Dominical Letter indicates the relation of the day of the week to the calendar of the year, depending on what day the first Sunday of January fell. If this fell on the fifth

(as it did in 1483), it was given the letter e since 1 January always had a; all dates marked with e were Sundays in that year; thus Richard III's birthday in 1483 fell on the Thursday. Leap years had two Sunday letters, one for the part of the year before 29 February, one for the rest of the year. 29 February had the same letter as 1 March (d). In 1452, a leap year, the letters were b and a (Richard III was born on a Monday).

116. Loiseleur, pp. 198–253; Steele, pp. 108–21 and references given there. The rhymes in the present Calendar are those printed by Steele on p.117, beginning *Prima dies mensis et septima truncat ut ensis* (The first day of the month and the seventh cut like a sword). These days were also called *dies mali* (evil days), whence 'dismal'.

117. The present Calendar only differs from the 'standard' Sarum Calendar printed in Wordsworth, *Ceremonies,* pp.3–14, in including St. Aldelmus (25 May), St. Eustace and his companions (red, 2 November) and St. Clement (red, 23 November); in lacking Sts. Tyburcius and Valentianus (19 April), the Translation of St. Edmund (9 June) and St. Barnabas (11 June) and in having St. Cuthbert in black instead of in red (20 March).

118. Edward's Translation (13 Oct., fig.28) was left untouched. The erasure at 5 January was perhaps done because that date also had the Octave of St. Thomas Becket, but other feasts of St. Thomas were left untouched.

119. See the discussion of 'Richard III's prayer', ch.6, below.

120. See the chapter on Ownership, ch.4, above.

121. For a complete Latin text of the Hours of the Virgin with an English translation and introduction, see e.g. *The Little Office of the Blessed Virgin Mary,* by a Master of Novices, Carmel of Plymouth 1983; for an English text of the Hours and of all the usual items in a book of hours of Sarum use, see Littlehales, vol.1, pp.1–89, where the text is identical to that of Richard's Hours except for the omission or inclusion of a few prayers and some minor details.

122. Nicholas Rogers informs us that the inclusion of a *memoria* to St. Sitha or Zita (of Lucca, festal day 27 April) is highly unusual before the sixteenth century. He has found only a few fifteenth-century instances and is still studying her cult in England.

123. *RH,* nos. 14725–6; *AH,* vol.30, pp.32–5, item 13 (followed by similar texts); Mone, vol.1, pp. 106–10, item 82; Daniel, vol.1, pp.337–8; Julian, p.886, lists translations e.g. Chambers, part 1, pp. 168–70. Simmons, pp.82–7, has the text of the poem, the versicles, responses and the accompanying prayer *Domine ihesu christe* with an English translation, commentary on pp.346–52. See also Littlehales, vol.1, pp.15, etc. (a fifteenth-century translation); Searle, *Fitzwilliam,* p.xliv; Stadlhuber, pp.307–8, notes 151–3, and *passim* on the Hours of the Passion in general; Wieck, *The Book of Hours,* p.162; Woolf, pp.235–6 on the English versions of *Patris sapientia,* and on the influence of the hymn, and Barratt, pp.266–8, 272–3. In BL Ms. Add. 37787, ff.96v ff. the rubric of this

text reads: The lord [John] XXII composed these hours and granted to all who say them devoutly 100 days of indulgence. It is sometimes ascribed to Giles of Rome (Aegidius Colonna, died 1316).

124. See preceding note and Hoskins, pp.122–3, 197.

125. *RH*, no.29551; *AH*, vol.30, pp.106–7, item 47 (followed by similar texts); *Horae Ebor.*, pp.xxxii–xxxiii and 47, n.1, 49, n.1, 52, n.1, etc.; Searle, *Fitzwilliam*, p.xliv; English translation in Chambers, part 1, pp. 170–3. The pity and grief Mary felt at her son's suffering was a popular object of devotion in the fifteenth century, see Wilmart, *Auteurs*, pp.505–36; Stadlhuber, pp.313–5; Woolf, pp.239–73; Pfaff, pp.97–103.

The Hours of the Cross (or the Passion) are common in books of hours of Sarum use, those of the Compassion are rare (*ibid.*, p.103, n.1); Nicholas Rogers informs us they are very rare before the middle of the fifteenth century. In the present ms. the quatrains of *Patris sapientia* are headed 'antiphon' and have a two-line initial in Lauds and only one-line initials at the other hours. The invariable prayer has a three-line initial in Lauds, one-line initials at the other hours. Each quatrain of *Matris cor* has a three-line initial, suggesting that this was felt to be the main part of these composite short hours. It has to be remembered that these very short offices contain no psalms or lessons and that they occur under various names and in various combinations.

126. Folio 52, the *Salve regina,* with veriscles, responses and the prayers *Omnipotens sempiterne deus qui gloriose virginis ac matris marie corpus* (ff.52v–53), and *Famulorum tuorum quesumus* (f.53). Folio 53v, *Gaude virgo mater christi que per aurem concepisti* (*AH*, vol. 15, p.96, item 68; only the first three lines of each stanza are given in the present ms.; that was the original text, compare Meersseman, vol.2, pp.38–40, 206–8), with versicles, responses and the prayer *Omnipotens sempiterne deus qui divina gabrielis salutacione.* On f.54 are two very short prayers, *In omni tribulacione* and *Meritis et precibus,* with antiphons, versicles and responses.

127. Psalms, 6, 31, 37, 50, 101, 129 and 142.

128. The Gradual Psalms were probably sung by pilgrims going up the fifteen steps (*gradus*) of the Temple in Jerusalem. Apocryphal medieval tradition had it that Mary dedicated herself as a girl to God's service, ascended these steps alone and sang the fifteen psalms as she went (Meersseman, vol.2, p.6 and references give there).

129. The saints invoked in the Litany are listed below. Spelling and capitals follow the ms.; all individual saints are preced by *Sancte* or *Sancta* in full in the ms. but these words have here been omitted; the vocative has been maintained, the few abbreviations extended: maria, dei genitrix, virgo virginum, michael, gabriel, raphael, Omnes sancti angeli et archangeli, Omnes sancti beatorum spirituum ordines, iohannes baptista, Omnes sancti patriarche et prophete, petre, paule, andrea, iacobe, iohannes, thoma, iacobe, philippe, bartholomee, mathee, symon, thadee, mathia, barnaba, marce, luca, marcialis, Omnes sancti apostoli et evangeliste, Omnes sancti discipuli domini, Omnes sancti innocentes,

stephane, line, clete, clemens, sixte, corneli, cypriane, laurenti, vincenti, fabiane, sebastiane, cosma, damiane, prime, feliciane, potenciane, grisogone, ypolite cum sociis tuis, georgi, gervasi, prothasi, iohannes, marcelline et petre, iohannes et paule, crispine et crispiniane, christophore, albane, edmunde, lamberte, Omnes sancti martires, Silvester, leo, ieronime, augustine, ysidore, hillari, nicholae, martine, ambrosi, gregori, germane, romane, vedaste, taurine, iuliane, cuthberte, egidi, leonarde, antoni, philiberte, audoene, albine, amande, ausberte, sampson, paterne, patrici, remigi, basili, brici, wilfride, pauline, machute, Omnes sancti confessores, Omnes sancti monachi et heremite, anna, maria magdalena, maria egypciaca, felicitas, perpetua, petronilla, agatha, agnes, cecilia, lucia, scolastica, genovefa, margareta, katerina, elisabeth, paschalia, affra, barbara, batildis, radegundis, fidis, tecla, christina, helena, praxedis, sotheris, prisca, editha, ositha, fides, spes, karitas, Omnes sancte virgines, Omnes sancti et sancte.

130. f.68v Deus cui proprium est misereri semper et parcere propiciare animabus famuli tui ...

f.69 Preces populi tui quesumus clementer exaudi ...

Deus cui proprium est misereri semper et parcere suscipe deprecacionem meam ...

Omnipotens sempiterne deus qui facis mirabilia magna solus ...

f.69v Deus qui caritatis dona per graciam sancti spiritus ...

Deus a quo sancta desideria recta consilia ...

Omnipotens sempiterne deus dirige actus nostros ...

Pretende domine famulis et famulabus tuis dexteram ...

f.70 Ure igne sancti spiritus renes nostros ...

Acciones nostras quesumus domine ...

Omnium sanctorum tuorum quesumus domine intercessionibus ...

Ineffabilem misericordiam tuam ...

f.70v Omnipotens sempiterne [often: mitissime] deus respice propicius ad preces nostras ...

Fidelium deus omnium conditor et redemptor ...

f.71 Absolve domine animas omnium fidelium defunctorum ...

Pietate tua quesumus domine ...

These prayers occur at the end of the Litany in many books of hours, with endless variations in wording, number and selection. See, for instance, Littlehales, pp.50–1.

Many of them are still used at the end of the Litany in the modern Roman Catholic Church.

131. Hoskins, p.172; see *Horae Ebor.,* pp. 114–5, for the 'argument' of each psalm.

132. Searle, *Fitzwilliam.* p.xlix. A similar story is told of St. Nicholas: ' ... when he came to the words *in manus tuas,* which means "into Thy hands I commit my spirit", he breathed forth his soul to the sound of heavenly music' (de Voragine, *The Golden Legend,* Dec.6, p.21).

133. *Deus qui sanctam crucem ascendisti,* which is very close to the collect used in the memorial on the Cross on f.31v (Hoskins, pp.109, 130, 163, 215); *Gracias tibi ago domine ihesu christe qui me indignum famulum tuum* ... (similar to *Lyell,* no. 196; in BL Ms. Harl. 211, ff.146–146v, a very similar prayer is acribed to St. Edmund of Abingdon). In the *Antidotarius,* ff.32v–33, the last prayer is to be said 'after rising in the morning'.

134. In the Sarum Missal this text is part of the *Commendatio anime,* Wickham Legg, pp.428–9.

135. Turner, 'The Prayer-Book', pp.360–3 and references and mss. given there. *LH,* vol. 1, p.xxviii; Hoskins, p.115; complete text and similar rubric in *Horae Ebor.,* pp.116–22. Searle, *Fitzwilliam,* p.xlviii (full rubric).

   Because it was desirable but also impossible for the layman to say the whole psalter every day – and not everyone could afford or obtain a Psalter – abridgements were made very early on. Bede had made one, adapting the lines of verse for use by the laity, and others followed. A rubric virtually identical to the one given here, but without mention of St. Jerome, is found in an eleventh-century ms. (Meersseman, vol.2, pp.7–8). These abridged texts possibly explain how stories of people saying the whole psalter daily should be interpreted; for example, John Rous on Henry Beauchamp, Duke of Warwick (died 1445): 'he wolde ... dayle sey the hole daved sawter with owt he had the gretter besiness he cowd hyt with owt the boke perfyzzle [perfectly]' (*The Rous Roll,* ed. Charles Ross, Gloucester 1980, item 54).

136. *Omnipotens et misericors deus clemenciam tuam suppliciter deprecor* ...; *Omnipotens sempiterne deus maiestatem tuam suppliciter deprecor* ...; *Omnipotens sempiterne deus miserere famulo tuo .N...* .

137. Identical to the first half of a prayer in BL Ms. Harl. 211, f.116v. For the Verses of St. Bernard, see *LH,* vol.1, p.xxx. Searle, *Fitzwilliam,* p.1.

138. It has proved impossible to find another copy of these texts, which obviously form one devotion. It is a trope on the *Kyrie* very similar to some of those printed in *AH,* vol.47, pp.45–216. – The words prose, sequence and trope all have more or less the same meaning. They are basically texts composed to help remember the music of the liturgy. The most important instance is the final syllable of the *Alleluia* which was on some occasions prolonged to a number of musical notes and many proses were written (in rhythmical prose) to assist the singers' memory. When these prose texts became more metrical they came to be called sequences, because they 'followed' the *Alleluia.* Trope is a more general name for supplementary phrases or verses to ecclesiastical chants. Julian, *Dictionary,* under 'Latin Hymnody', 'Prose', 'Sequence' and 'Trope'.

139. No other copy of these texts has been found.

140. See note 138.

141. *RH,* no.9728; Walther, no.9850; compare *Lyell,* no.202; *AH,* vol.50, pp.558–68, item 381, has the text with some lines lacking and others added, as well as other versions and the music of the text.

142. Raby, pp.263–4; Szövérffy, vol.1, p.408; *Ancrene Riwle,* p.11; *LH,* vol.1, pp.155, 340; Mone, vol.1, pp.359–61, item 265; *Lyell,* no.216; *RH,* no.9910; Walther, no.9997; translation in Crippen, pp.77–80. In BL Ms.Harl. 211 ff. 128v–129, the prayer is said to be 'against the wiles of evil spirits'. For Berengar see R. W. Southern, 'Lanfranc of Bec and Berengar of Tours', in *Studies in Medieval History presented to F. M. Powicke,* ed. R. W. Hunt *et al.,* Oxford 1948, pp.27–48.

143. The first stanza (*Omnibus* ...) has a four-line initial, the other have three-line ones, and each is prefaced by a short rubric: *Ad crucem christi. Triumphale signum crucis, tu seductos nos reducis* ... (To the Cross of Christ. O triumphant sign of the Cross, you lead us back who have been led astray ..., f. 132), *Ad caput ihesu christi. Ave caput inclinatum, despective coronatum* ... (To the head of Christ. Hail, bowed head, shamefully crowned ..., f.132v), *Ad vulnus dextre manus. Salve vulnus dextre manus, velut phison rivus planus* ... (To the wound of the right hand. Hail, wound of the right hand, like the wide river Phison ..., f.132v), *Ad vulnus sinistre manus. Ave tu sinistra manus, perforata tu fuisti* ... (To the wound of the left hand. Hail, left hand, you were pierced ... f.133), [rubric lacking] *O fons aque paradisi, a quo quatuor divisi dulces fluunt rivuli* ... ([To the wound in the side.] O source of the water of paradise, from which four separate sweet rivers flow ..., f. 133), *Ad vulnus dextri pedis christi. Salve vulnus dextri pedis, tu cruoris rivum edis* ... (To the wound of the right foot of Christ. Hail, wound of the right foot, you bring forth a stream of blood ..., f.133v), *Ad vulnus sinistri pedis. Levi pedis perforati, ave vulnus in quo pati deus homo voluit* ... (To the wound of the left foot. Hail, wound of the pierced left foot, by which God was willing to suffer as Man ..., f.133v), *Ad virginem mariam. O maria plasma nati, que vidisti ihesum pati* ... (To the virgin Mary. O Mary, creature of your son, who saw Jesus suffer ..., f. 134), *Ad iohannem evangelistam. Iohannes evangelista, tu sacrarii sacrista in quo deus iacuit* ... (To John the Evangelist. John the Evangelist, you are the keeper of the shrine in which God lay ..., f. 134); *AH,* vol.31, pp.87–9, item 68 (it was a very popular text, *AH* records 25 mss., but many more copies survive); *RH,* no. 14081; *Lyell,* no.309; *LH,* vol.1, pp.247, 321; Wilmart, *Auteurs,* pp.527, 584; Gougaud, *Devotional ... Practices,,* p.78. See also Gray, pages given and esp. p.132.

144. *Lyell,* no.316; the prayer also follows *Omnibus consideratis* in Bodleian Library, Ms. Lat. liturg. f.9, f.60, and Ms. Rawl. liturg. d.1, f.108v; BL Ms. Royal 2 A viii, f.56; Ms. Harl. 211, f.138v, and Ms. Harl. 5315, f.87.

145. *Hoskins,* p.127; *Lyell,* p.65 and nos. 143, 245; *Anddotarius,* f.38 (*oratio Sancti Bernardi ad Jhesum*); *LH,* vol.1, p. 77, 356 (with ascription); vol.2, p.79; Leroquais, *Bréviaires,* vol.3, p.393.

146. No other copy of this text has been found.

147. Leroquais printed the text in full, *LH,* vol.2, p.342. *LH,* vol.1, pp.3, 111, etc.; vol.2, pp.46, 52, etc. and *PL,* vol.94, cols. 561–2 (with variant readings); *Lyell,* no. 159; Meertens, vol.2, pp.111–4; *Horae Ebor.,* pp.140–2, has a rubric

similar to the one in Richard III's Hours, but Bede is not named; *Antidotarius,*
ff.45v–46 (rubric with Bede's name); Haimerl, pp.74, 80, 86, 92, 95. Bennett,
Devotional Pieces, p.240, has a medieval English translation. See Barratt,
pp.276–8, and Woolf, pp.219–22, on the English versions. Wilmart, 'Le grand
poème', pp.273–4 and notes, discusses the prayer in the context of other
writings on the Seven Words. – The 'effect' of the prayer is not always the
same, see e.g. Haimerl, pp.57, 95.

148. Prayers said at, before or after the elevation of the host during mass are of
a special intensity; many survive in the vernacular: 'The consecration and
elevation are the most solemn and sacred points of the entire service, and,
since in times of great emotion the natural tendency is to revert to the mother
tongue, ejaculations and prayers in the vernacular arose to meet the demands of
public worship', Robbins, p.131.

149. *Hoskins,* p.123; *LH,* vol.1, pp.xxxi, 269 (?), 336; vol.2, pp.100, 252 (?), 443;
Haimerl, pp.80, 86,124; Wilmart, *Auteurs,* p.378, n.1 (12); Meertens, vol.1,
pp. 143–5 (quoting various rubrics); *Antidotarius,* ff.27v–28 (with rubric). The
text often has *amantissime* instead of *piissime,* and *eximiam caritatem,* and there
are many other variations of detail (see *Darmstadt,* vol.3, index: *Precamur te* and
Precor te).

150. University of London Ms. 519, f.128; *LH* vol.1, p.xxxi; Hoskins, p.123 (and
compare p.152); *Antidotarius,* f.27v (with rubric). See also Breeze, pp.88, 91 and
notes and references. In the context of this prayer the number of the wounds is
calculated at 6,666.

151. *Lyell,* no. 157; *Horae Ebor.,* pp.72, 177 (with similar rubric); Hoskins, p.111;
Haimerl, pp.57, 94, 126; *LH,* vol.1, pp.36, 40, etc.; vol.2, pp.25, 62, etc.;
Antidotarius, f.30 (with rubric); Meertens, vol.3, pp.7–8. Wilmart, *Auteurs,*
p.378, n.1 (10); Robbins, p.139 and n.20. The text sometimes reads *sanctissimam
carnem.* – The rubric in Richard III's Hours probably read: *Cuilibet dicenti hanc
oracionem sequentem inter elevacionem corporis christi et tercium agnus dei per papam
bonifacium sextum duo milia annorum indulgencie conceduntur ad supplicacionem philippi
regis francie.* Boniface VIII (1294–1303) and Philip IV, the Fair, are meant.

152. *Lyell,* pp.63–4 (rubric given), no. 123; Hoskins, pp.112 (... *pro perditione* ...[!]),
152 (wrong rubric); *Horae Ebor.,* pp.83, 177 (with a longer ending); Meertens,
vol.1, pp. 127–8 and notes; *Antidotarius,* f.38v; *LH,* vol.1, pp.41, 45, 122,
153; vol.2, pp.26, 108, 344; *Darmstadt,* vol.3, pp.28, 62,105. The text is either
ascribed to Boniface VIII or said to have been 'confirmed' by John XXII.
Alternative *incipit* are *Domine Jesu Christe (fili Dei vivi) qui* ... and *Gracias tibi ago
domine Jesu Christe qui* ...

153. For this prayer see also the discussion of 'Richard III's prayer' ch.6, below.
In many instances the text is connected with St. Michael, e.g. part of a
memorial of him and/or illustrated by a miniature depicting him: *LH,* vol.1,
pp.178,299,329; vol.2, pp.47,219, etc.; *Lyell,* nos 93, 94, 95; Hoskins, pp.114,
124 (long rubric); *Horae Ebor.,* p.125; Haimerl, pp.73,91,104 (called morning

prayer or *Segenspruch*); *Antidotarius,* ff.30v–31 (two rubrics). Bennett, *Devotional Pieces,* p.247 (medieval English translation).

154. *RH,* no.18189; Mone, vol.1, pp.155–8, items 119, 120; *Lyell,* no.357; Hoskins, p.125 (with rubric); *Horae Ebor.,* pp. 174–5; Daniel, vol.1, p.341; vol.2, pp.232, etc.; *LH,* vol.1, pp.16, 100. etc.; vol.2, pp.13, 24, etc. and 349–50 (full text of hymn and prayer). For a modern English translation Chambers, part 2, pp. 115–6. See also Flora Lewis, 'The Veronica: Image, Legend and Viewer', in *England in the Thirteenth Century, Proceedings of the 1984 Harlaxton Symposium,* ed. W. M. Ormrod, Woodbridge 1985, pp.100–6.

155. *Lyell,* no. 115; Hoskins, p.127; *Horae Ebor.,* pp. 174–5; Meertens, vol.2, pp.73–8 and notes; *Antidotarius,* f.52v; *LH,* vol.1, pp.183, 323; vol.2, pp.13, 24, 58. Together the hymn, the prayer and the psalm with verisicles and responses form a private 'little office' of the vernicle, in part identical with the one printed in S. Corbin, 'Les Offices de la Sainte Face', *Bulletin des études portugaises,* new series, vol.11 (1947), pp.1–62, esp. pp.28–29.

156. No other copy of this text has been found.

157. Though different in many details this text is very similar to prayers to the cross printed in Gjerløw, p.128 and references given there; Wilmart, 'Prières', pp.23–4, 51–2 and 'L'office', p.422; *Horae Ebor.,* p.114; *LH,* vol.2, pp.208, 299; Leroquais, *Psautiers,* vol.1, p.140.

158. Hoskins, pp.135, 354; *LH,* vol.1, pp.258, 273; vol.2, pp.37, 39, 232; *Antidotarius,* f. 14; Haimerl, pp.90, 126. Wilmart, *Auteurs,* p.381, n.2 (1). The text is virtually identical to one of the prayers used in the preparation for the mass today. The rubric in the present ms. reads: 'This prayer should be said before seeing the sacrament and it is beneficial to say it daily'.

159. Hoskins, pp.145, 354; *LH,* vol.1, pp.156 (?), 182, 237, etc.; Haimerl, p.126; *Lyell,* no.312. Wilmart, *Auteurs,* p.381, n.2 (2); according to Wilmart the prayer was not made by Aquinas. The beginning of the text varies but it is easily identifiable.

160. No other copy of this text has been found.

161. *Lyell,* pp.62–3; *LH,* vol.1, p.98; Leroquais, *Bréviaires,* vol.3, p.390; *Horae Ebor.,* pp.76–80; Hoskins, pp.111,116, 165, 171, 196, 211, 223; Meertens, vol.2, pp.15–21; *Antidotarius,* ff.47v–50. Maskell, vol.3, pp.275–82. For a discussion see Wilmart, 'Le grand poéme', pp.274–8; Rogers, 'About the 15 "O"s', *passim;* Bennett, *Devotional Pieces,* pp. 170–80 (medieval English translation). Meier-Ewert, *passim,* on the English translations by Caxton and others.

162. In other mss. these prayers occur as one; *Lyell,* no. 152 and mss. referred to there. The text sometimes begins *Domine* or *O Iesu.*

163. For this and other 'farced' versions, see Mone, vol.2, pp.203–14, esp. p.208; Woolf, p.282; Julian, pp.991–2. For this devotion: *Lyell,* no.358; Hoskins, p.133; *RH,* no.18318. For the *Salve Regina* itself: Thurston, pp.115–45.

164. *Lyell,* no. 106; Hoskins, p.133 (and pp.126, 143 in another marian context); Haimerl, p.127; Wordsworth, *Ceremonies,* p.122 and n.1. In the *Ancrene Riwle*

it follows after a devotion on the Five Joys of Mary. The prayer is still in use today.

165. For the connection of Sts. Mary and John, see Gougaud, *Devotional Practices,* p.78; Wilmart, *Auteurs,* pp.507–8 and also the prayer *Omnibus consideratis,* ff. 132–134 above. Bennett, *Poetry,* p.97.

166. See especially Wilmart, 'La Prière à Notre-Dame', *passim,* and *Auteurs,* pp.474–504, where the story of St. Edmund is told, and that of a young man whose soul was saved by St. John because he had said the prayer on fifteen consecutive days. *LH,* vol.1, pp.xxiv–xxv and *passim*; vol.2, pp.346–7 (full text); Wieck, *The Book of Hours,* ch.viii *passim,* and p.164 (English translation). The text in Richard III's Hours is virtually identical with the one printed by Leroquais and translated by Wieck. See also *Lyell,* no.264; *Horae Ebor.,* pp.67–8; Hoskins, pp.111, 191, 335, 361 (?); *Antidotarius,* ff. 52–52v and ff.61v–62v (both with long rubric); Barré, pp.194–7; Woolf, pp.222, 282, 394. In *PL,* vol. 158, cols.959–60, the text is printed among works ascribed to St. Anselm. There exists a version addressed to Mary only and the text is often illustrated by a *Pietà. –* In the present ms. both the *O intemerata* and the *Obsecro te* have masculine forms.

167. *LH,* vol.1, pp.xxiv–xxv and *passim;* Wieck, *The Book of Hours,* ch. viii, *passim* and pp. 163–4 (English translation); *Lyell,* nos.295, 365; *Horae Ebor.,* pp.66–7; Hoskins, p.355; Woolf, pp.282, 394.

168. This prayer continues ... *virgo maria per amorem unigeniti filii intercedas pro me peccatore* ... and until f.160v, line 6, it is virtually identical to a marian devotion in Meersseman, vol.2, p.240, and one in Barré, p.276 (tenth century). The next section beginning *O dulcissima maria ornamentum seculi. O pia domina. O margarita celestis sponsi.* (O sweetest Mary, ornament of the world. O merciful lady. O pearl of the heavenly bridegroom, ff.160v–161), is the salutation (*Per-te-Oration*) printed in Meersseman, vol.2, p.160, and Barre, p.277. Apart from the Virgin's names it also celebrates her actions: 'By you (*Per te*) ... the gates of paradise were opened. By you peace was made between angels and men ... All the apostles, martyrs and confessors, virgins and all the hosts of heaven obey you'.

169. No other copy of this suffrage has been found.

170. *Horae Ebor.,* p.64; Hoskins, pp.110, 164, 217; *Lyell,* p.69 (Ms. Lyell 30, ff.170v–171); *Antidotarius,* f.65.

171. *Lyell,* p.68 (Ms. Lyell 30, f.159v) and ms. references given there.

172. *RH,* no.21899; Walther, nos.20560–1; Mone, vol.2, pp. 165–9, item 457; *LH,* vol.1, pp.46, 248; Leroquais, *Bréviaires,* vol.2, p.324; *Antidotarius,* ff.64–5; Wilmart, *Auteurs,* p.329, n.1; Meersseman, vol.2, pp. 195–9. For the author, Philippe de Grève, see Raby, pp.395–401; Szövérffy, vol.2, pp. 192–205; *AH,* vol.50, pp.528–32.

173. BL Ms. Royal 2 A viii, f.54; BL Ms. Add. 43683, ff.18v–19.

174. Meersseman, vol.1, pp.94–6; *theoteca* is possibly an error of the present ms. for *theotes* (Greek 'divine'). *LH,* vol.2, p.208. *Lyell,* p.67 (Ms. Lyell 30, ff.

123–125v), where *Ave Maria* was meant to be said before every name. The rubric in BL Ms. Add. 22720, ff.45–6, specifies that *Ave* should be said before every name. Bodleian Library Ms. Canon. Liturg. 223, f.31v, has a cross written between every two names where the sign of the cross is to be made and the prayer is preceded by one on the names of Christ. Bodleian Library Ms. Canon. Liturg. 251, ff.226–227, calls it merely 'a devout prayer'. The first name is variously given as *diva, digna* or *domina.*

175. *Lyell,* nos.175, 349 and references given there, esp. Wilmart, 'Le manuel', p.279 and n.5; Gougaud, 'Etude', *passim.* The text can also begin *Sis mihi quaeso.*

176. Meersseman, vol.2, pp.34–8 and 190–3; the text in Richard III's Hours is to all intents and purposes identical to the one printed *ibid.,* p.193. See also Woolf, p.135. On the Five Joys of Mary, Wilmart, *Auteurs,* pp.326–36, and Woolf, ch.iv, both on the origins and the vernacular texts of the devotion.

177. *LH,* vol.1, pp.76, 99, etc.; vol.2, pp.7, 8, etc.; Leroquais, *Psautiers,* vol.1, pp.109, 209; Mone, vol.1, pp.5–6, item 323; *RH,* no.1744; Walther, no.1904; Hoskins, p.119. Bennett, *Devotional Pieces,* p.287 (medieval English translation).

178. *LH,* vol.1, pp.76, 99, etc.; vol.2, pp.7, 8, etc.; Bennett, *Devotional Pieces,* pp.287–8 (medieval English translation).

179. The text in Richard III's Hours is virtually identical with *AH,* vol.31, pp. 171–2, item 165, but the scribe omitted the last couple of lines of stanza 7. See also BL Ms. Add. 37787, ff.164v–165 and Ms. Harl. 2894, ff.45–6. For the five 'great sorrows' see Wilmart, *Auteurs,* p.513 and n.4; Woolf, pp.268–71.

180. This text is frequently connected with the preceding one; for references see the preceding note.

181. *Lyell,* nos.253, 254 and references given there; Leroquais, *Bréviaires,* vol.1, p.18. A variant incipit is *O domina misericordissima.*

182. No other copy of the metrical prayer has been found. The prose text is very similar to twelfth-century prayers, used to conclude longer devotions to the Virgin, printed in Meersseman, vol.2, pp.178, 231, 240.

183. A great number of farced *Ave Marias* is printed in *AH,* vol.30, pp. 190–281, and Mone, vol.2, pp.91–114, but the present one is not among them. See *Lyell,* no.47 and references given there; also BL Ms. Harl. 2341, f.143, a copy virtually identical to Richard III's, and *LH,* vol.1, p.252. Many similar prayers in vernacular languages are extant.

184. No other copy of this prayer has been found.

185. Wilmart, *Auteurs,* p.328 and n.4; only one copy of the text was known to Wilmart, in a psalter written for a religious at Shaftesbury towards the end of the twelfth century, BL Ms. Lansdowne 383, f.166. Barré, pp.281–4, and Meersseman, vol.2, pp. 162–3, add a few other twelfth- and thirteenth-century mss, with very similar salutations. The text was printed by Egerton Beck, 'A Twelfth-Century Salutation to Our Lady', *The Downside Review,* vol.42 (1924), pp.184–5.

186. *Lyell,* no.366 and mss. and references given there; *LH,* vol.1, pp.182, 356; vol.2, p.299.

187. *AH,* vol. 15, p.138, item 12, has all stanzas; *RH,* no. 12861; Walther, no. 12564. Also Bodleian Library, Ms. Bodley 40, f.41v (all stanzas).

188. *AH,* vol.54, pp.312–8, item 201; *Horae Ebor.,* pp.134–5; Hoskins, pp.119, 355, 375; *Lyell,* no.352; *RH,* no. 18018. Julian, *Dictionary,* lists translations; Raby, pp.437–43; Wieck, *The Book of Hours,* pp. 104–5. Nicholas Rogers informs us that the *Stabat mater* is quite uncommon in fifteenth-century English books of hours.

189. Barré, pp. 185–93 and notes ('La Prière de Théophile'); the text in Richard III's Hours is virtually identical to the one printed by Barré, pp. 186–8. The prayer is based on the *Publica Theophili Penitentia,* a Latin translation of a Greek text, and dates from the eleventh century. See also *LH,* vol.1, p.320; *Darmstadt,* vol.3, p.83. For the Theophilus legend see e.g. H. S. D. Ward, *Catalogue of Romances in the British Museum,* vol.2, pp.595–7; de Voragine, *The Golden Legend,* pp.528–9, September 8, the Nativity of the Virgin.

190. Compare folio 170v, above, and n.183. This text does not occur in *AH* or Mone either.

191. Wilmart, *Auteurs,* p.582, n.1, quotes the only copy known to him (BL Ms. Royal 2 A xxii, f.203, the twelfth-century Westminster Psalter). The present text is almost identical, but slightly longer. It also occurs in 'Queen Melisende's Psalter' (1131–43), see H. Buchthal, *Miniature Painting in the Latin Kingdom of Jerusalem,* Oxford 1957, p.134.

192. *Lyell,* no.375, and mss. referred to there. The text is printed in *Matthaei Parisiensis Chronica Majora,* ed. H. R. Luard, 7 vols., Rolls Series 1872–84, vol.6 *Additamenta,* pp. 127–8, with a description of St. Edmund's devotion to the virginal St. John. See also the *O intemerata,* ff.156v–158, and n.166.

193. No other copy of this suffrage has been found.

194. *Salve sancte ioachim* is printed *AH,* vol.28, p.302, item 123. No other copy of the collect has been found but it is probably not rare.

195. Stadlhuber, p.284; the text occurs in the prayer book of Charles the Bald (died 877), where it is called 'a prayer for the tweifth hour', that is, the last hour of daylight, *PL,* vol. 101, cols.507–8, and *Liber precationum quas Carolus Calvus Imperator…,* ed. F. Ninguarda, Ingolstadt 1583, p.126.

196. No other copy of this prayer has been found. Among the many prayers to the guardian angel quoted by Wilmart, *Auteurs,* pp.537–58, none even resembles the present text.

197. The full Latin text reads: [rubric] De beato ioseph. Oracio [text] Deus qui prudenciam beato ioseph in domo domini sui et coram pharaone dedisti et eum a fraterno odio et invidia non solum liberasti, sed in honore sublimasti. Precor te domine deus omnipotens ut me famulum tuum .N. ab insidiis inimicorum meorum et omnium christianorum gratiam invenire concedas. Per christum. – We are grateful to Dom Eligius Dekkers for giving us his thoughts on the prayer and its purpose. The conclusions are our own.

198. *Lyell,* no.213, and mss. referred to there.

199. *Lyell*, nos.349 (and 175) and mss. and variants referred to there.
200. For more details see the present authors' 'Richard III and St. Julian: a new Myth'.
201. For St. Julian, his legend and other suffrages see de Voragine, *The Golden Legend*, pp. 128–31, 27 January; 'La Légende de St. Julien l'Hospitalier', *Analecta Bollandiana*, vol.63 (1945), pp. 145–219 and references given there.
202. Words beginning *perem* ... or *peren* ... can probably be excluded because the scribe would have added an abbreviation sign over the second e. *Peregrinari* was M. R. James' conjecture (*Lambeth*, p.653).
203. James, *Lambeth*, p.653. For the prayer see also *Lyell*, no. 169.
204. There are several devotions for which the name 'litany' is used but it was essentially an earnest entreaty to the deity, said or sung publicly and deriving from pre-Christian custom. The tone of such begging prayers is one of great penitence and humility, beseeching God in repetitive phrases and answers for his protection against disasters that concerned the community as a whole: the blighting of crops, pestilence and war. The formula had developed from, and is closely connected with, the *Kyrie eleison,* and litanies always contain this phrase once or several times (up to seven). Because of their purpose and contents they came to be used especially during processions, for instance those of 25 April and the three 'great days of the Cross'.

A litany is a responsorial prayer and consists of a series of saints' names, or a list of the names and titles of Christ or the Virgin, which are intoned by the leader, answered by brief pleas of the people (intercede for us; hear us; pray for us) and followed by short exclamatory entreaties of a more specific nature, which are again answered and completed by the community. A lengthy dialogue of versicles and responses and, at the end, a number of prayers for various purposes, are frequent components of a litany.

Apart from pre-Christian begging prayers and a natural inclination of man to plead with his gods in repetitive formulas, psalm 135, *Confitemini domino* (Praise the lord), in which every line celebrating God's deeds and goodness is answered by 'his mercy lasts for ever', is thought to have inspired the composition of litanies. Of the many litanies composed since the beginnings of the church only a few were eventually approved by the pope or integrated into the liturgy: the Great Litany or Litany of Saints, the Litany of Loreto (of St. Mary) and later that of the Holy Name of Jesus. Most were forbidden for public use by Pope Clement VIII in 1601, because they contained 'improper, dangerous and erroneous' material. Perhaps a Catholic owner around this time was moved to cut out the more offending pages of Richard III's own text.
205. We are grateful to Dom Eligius Dekkers for help and suggestions on this matter.
206. M. Frost, 'A prayer book from St. Emmeran, Ratisbon', *The Journal of Theological Studies,* vol.30 (1929), pp.32– 45, esp. pp.41–2.
207. *Ibid.,* p.41; see e.g. Hoskins, p.362, among 'Prayers and orisons to be said after the Litanies, according to the diversity of times'.

208. Dom Eligius Dekkers informs us that the words *Dominus vobiscum* and *Et cum spiritu tuo* were probably omitted in this layman's devotion because these words were to be said only by a priest or deacon; when no priest was present they were not pronounced.

209. *The Gregorian Sacramentary under Charles the Great,* ed. H. A. Wilson, Henry Bradshaw Society vol.49, London 1915, p.220, under *Benedictiones variae,* item cxvii *Oratio quando aqua spargitur in domo;* W. Bright, *Ancient Collects and other prayers ...,* Oxford 1857, p.89.

210. E.g. *Missale Romanum Mediolani 1474,* ed. R. Lippe, Henry Bradshaw Society vol.17, London 1899, in the mass *contra paganos; ibid.* vol.33, London 1907, in the mass *pro recuperatione terre sancte* (for the recapture of the holy land); Hoskins, p.352, among *Preces et orationes dicendae post Litanias pro diversitate temporum: Contra paganos,* and p.363 for the same in English.

211. E.g. *Missale Romanum* (see preceding note), vol.33, p.327, in the mass *pro vitanda mortalitate.* The prayer is in Edinburgh, University Library Ms. 309, f.23

212. See L. von Pastor, *Geschichte der Päpste,* 16 vols., Freiburg im Breisgau 1886–1933, vol.3, p.209 and n.2; *Annales Ecclesiastici ab anno quo desinit Card. Caes. Baronius usque ad annum MDXXXIV...,* ed. O. Raynaldus, vol.XIX, pp.343–4, no.61, 1484 November 21. Among those to whom the letter was sent was 'the King of England'.

The 'Prayer of Richard III'

213. *The Song of Roland,* translated by Dorothy L. Sayers, Harmondsworth 1957, lines 3100–2; 3104–7; p.170.

214. *Ibid.,* lines 2385–6; p. 142.

215. Gaultier, *La Chevalerie,* pp.539–45; he also calls these prayers 'soldiers' prayers'. There are many instances of people using similar formulas in French epic poetry, see Koch, *An Analysis,* especially chapter 5. Sister Koch's work is exhaustive, gives many quotations and references and discusses the origin of the formula. The close association of these 'lists' of examples with death and the dying is clear from the situations in which the literary works use the formula, from the illustrations of the stories in the catacombs, from the prayers in which they are used and from their place in the modern Catholic liturgy, that is, the *Ordo Commendationis animae,* the words spoken by the priest over the dying, commending the departing soul to God and asking, among others, St. Michael to receive it: *Libera, Domine, animam servi tui (ancillae tuae), sicut liberasti Danielem de lacu leonum, ... sicut liberasti Susannam de falso crimine, ...* These either go back to the same very old source, or the prayer was inspired by the well-known liturgical text, as other prayers were.

216. The longest and most interesting of such prayers (listed in Gougaud, 'Etude', pp.3–27) is the version known as the *Oratio Sancti Brandani,* probably of the ninth century. It is in effect a long detailed narration of biblical events, starting with the creation of the world and ending with the life of Christ. It calls on all

the ranks of the angelic hierarchy, all the apostles and all the nameless faithful to save the person praying from danger on land and sea, from every kind of animal, from fire and earthquakes and all natural dangers, from poison and hate, and from all visible and invisible danger by day and by night. Even more than Richard III's prayer it obviously desires to cover every eventuality. This 'prayer of St. Brendan' survives in some 35 Latin and vernacular copies on the continent and in England, see Salmon, 'Oratio Brandani', *passim*. – Many of the elements in Richard III's prayer also appear in the eleventh-century 'Office of the Crucifix', see Wilmart, 'L'office', *passim*.

217. Fourteenth-century mss. containing the prayer traced so far:

BN Ms. latin 757, hours and missal, 1385–90, North Italy.

Oxford, Bodleian Library Ms. Canon. Liturg. 251, hours, 1380s, made in Bruges for Catalan client.

BN Ms. Smith-Lesouëf 22, hours and missal, 1390, North Italy.

BN Ms. latin 1281, breviary, Franciscan, first half of the fourteenth century, Italy; the prayer was added later in the fourteenth or fifteenth century.

BN Ms. latin 13261, hours, Parisian, end fourteenth century; it is not certain when the prayer was written.

Brussels, Bibliothèque Royale Ms. 11035–37, Hours of Philip the Bold, 1380–90, prayer perhaps added later.

BN Ms. latin 18014, Hours of John, Duke of Berry, end of fourteenth century. The last named ms. is one of the books of hours owned by the Duke of Berry, better known for his commission of his 'Très Riches Heures'. The so-called 'Petites Heures du Duc de Berry' contain a curiously corrupt version of the prayer (ff.115v–117); *LH*, vol.2, pp. 175-87). It is simply headed *oroyson* and begins *Deus qui de sinu patris missus es in mundum* ... It is part of the original book and not inserted later. No part of the text allows of any conclusion about its relation to other mss. It is full of errors caused by misreading and after about two-thirds (after the mention of Achitophel) becomes entirely different, bearing no resemblance to any of the other copies studied. There are many fifteenth- and sixteenth-century mss. containing 'the prayer of Richard III'. Some have been studied 'in the flesh', others from photocopies. The existence of many others may be concluded or assumed from their descriptions in catalogues – which are sometimes very inadequate – but these have not all been pursued. It is not thought relevant to list them all. The more interesting ones are mentioned or discussed in the text or the notes below. See also Sonet, *Répertoire,* and Sinclair, *Prières,* nos. 1561, 1562, 2183 and 2205–6, Rézeau, *Répertoire,* the same nos. and R910, for French texts (and a few Latin ones).

218. One is BN Ms. latin 757, book of hours and missal ('une combinaison assez rare' according to *LH*, vol. 1, p.1.) The ms. is described *ibid.,* pp.1–7, and also in Avril, *Dix siècles d'enluminure,* item 83, pp.96–8, plate 83; it is dated 1385–90 and its main interest lies in its Italian illumination (Padua or Milan). The prayer is on ff.218–220 in the first part, the book of hours. It is remarkable that

Ms.757 also appears to contain the earliest known copy of the prayer of the Seven Words of Christ on the cross, which is usually ascribed to Bede and is included in Richard's hours (ff.136v–138, see above, ch.6). The other, closely related, ms. is BN Smith-Lesouëf Ms. 22, book of hours and missal of the use of Rome. This was probably made later than Ms.757 but in the same workshop, and it contains the prayer on ff.214–217v, in the missal. Another ms. in the same library, also of Italian origin, Ms.latin 1281 (see Leroquais, *Les Bréviaires,* vol.3, pp. 122–3), has the prayer on ff.1–3. This Franciscan breviary dates from the first half of the fourteenth century but the prayer was added later – which is not unusual with this text – at an unknown date in the fourteenth or fifteenth century.

219. Apart from the fact that two of the oldest mss. containing the prayer that have been traced are Italian, it has also to be mentioned that many of the volumes in British libraries which contain it appear to be of Italian provenance as well (e.g. Oxford, Bodleian Library, Mss. Douce 8, Lyell 82, Canon. Liturg. 16, 25 and 220; Cambridge, Fitzwilliam Museum, Mss. 152, 156 and MacClean 72; Cardiff, Public Library, Ms. I.373) as are many others in continental collections.

220. Of course, this cannot be called unique in any way; it is merely a question of emphasis; compare the 'most sweet Lord Jesus Christ' with which the prayer begins. See Haimerl, p. 35.

221. Oxford, Bodleian Library Ms. Canon, Liturg. 251. We are grateful to Nicholas Rogers for bringing the book to our attention.

222. Brussels, Bibliothèque Royale Albert I, Ms. 11035–37 (the prayer with its additions is on ff.64–67) and Cambridge, Fitzwilliam Museum, Ms. 3–1954. The original book had become unwieldy by 1450 and was divided. The earlier part eventually came to England and is now in the Fitzwilliam: Gaspar and Lyna, *Les principaux manuscrits,* pt. 1, no.175, pp.419–23; Lyna, 'Un livre de prières', *passim;* Wormald and Giles, 'Description', *passim;* de Winter, 'The Grandes Heures', *passim,* and *La Bibliothèque,* pp. 182–94. At the time of its production in 1376 the book already contained 'oroisons et autres choses', but ff.63v–67 are in a different hand and the initials on these folios were not painted. The next item is again in a different hand, probably that of Jean Miélot, scribe and author in Philip the Good's time. The memorial to St. Pierre de Luxembourg on f.62v cannot have been written before 1387, the year of his death. The composition of the Ms. is very complicated and the exact date of each item's production cannot be established.

223. See Searle, *The Illuminated Manuscripts,* p.xv and James, *Catalogue ... Fitzwilliam Museum,* p.xxxviii; it appears to be accidental that a comparatively large number of mss. in the Fitzwilliam Museum contain 'the' prayer, enabling both Searle and James to list it among the 'usual' contents of books of hours. Salmon, 'Oratio Brandani', p.xxxvii, mentions the prayer very briefly: '... une autre prière du même genre, attribuée à S. Augustin, mais n'ayant assurement rien à voir avec le grand Docteur'. In one case, probably through a scribal error,

the text is attributed to St. Jerome: Uppsala, Universitetsbibliothek Ms. C 80, ff.62–63. We are grateful to Mrs. Margarete Andersson-Schmitt for information and photocopies. See *Mittelalterliche Handschriften der Universitätsbibliothek Uppsala. Katalog über die C-Sammlung,* M. Andersson-Schmitt and M. Hedlund, vol. 1, Stockholm 1988, vol.2 forthcoming. The Ms. containing the prayer is fifteenth-century, made in Italy.

224.The text, with some unlikly readings, is printed *PL,* vol.101, col.476–9; it does contain some of the biblical *exempla,* but it is completely different after the first few words. It occurs in the collection *De psalmorum usu,* incorrectly ascribed to Alcuin of York (*PL,* vol.101, col.465–508), and probably made in Italy *c.* 850 for monastic use; see Wilmart, 'Le manuel', pp.262–5 and notes. See also *Die handschriftliche Ueberlieferung,* I *Italien,* vol. 1, p.404; II *Grossbritannien und Irland,* vol.2, p.117; III *Polen,* pp. 126–7; and de Vreese, *Over handschriften,* p.93. The authors of several of these works appear to regard 'Alcuin's' text and Richard III's prayer as one text or two versions of one.

225.See chapter 5, Contents, above (ff. 180–181).

226.The prayer-book of Alexander is BL. Ms. Add. 38603; the prayer is on ff.57v–58, its main rubric is at the end. Alexander was born in 1461, became King of Poland in 1501 and died in 1506; he was a cultured man with a humanist education. – Interesting rubrics to the prayer are in Oxford, Bodleian Library, Ms. Don. d.85, f.119v, and Ms. Canon. Pat. Lat. 10, f.46v.

227.Similar promises are made at the beginning of many prayers. Some will protect the faithful against evil on the day they are said, and even if the person who pronounced it dies on that day his soul cannot go to hell. Some guarantee that one will have foreknowledge of one's death or not die unconfessed, others give protection against every conceivable human or diabolical evil and any disaster on sea or on land. For example, another prayer sometimes attributed to St. Augustine and beginning *Deus propitius esto mihi peccatori et sis custos meus omnibus diebus vite mee Deus Abraham. Deus Isaac. Deus Iacob* ('God be merciful to me, a sinner, and be my guardian all the days of my life, God of Abraham, God of Isaac, God of Jacob') was held to be very effective in all kinds of physical trouble; in fire and in water, in battle and at trial, it would give protection against a sudden and evil death. In the present Ms. this text is only headed 'A devout prayer' (ff.139v–141, see above ch.5); see Hoskins, p.124 for its rubric and pp.201–3, where a primer of 1535 is quoted which fulminates against the 'vain promises' of the rubric of this and other prayers. In one Ms. (Cambridge, Fitzwilliam Museum Ms. 71) a later hand added: *deleatur ista rubrica* ('this rubric must be deleted') against the heading of *Deus propitius esto,* but no such warning was given in the case of Richard III's prayer in the same Ms. The rubric is also in *LH,* vol.2, p.219, where it is claimed that the text was revealed to St. Augustine by the Holy Ghost and, apart from its other merits mentioned above, it also helped against robbery and in childbirth. Compare Hanham, 'A Medieval Scots merchant's handbook', pp.114–5, in which the text of a superstitious amalgam of this and other prayers is printed. This was jotted down in abominable Latin among the notes of a fifteenth-century merchant and shows to what level such texts and their users could descend. – For such prayers and their 'power' see also Gougaud, 'La prière', who quotes a Ms. in which *Deus propitius esto* is said to have been spoken by Charlemagne before battle.

228. The full (French) rubric reads: 'St. Augustine made the prayer that follows; if someone is in trouble or distress let him say it or let it be said (for him) on thirty consecutive days in honour of God and Our Lady and he shall be uplifted in such a way that his sadness will turn to joy. And this has been proved several times and it works for him who says it or who has it said for him'. The Dukes of Burgundy's text is the only one to have the third person singular. It reads, e.g.: 'And so, Lord, deign to save *him* from all anxiety in which *he* is placed', though towards the end it changes (back?) to the first person.

229. In one case pope John XXII is said to have granted to whoever spoke the prayer *Domine Iesu Christe salus et liberatio fidelium* ('Lord Jesus Christ, salvation and deliverance of the faithful') while passing through a churchyard, as many indulgences as there were people buried there (Hoskins, pp.123 and 128). The most extreme examples of up to 800,000 years are given by *LH*, vol.1, p.xxxi.

230. The senselessness of other erasures in the prayer itself in this ms. (BN, Ms. latin 1354) suggests a child may have been responsible.

231. For Alexander of Poland see above and note 226. Maximilian's text occurs on f.27ff. of his so-called 'older prayer-book'. It is in the first, more or less 'original', part; Maximilian is said to have had great influence on the composition of the book as a whole and on the choice of its contents. It was probably produced in Bruges, between his coronation as King of the Romans on 9 April 1486 and his imprisonment by the people of Bruges from 5 February to 16 May 1488; see Hilger, *Das Aeltere Gebetbuch, passim,* and Thoss, *Flaemische Buchmalerei,* item 67, pp. 104–6 and plate 88.

232. Frederick I (Federico) of Aragon, born 1451 or 2, crowned King of Naples 1497. Led a very active military life, fighting on land and sea; tried to prevent the French invasion of Italy. Deprived of his kingdom by Louis XII, he lived in exile in Tours, where he died in 1504. His book of hours was written in Italy and illuminated in Tours. *LH*, vol.1, pp.xxv–xxxvi and 328–9; *Lexicon des Mittelalters,* München/Zürich 1980– (in progress), col.944; Wilmart, *Auteurs,* p.377.

233. Perhaps the addition was made when the book was rebound in the sixteenth century (the lines are untouched by the binder's rigorous cropping). – *Dulcissime Domine Iesu Christe* are the usual opening words of the prayer, with or without O. *Dulcissime* is sometimes omitted, as in the hours of Philip the Bold (see above); *O dilectissime* occurs (Bodleian Library, Ms. Don. d.85, f.119v); *(O) domine et dulcissime ihesu christe* (Fitzwilliam Museum, Ms. 152, f.140 and Bodleian Library, Ms. Canon. Pat. Lat. 10, f.46v); *Domine Ihesu Christe dulcissime*

(Bodleian Library, Ms. Canon. Liturg. 220, f.138) An unusual variant is found in New York, Pierpont Morgan Library, Ms. 893, the Hours and Psalter of Henry Beauchamp, ff.237v–239v; the first lines are very similar to Richard III's text: *Domine iesu christe fill dei vivi qui de sinu patris missus fuisti in mundum peccata relaxare, peccatores solvere, captivos in carcere positos redimere.* These words are followed by *Exaudi me miserum peccatorem* ... and an entirely different prayer; see Warner, *Descriptive Catalogue,* vol.1, p.65, item 18; this is one of the items in the ms. said to have been added in Italy. – It is not unusual that parts of 'different' prayers became attached to each other, or that segments of one text came to lead a separate life. It makes them very elusive.

234. E.g.: *O tres doulx seigneur Jhesuchrist, filz de Dieu vif qui du saing* (sic) *du Pere tout puissant es envoyes en ce monde* ..., (Châlons-sur-Marne, Bibliothèque Municipale, Ms. 22, f.158, quoted in Sonet, *Répertoire,* p.273, no. 1561); *O alre suetste here Jesu christe, gewaer god en gewaer gods soon, die utten schoot des almachtigen gods dijns heijligen vaders in dese werlt geseijnt biste* ..., (Utrecht, Rijksmuseum Het Catharijneconvent, Ms. Bisschoppelijk Museum Haarlem 107, f.41); *Sanfft modichste here Jesu christe der von dem schois des almechtigen vaders komen bis in dise werelt* ..., (Cologne, Stadtarchiv, Ms. 1899, f.159).

235. *Ex informatione* Dom Eligius Dekkers.

236. Once these errors have been realised 'Richard III's prayer' becomes easier to trace, though confusion with the other text mentioned earlier as ascribed to St. Augustine is unavoidable when too short an *incipit* is given in catalogue or index.

237. Compare also Luke 4:18–9

238. In BN Ms. latin 575 between the lines and over the word *positus* the scribe neatly added in Latin in very small script 'or *posita* if you are a woman'.

239. The presence of *dolor* here and on f.182 may have some meaning, far more than the use of the present tense emphasised by Tudor-Craig, *Richard III,* p.27. The present tense is in fact common usage in such prayers.

240. The Hague, Koninklijke Bibliotheek, Ms. 78 J.49, ff.305–317, French text, written in Northern France, c.1450 and Edinburgh, University Library, Ms. 309, ff.21–23, Latin text, written in France (Paris?), end of the fifteenth century.

241. *custodia* became *concordia* and *posita incredulitate* became (*post-*) *posita crudelitate* and *proscripta hereditate.* Total confusion eventually led to reorganisation and the standardised text reads: *et ex pietate tua, crudeli passione nobis paradisum* ... *mercatus es.* – No conclusion can be drawn about the relation of any mss., there are too few data.

242. The separate mention of Esau and Jacob suggests the existence of a separate textual tradition and a different prayer, since they are pointlessly mentioned again in the series as a whole. Abraham departs from the city of Ur (Gen. 11:31); Isaac's sacrifice (Gen.22:1–19); Jacob and Esau (Gen.25:19–34; 27; 28:1–5); Joseph and his brothers (Gen.37); Noah (Gen.6:14–22; 7; 8:1–19);

Lot (Gen. 19:1–28); Moses and Aaron (Ex.); Saul on Mount Gilboa (I Sam.31?; Saul died on Mount Gilboa and the description of this as a deliverance is inexplicable. The most likely solution is that the original text had: *David de manu Saul et Golie gigantis* and that *de manu* was corrupted to *de monte* and *Golie* to *Gelboe,* as well as surviving in the proper order; the standardized sixteenth-century text omits *Gelboe* altogether); David and Goliath (I Sam. 17:38–51); Susanna (Additions to Daniel 13, Apocrypha); Judith (Judith, Apocrypha); Daniel (Dan.6); the three young men in the burning furnace (Dan.3; in some copies of the prayer their names are given); Jonah (Jonah 2); the daughter of the Canaanite woman (Matt. 15:21–8; Mark 7:24–30); Adam (i.e. the 'Harrowing of Hell', Christ's traditional descent into hell after his crucifixion to overcome the devil and deliver the souls of Old Testament saints, confined there because they had not had the benefit of the Christian sacraments. The medieval tradition is based on the Gospel of Nicodemus, retold in de Voragine, *The Golden Legend,* pp.221–3, under the Resurrection); Peter and Paul (probably and more correctly, as in some versions of the prayer, Peter should in fact be remembered for his deliverance from prison (Acts 12:1–12) and Paul for being saved after he had been shipwrecked (Acts 27)). Not all copies of the prayer include all the stories. A few end with the legend of John the Evangelist: his miraculous emergence, rejuvenated, from the cauldron of boiling oil and his preservation after drinking from the poisoned cup (de Voragine, *The Golden Legend,* p.61, December 27). One book of hours, made in London about 1460, Cambridge, Fitzwilliam Museum Ms. 375, has the addition 'and the blessed Margaret from the mouth of the dragon' (de Voragine, *The Golden Legend,* p.353, July 20). This suggests that the book's owner was called Margaret. The hours that may have belonged to Richard III's sister, Anne, Duchess of Exeter, Cambridge, Sidney Sussex College Ms. 37 (see note 267 below), has an interesting and apparently unique additional series of 'deliverances' in which the prophet Elijah figures largely: how he was saved from Jezebel (I Kings 19:4–8), won the contest with the priests of Baal (I Kings 18:17–40) and how he was saved from 'common death' (II Kings 2:9–15). The series also includes David and Abigail (I Sam.25) and Job, apart from the 'usual' *exempla.*

243. *Navigatio Sancti Brendani Abbatis,* ed. J. Selmer, Notre Dame, Indiana, 1959, p.45; *Lives of the Saints,* ed. and transl. J. F. Webb, Harmondsworth 1981, p.53.

244. *Ex informatione* Brother P. J. Berkhout.

245. Compare Tudor-Craig, *Richard III,* p.27. Susanna is part of the series of Old Testament deliverances and as such occurs in most copies of the prayer: the story is not unique to Richard III's text and tells us nothing about his guilt or innocence of the crimes he has at one time or another been accused of. The words *may* have had a special significance for him – as Achitophel and his evil counsel *may* have reminded him of the Duke of Buckingham's rebellion in the autumn of 1483 (for Achitophel see 2 Sam.15; 16; 17 and Pss.40, 8–9 and 54, 11–5). Compare David's outburst in psalm 54 'But it is you, my companion

and close friend' to the lines added in Richard's own hand to the letter about Buckingham: 'the malysse of hym that hadde best cawse to be trewe' (printed in Hammond and Sutton, *Richard III. The Road,* p.145).

246. Tractatus de Regimine Principum ad Regem Henricum Sextum, in Genet, *Four English Political Tracts,* p.54.

247. See also the next note. So common was the addition of *.N. after famulus tuus* that in one copy of the prayer the words *famulos tuos Moyses et Aaron* made the scribe automatically add *.N.* after *tuos,* in spite of the fact that the 'servants' are named and are part of the story (Rome, Apostolic Library, Ms. Ottob.524, f.2v).

248. It occurs on ff.135v–136, 165,159v, 122,122v, 156v and 157. In one prayer the reader is able to insert twice the name of the enemy to whom he wishes to be reconciled (f.180: make peace between me and .N.; avert from me the anger and the fury of .N.). The occurrence of only the masculine form in every instance in the original part of the hours of Richard III makes it less likely, though not impossible, that it was made for a woman (compare Tudor-Craig, *Richard III,* p.27 and Jones, 'A Study', p.28). The hours made for Margaret Beauchamp, for example, has masculine forms only in its text (see below).

249. St. Michael is also the first to be named in a prayer of the *Ordo Commendationis animae* (see n.215 above) in which the priest prays that the heavens will open to receive the soul of the dying.

250. *Song of Roland,* lines 2393–4.

251. See note 245.

252. For the next paragraph see Wilmart, 'Le grand poème', *passim,* a survey of the devotion to the Seven Words and its expression.

253. Meertens, part 2, p.110. In the English translation of Mechtild of Hackeborn's *Liber specialis gratiae* – of which Richard III and his wife owned a copy (see Sutton and Visser-Fuchs, 'Richard III's Books: I,' *passim*) – Christ says (f.138): 'Ande than I straykede owte myn aarmes and myne handdys to be naylede with herde nayles ande I sange songys of a wonderfull sostenesse (sweetness) in the chambur of luffe and that was on the crosse'.

254. Wilmart, 'Le grand poème', p.274, n.3, notes that Bede's name is usually not mentioned in English books of hours.

255. See ch.6, Richard III's Piety, below; Hammond and Sutton, *Richard III. The Road,* pp.75–80.

256. E.g. in the Hours of Philip the Bold, Frederick of Aragon and Paul Deschamps.

257. Psalm 135 is a psalm of praise and thanksgiving. A long series of brief celebrations of God's great deeds, it is unique by reason of its responsorial character. It is said to have inspired the litanies of the later liturgy. Its style is simple; like the litanies it expresses in simple words strong religious feelings, gratitude and fear, and seems to accord well with the prayer discussed here.

258. Danzig, Gdánska Polskiej Akademii Nauk, Cod.2119, ff.73v–77v.

259. Cologne, Sammlung Ludwig, Ms. IX, 12, ff.286–293. Now at the J. Paul Getty Museum, Malibu, California, *ex informatione* R. S. Wieck.
260. Cambridge, University Library, Ms. Add. 1845, ff.64–95.
261. Rome, Apostolic Library, Ms. Ottob. lat. 524, ff.1–6v.
262. See *Lyell,* no. 169.
263. Rome, Apostolic Library, Ms. Ross. 64, ff.94v–100v; in this ms. the prayer is followed by psalm 135. The authors are indebted to Fr. L. E. Boyle, O.P., Prefect of the Vatican Library, for copies of the relevant pages of the mss.
264. Brussels, Bibliothèque Royale Albert I, Ms. IV 95, Hours of Paul Deschamps (Pauwels van Overtvelt); see *Vijftien Jaar Aanwinsten,* Koninklijke Bibliotheek Albert I, Brussel 1969, item 84, pp.106 and ills., and *Vlaamse Kunst op Perkament* (Catalogue of an exhibition at the Gruuthuse Museum, Bruges), Bruges 1981, item 116, pp.273–4 and ill.32, where the miniature of the Trinity is tentatively ascribed to the school of van Eyck. The prayer plus additions is called *Memoria de sancta Trinitate* in this ms.
265. Cambridge, Fitzwilliam Museum, Ms. 40–1950, Hours of John Talbot, 'Oroison devote pour tribulation' (f.65v), and Ms. 41–1950, Hours of Margaret Beauchamp, no rubric (f.79).

   Another ms. of the same date that *may* contain the prayer is the Hours of John, Duke of Bedford, described in E. F. Bosanquet, 'The Personal Prayer-Book of John of Lancaster, Duke of Bedford, K.G.', *The Library,* 4th series, vol. 13 (1932–3), pp. 148–55. This ms. is in a private collection at the moment and cannot be consulted.
266. Cambridge, Fitzwilliam Museum Ms. 375, Sarum Hours, London calendar, made in London *c.* 1460, artist under strong French influence. We are most grateful to Nicholas Rogers for part of this information.
267. Cambridge, Sidney Sussex College Ms. 37, Sarum Hours, produced in London in the early 1460s, illuminated in the Caesar Master tradition. On f.115v a woman is depicted kneeling before the Virgin. Her armorial mantle appears to have the leopards of England on red and a border of blue with the golden lilies of France, which may be those of Anne Plantagenet, wife of Henry Holand, second Duke of Exeter (1439–1475/6). We are most grateful to Nicholas Rogers for pointing out this ms. and the possible identity of the lady.
268. *Officium Beatae Mariae Virginis* …, printed in Rome 1571 and *The Primer and Office of The Blessed Virgin Marie, in Latin and English* …, edited by Richard Verstegen, printed by Arnold Conings, Antwerp 1599. A number of copies survive of the latter, e.g. in the Museum Plantin-Moretus, Antwerp (R. 49–39), Lambeth Palace, London (1599.4 and 1599.22) and several in the British Library. See Hoskins, nos.266 and 267, pp.355 and 361.
269. In this edition of the text of the prayer abbreviations have been silently extended. Foliation and erased words and letters are in square brackets. The punctuation of the ms. has been printed as commas. Capitalisation follows the ms.

270. *O dulcissime ... peccato-* is a reconstruction of the text based on comparison with other copies of the prayer made in the same decades. The initial O probably filled a three- or four-line square space. The sixteenth-century addition reads: *Clementissime domine Jesu christe vere deus qui a summi patris omnipotentis sede missus es in mundum peccata relaxare, peccatores* (for this and for the missing rubric that headed the prayer and explained its use and powers see the discussion of the text above).

271. *Perpetua,* struck through and restored by the scribe.

272. This is a literal translation which includes the errors and oddities of the Latin text (for details see the discussion of the prayer above). There is a short description of the prayer and a full medieval French translation in H. M. Rochais, 'Prières et moralités en vieux français, Ms. Ligugé 18', *Mélanges de science réligieuse,* vol.14 (1957), pp.151–66 (154–5 and 157).

Richard III's Piety

273. Some of the older general studies remain helpful: Manning, Hurnard, Huizinga and McFarlane. Studies on particular communities and individuals used are: Tanner (Norwich), Thompson (London), Vale (Yorkshire), Heath (Hull), Fleming (Kent), Armstrong (Cecily Neville), Rosenthal (Richard, Duke of York), Pantin (an unknown layman), Chesney (Margaret of York), Catto (Henry V), Underwood (Margaret Beaufort), Hicks (Hungerfords), Lovatt (Henry VI via Blacman), Goodman (Henry VII).

There is no particular study on the piety of Edward IV; he has received some praise from the Crowland chronicler, but mainly criticism from both him (pp. 150–3) and Ross, *Edward IV,* pp.268–9, 273–6, despite his lavish foundation of St. George's Chapel, Windsor. The Crowland chronicler resents Edward's taxing of the church.

274. For instance the very different conclusions about Henry VII reached by David Knowles and R. L. Storey, cited Goodman, 'Henry VII', p.115. Some statements about Richard III will be discussed below.

275. See e.g. Monitor, 'Frömmigkeit', *passim,* for the problems of research and how to define piety.

276. Mols, 'Emploi et valeur', *passim.* C. Burgess, 'Late medieval wills', typescript lent by author.

277. For instance, Monitor, 'Frömmigkeit', p.6 on scepticism about visible acts of piety, an attitude prevalent since the Reformation (at least). Richard III, of course, is very much the subject of controversy and scepticism, e.g. Richmond, 'Religion', p.201, is 'unnerved' by the fact that Ross (*Richard III*, p.128), calls Richard 'a genuinely pious and religious man', and says that this 'is like calling Joseph Stalin a genuinely devout Marxist'!

278. Vale, 'Piety', p.28; Thompson, 'Piety and Charity', p.180 and *passim.*

279. An attractive contemporary pictorial example is the series of miniatures of Margaret of York, Duchess of Burgundy, performing the Acts of Mercy while Christ looks on (Nicolas Finet, *Benois seront les miséricordieux*, Brussels, Bibliothèque Royale, Ms. 9296, f.1). Some seventy years earlier Langland wrote of Christ who 'in poor man's apparel pursueth us ever', cited Bennett, *Poetry*, pp.60–1. See also de Voragine, *The Golden Legend*, p.121, on St. John the Almoner, who carefully remembered how Christ might be anywhere.

280. Richard III's piety has only received more than a passing glance comparatively recently. For all aspects discussed and further references see Ross, *Richard III*, pp. 128–38; Sutton, 'A Curious Searcher', pp.64–70; Dobson, 'Richard III and the Church', *passim*.

   Richard's earliest friendly biographer, George Buck, included piety as one of the seven virtues of a king (and proceeded to show Richard possessed all seven), but scarcely distinguished between charity and piety and building works (Buck, *The History*, pp.201–4). Caroline Halsted actually acknowledged defeat and declined – perhaps wisely – to assess the piety of a byegone age (Halsted, *Richard III*, vol.1, pp.335–8; vol.2, pp.296–8). She had, in 1844, little information on such religious activities as the founding of Middleham College. Paul Murray Kendall (*Richard III*, p.320) was more courageous on the issue. He concluded Richard had a 'powerful and more private' religious experience than conventional piety, but he placed too much importance on his owning a 'Lollard' New Testament. His picture of Richard is flawed for present-day readers by his '1955' understanding of a virtually unresearched period, but nevertheless it is much repeated by novelists and historians, e.g. Lander, *Government*, pp.328–30.

281. A similar apparent incompatibility has been noted in the behaviour of other rulers, e.g. Henry V's noted piety compared with his ruthless refusal to succour the helpless people turned out to starve by the citizens of Rouen during his siege of that town.

282. E.g. Polydore Vergil and Charles Ross. Charles Ross was clearly aware of the dangers of making the charge of hypocrisy and reluctant to adopt Vergil's stance. The development of his argument is interesting when examined in detail. Vergil explained Richard's good government very simply: Richard found that the murder of his nephews made him unpopular; he became so fearful and anxious to appease God and his critics that he took up a 'new form of life' in order to be thought 'righteous', 'liberal', etc. He became 'suddenly good' (pp.191–2). Ross considered that Vergil was reporting the 'truth as he knew it' or as he was told it (*Richard III*, p.xxvi) and set out to examine this idea. He inclined to find hypocrisy in Richard's behaviour over the execution of Clarence and describes his sympathy to Desmond as 'tongue-in-cheek' (pp.32–4 and n.37). He finds Richard's piety genuine (pp. 128–36), but his sexual virtue hypocritical (pp.136–8). In all these cases Ross is expressing his own opinion (not Vergil's). In the rumour of Richard's proposed marriage

to his niece (and the King's denial of it) as told in the Crowland Chronicle, Ross finds the true reflection of contemporary opinion that Richard was a hypocrite and that Vergil was right (p.146). From this point on Ross is clear: the usurpation made Richard desperate to commend himself (pp. 147–8), and particularly by his administration of justice (pp. 173–5) and in his parliament (pp.187–9). For Ross Vergil is the true revelation of the usurper (p.190).

Ross' resurrection of the hypocrisy theme has been enthusiastically imitated in G. St. Aubyn, *The Year of Three Kings 1483,* London 1983, and D. Seward, *Richard III, England's Black Legend,* London 1983.

283. Aristotle, *Politics,* book 5, 9, 10–20. Greek *tyrannis* and medieval/modern 'tyrant' do not have exactly the same meaning. A *tyrannis* is not necessarily a bad ruler – though Aristotle, who was interested in practical politics, knew from history and experience that he only too often was. What we are concerned with here is the influence of the word-plus-image on later thinkers, and their interpretation. Neither Aristotle's nor his imitators' terms can be defined with mathematical precision, but the later interpreters had the authority of the image's philosophical origins behind them. See also U. Baumann, 'Thomas More and the Classical Tyrant', *Moreana,* vol.22 (1985), pp.108–27, where, however, the intermediate period and the use of the word between classical times and the Renaissance are not discussed.

284. Giles of Rome, *De Regimine Principum,* book 3, part 2, ch.9.

285. For Tacitus, see B. Walker, *The Annals of Tacitus. A Study in the Writing of History,* Manchester 1968, esp. Ch.6, Fact and Impression. Thomas More in his *History of Richard III* used such elements to great effect and Richard's reputation will probably never recover from this onslaught (as the Emperor Tiberius' image will always be coloured by the pictures given by Suetonius and Tacitus); see More, *Complete Works,* vol.2, pp.1xxxviii–xcvii. See also Buck, *The History,* pp. 126–8, for an attempt to remonstrate against such methods.

286. Several other elements doubtless helped to make the picture of Richard III as it has prevailed since the accession of the Tudors. One is reminded of the ambitious tyrants staged by Seneca, the heathen kings who persecute Christians in medieval lives of saints and of King Herod, known to every churchgoer as the slaughterer of the Innocents. Richard's career was probably, even during his life time, seen as a modern *exemplum.* A king who loses his only son and his wife as well must have committed unspeakable crimes to deserve such a fate. His death in battle served to make this line of thought even more acceptable.

287. Ross, *Richard III,* pp. 136–8; Lander, *Government,* p.329. The documents are both printed in Hammond and Sutton, *Richard III. The Road,* pp. 146–7 and 189–90. It *is* intriguing that the rebels who are the subject of the first document, are twice called 'traitors, *adulterers and bawds*' (our italics). The reason must lie in the fact that Mistress Shore and her supposed lover, the Marquis of

Dorset, were among those named. The other document is an official injunction to bishops to do their duty as regards the morality of their flocks.

288. Louis XI of France cast doubts on Margaret of York's morals to try to prevent her marriage to Charles the Bold. Charles himself was accused of homosexuality by former servants who had gone over to the King, and in his turn he accused Louis of murdering his (Louis') brother, the Duke of Guienne, by poison and magic, and of attempting to murder Charles himself (Vaughan, *Charles*, pp.48, 239 and 77). John, Count of Armagnac, and James III of Scotland were said to have committed incest with their sisters.

289. Vale, *Piety*, pp.29, 31. Carey, 'Devout Literate Laypeople', pp.361–81. And see Jolliffe, *Check-list of Middle English Prose Writings of Spiritual Guidance*: the mere existence of so many works of that nature is significant.

290. For the 'meddled life' see Pantin, 'Instructions'; Bennett, *Poetry*, esp. pp.59–61; Hirsh, 'Prayer and Meditation', pp.57–8; Wieck, *The Book of Hours*, pp.40–4; Chesney, 'Notes on some Treatises', *passim*.

291. Goodman, 'Henry VII', pp.116–7.

292. Olivier de La Marche in his *État de la Maison du Due Charles de Bourgoigne* (ed. Beaune and d'Arbaumont, vol.4, pp.2–3). La Marche in his discussion of the Duke's public piety evidently finds no fault with this and other examples of an efficient and bureaucratic approach.

293. Raine, 'The Statutes', p.160 (the relevant text is quoted in the discussion of 'Richard III's prayer' above). The preamble is quoted with approval by Ross, who perhaps over-emphasises its implications and uniqueness.

294. The 'jeopardies' and 'perils' Gloucester says God saved him from echo in a humbler vein the 'great perils, dangers and difficulties' that Edward IV and Richard had survived to report officially to their brother-in-law, Charles of Burgundy (Paris, BN Ms. français 3887, ff.114-116v).

295. See above, ch.5, the description of the contents of the hours (ff. 1 and 180–184v), and ch.6, the discussion of 'the prayer of Richard III'.

296. Ross, *Richard III*, p.129.

297. Lander, *Government*, pp.329–30.

298. Lander, *Government*, p.330; all his conclusions appear to be based on Tudor-Craig, *Richard III*, p.27.

299. Richard is traditionally held to have called Nottingham Castle his 'castle of care', the place where he learnt of his son's death, anticipated his wife's death and waited for news of invasion in 1485. The 'castle of care' (despair) and the 'tower of truth' nearby are images used at the beginning of Langland's *Piers Plowman*, which it is possible that Richard was quoting. This is all conjectural, but the connections are not entirely to be dismissed. The progress from castle to tower is undoubtedly paralleled in the comfort offered by the prayer. See Sutton 'Richard III's Castle of Care', pp.303–6 and the possible rubrics of 'Richard III's prayer' discussed above.

300. Bennett, *Poetry*, esp. chs.2, 3 and 4.

301. E.g. Bossy, *Christianity*, pp. 11–23, on saints as mediators.

302. Raine, 'The Statutes', pp.161–2 and *passim*; Melhuish, *The College*, p.7; Searle, *History of Queens' College*, p.89.

303. Sutton, 'A Curious Searcher', pp.65–6; Dobson, 'Richard III and the Church', p.141.

304. For the Holy Oil see Sutton and Hammond, *The Coronation*, pp.5–10, and references given there. For the reburial of Henry VI see White, 'The Death', pp. 110–3.

305. Richard's well known remark on crusading, made to a visitor from Germany in 1484, is quoted by Ross, *Richard III*, p.142; a better and more literal translation of the German (and only surviving) version of Richard's words would read: 'I *would certainly* with my people alone and without the help of other princes, *easily* drive away not only the Turk but all my enemies' (our italics). Biographers of Richard III have so far literally repeated C. A. J. Armstrong's translation (in his edition of Dominic Mancini, *The Usurpation of Richard III*, Gloucester 1984, p.137) and missed out on the King's evident self-confidence in the matter; there is also a note of naivety in his remark. – Further evidence of Richard's involvement may perhaps be found in one of the devotions added later to the present ms., 'the "litany" of Richard III'. *If* this was added for Richard it suggests that he was concerned about the international situation and the threat from the East and was happy to have his concern expressed in purely conventional devotional terms in a composite prayer. The evidence about the original contents of this prayer, its purpose and connection with the King, is tenuous, however, and no conclusions will be drawn from it concerning his piety. See above, ch.5, Contents, the description of the last folio of the ms.

306. For the King's Evil see Sutton and Hammond, *The Coronation*, pp.6–7, and references given there.

307. Bennett, *Poetry*, esp. ch.2; and see Catto, 'Henry V', pp. 107–15.

308. Ross, *Richard III*, pp. 128–9.

309. Kendall, *Richard III*, p.320 and also pp.314, 316.

310. Lander, *Government*, p.328; Lander's argument is further bedevilled by his inclusion of a book made for Richard II as one of Richard III's (William Sudbury's *Tractatus de sanguine Christi precioso*). This mistake derives from the first edition of the catalogue of the National Portrait Gallery exhibition on Richard III (see Tudor-Craig, *Richard III*), corrected in the second edition.

311. See the series of articles on Richard's books by the present authors, and the concluding article on his 'library' as a whole to be in *The Ricardian* 1991.

312. See Hammond, 'Richard III's Books: III'.

313. Vegetius' *De Re Militari*.

314. *History of the World*, book 2, ch.21, section 6, p.311.

Bibliography

Manuscript Sources

Altenburg,   Benedictine Abbey of Altenburg Ms. AB 6 C 4, hours

Berkeley   Nevill Hours (set of slides held by the Bodleian Library)
  Castle,

Blackburn,   Museum and Art Galleries, Hart Ms. 21018, hours

Brussels,   Bibliothèque Royale Albert I Ms. 11035–37, Hours of Philip the Bold
                                    IV 95, Hours of Paul Deschamps

Cambridge,   Corpus Christi College Ms. 537, prayers
                Gonville and Gaius College Ms. 148/198, psalter

Fitzwilliam Museum	Ms. 60,	hours
	71,	hours
	152,	hours
	156,	hours
	375,	hours
	40–1950,	Hours of John Talbot
	41–1950,	Hours of Margaret Beauchamp
	3–1954,	Hours of Philip the Bold
MacClean Ms. 72,		hours

Sidney Sussex College Ms. 37, Hours of Anne Plantagenet, Duchess of Exeter (?)

Cardiff,   Public Library Ms. I 373, hours

152

Edinburgh,   National Library of Scotland, Blairs College Ms. 7, hours
Advocates Ms.18.6.5, psalter and hours

University Library   Ms. 39, hours

42, hours

43, hours

309, hours

Estate of Late Major J. A. Abbey Ms. JA 7398, Hours of the Duchess of Clarence
(photographs held by the Conway Library)

Le Mans,   Bibliothèque Municipale Ms. A 184, breviary

London,   British Library Ms.   16998, prayers and offices
Add.

22720, prayers

37787, prayers

38603, prayers of Alexander,
Prince of Poland

42131, Hours and Psalter of
John, Duke of Bedford

50001, Hours of Elizabeth the
Queen

65001, Hours of Katherine de
Valois

Ms.Harl.211, prayers

2341, hours and prayers

2887, hours

2894, prayers

Ms. Royal 2 A xviii, Beauchamp Hours (with
additions that were
once part of the psalter
that is now Rennes,
Bibliothèque Municipale
Ms. 22)

2 B viii, Psalter of 'Princess Joan'

Ms. Sloane 2863, hours

Ms. Stowe 16, hours

	Lambeth Palace	Ms. 459,	hours
		474,	Hours of Richard III
	University College	Ms. 19,	prayers
	University of London	Ms. 519,	hours
New York,	Pierpont Morgan Library	M. 815,	Hours of Henry VII
		M.893,	Hours and Psalter of Henry, Duke of Warwick
Oxford,	Bodleian Library,	Ms. Bodely 113,	hours
		264,	Livre du Graunt Cam
		Canon. Liturg. 16,	psalms and prayers
		25,	prayers and hymns
		116,	hours
		220,	hours
		251,	hours
		Canon. Pat. Lat.10,	theological miscellany
		Don.d.85,	psalter
		Douce 8,	offices and prayers
		Gough Liturg.6,	hours
		Lat. liturgy. f.2,	hours (and Marbod, 'On precious stones')
		Lyell 82,	prayers
		Rawl. liturg. d.1,	hours
		Rawl. liturg. e.28,	hours
Paris,	Bibliothèque Nationale,		
		Ms. latin 757,	hours and missal
		921,	hours
		1281,	breviary
		1354,	hours
		1426 A,	hours
		1428,	hours and prayers
		1430,	hours and prayers

		10532,	Hours of Frederic of Aragon
		10565,	hours
		10567,	Hours of William of Baden
		13261,	hours
		18014,	Little Hours of John of Berri
		Ms. Smith-Lesouëf 22,	hours and missal
Rennes,	Bibliothèque Municipale	Ms. 22,	Beaufort Psalter
Rome,	Apostolic Library		
		Ms. Ottob. lat. 524,	prayers
		Ms. Ross. 64,	hours
The Hague,	Koninklijke Bibliotheek	Ms. 78 J 49,	hours and prayers
Uppsala,	Universitetsbibliothek Ms.C 80, works concerning, and ascribed to, St. Jerome		
Utrecht,	Rijksmuseum Het Catharijneconvent		Ms. Bisschoppelijk Museum Haarlem 107, hours

Secondary Sources

Achten, G. and E. Bliembach, *Das christliche Gebetbuch im Mittelalter: Andachts-und Stundenbücher in Handschrift und Frühdruck,* Staatsbibliothek Preussischer Kulturbesitz, Ausstellungskataloge 13, Wiesbaden 1987.

Adams, Frederick B., *Ninth Report to the Fellows of the Pierpont Morgan Library 1958 and 1959,* New York 1959.

Alexander, J. J. G. *et al., Medieval and Early Renaissance Treasures in the North-West,* Whitworth Art Gallery, Manchester 1976.

Alexander, J. J. G., and C. M. Kauffmann, *English Illuminated Manuscripts 700–1500,* Exhibition Catalogue 1973, Bibliothèque Royale Albert I, Brussels 1973.

Alexander, J. J. G., 'William Abell "lymnour" and Fifteenth-Century English Illumination', in *Kunsthistorische Forschungen Otto Pächt zu seinem 70. Geburtstag,* Residenz Verlag 1973, pp. 166–172.

Analecta Hymnica Medii Aevi, ed. C. Blume, G. M. Dreves, H. M. Bannister, 55 vols., Leipzig 1886–1922.

Ancrene Riwle, The English Text of the Ancrene Riwle, British Museum Ms. Cotton
  Nero A. XIV, ed. Mabel Day, Early English Text Society, OS. vol. 229 (1952,
  for 1946).
Armstrong, C. A. J., 'The Piety of Cicely, Duchess of York: A Study in Late
  Medieval Culture', *For Hilaire Belloc: Essays in Honour of his 72nd Birthday,* ed.
  D. Woodruff, London 1942, pp. 73–94.
Avril, F., *Dix siècles d'enluminure italienne VIe–XVIe siècles* (Catalogue of an exhibition
  at the National Library, Paris), Paris 1984.
Barratt, Alexandra, 'The Prymer and its Influence on fifteenth-century English
  Passion Lyrics', *Medium Aevum,* vol. 44 (1975) pp. 264–79.
Barré, H., *Prières anciennes de l'Occident à la Mère du Sauveur,* Paris 1963.
Bennett, J. A. W., *Devotional Pieces in Verse and Prose from MS Arundel 285 and MS
  Harleian 6919,* Scottish Text Society, 3rd series, vol.23, Edinburgh 1955.
——, *Poetry of the Passion,* Oxford 1982.
Bindman, David, ed., *The Thames and Hudson Encyclopaedia of British Art,*
  London 1985.
Bossy, John, *Christianity in the West 1400–1700,* Oxford 1985.
Breeze, A., 'The Number of Christ's Wounds', *Bulletin of the Board of Celtic Studies,*
  vol. 32(1985), pp. 84–91.
Brown, T. J., G. M. Meredith-Owens and D. H. Turner, 'Manuscripts from the
  Dyson Perrins Collection', *British Museum Quarterly,* vol. 23 (1961), pp. 27–38.
Buck, Sir George, *The History of King Richard the Third (1619),* ed. A. N. Kincaid,
  Gloucester 1979.
Burgess, C., 'Late medieval wills and pious convention: testamentary evidence
  reconsidered', typescript.
Calkins, R. G., *The Distribution of Labour: the Illuminators of the Hours of Catherine of
  Cleves and their Workshop,* Transactions of the American Philosophical Society,
  vol. 69, part 5 (1979).
——, *Illuminated Books of the Middle Ages,* London 1983.
Carey, Hilary M., 'Devout Literate Laypeople and the Pursuit of the Mixed Life in
  Later Medieval England', *Journal of Religious History,* vol. 14 (1987), pp. 361–81.
Catto, Jeremy, 'Religious change under Henry V' in *Henry V. The Practice of
  Kingship,* ed. G. L. Harriss, Oxford 1985, pp. 87–115.
Chambers, J. D., *Lauda Syon. Ancient Latin Hymns of the English and other Churches,*
  2 parts, London 1866.
Chesney, Kathleen, 'Notes on some treatises of devotion intended for Margaret
  of York (ms. Douce 365)', *Medium Aevum,* vol. 20 (1951), pp. 11–39.
Chevalier, U., *Repertorium Hymnologicum: Catalogue des chants, hymnes, proses,
  séquences, tropes en usage dans l'église latine depuis les origines jusqu'à nos jours,* 6 vols.,
  Louvain 1892–1912.
Craigie, W. A., '"Champ" and "Vynet"', *Notes and Queries,* vol. 148, March 1925,
  p. 171.

Crawford, Anne, 'The Piety of Late Medieval English Queens', in *The Church in Pre-Reformation Society. Essays in honour of F. R. H. Du Boulay,* ed. C. M. Barron and C. Harper-Bill, Woodbridge 1985, pp. 48–57.

Crippen, T. C., *Ancient Hymns and Poems,* London 1868.

Christianson, C. Paul, *Memorials of the Book Trade in Medieval London. The Archives of Old London Bridge,* Woodbridge 1987.

The Crowland Chronicle Continuations 1459–1486, ed. Nicholas Pronay and John Cox, Richard III and Yorkist History Trust, London 1986.

Daniel, H. A., ed., *Thesaurus Hymnologicus,* 5 vols in 2, Halle/Leipzig 1845–56.

De Hamel, Christopher, *A History of Illuminated Manuscripts,* Oxford 1986.

De La Mare, Albinia, *Catalogue of the Collection of Medieval Manuscripts bequeathed to the Bodleian Library, Oxford, by James P. R. Lyell,* Oxford 1971.

Delaissé, L. M. J., 'La Miniature en Angleterre à la Fin du XlVe Siècle', *Scriptorium,* vol. 8 (1954), pp. 128–135.

——, 'The Importance of Books of Hours for the History of the Medieval Book', in *Gatherings for Dorothy E. Miner,* ed. U. E. McCracken, L. M. C. Randall and R. H. Randall, Baltimore 1973, pp. 203–225.

Dennison, Lynda, 'The Stylistic Sources, Dating and Developments of the Bohun Workshop, *ca.* 1340–1400', unpublished Ph.D. thesis, University of London 1988.

De Vreese, W., *Over Handschriften en Handschriftkunde,* Zwolle 1962.

De Winter, P. M. 'The *Grandes Heures* of Philip the Bold, Duke of Burgundy: The De Vreese, W., *Over Handschriften en Handschriftkunde,* Zwolle 1962.

De Winter, P. M. 'The *Grandes Heures* of Philip the Bold, Duke of Burgundy: The Copyist Jean l'Avenant and his Patrons at the French Court', *Speculum,* vol. 57 (1982), pp. 786–842.

——, *La Bibliothèque de Philippe le Hardi, Due de Bourgogne ...,* Paris 1985.

Diringer, David, *The Illuminated Book: Its History and Production,* London 1967, (2nd edn.).

Dobson, R. B., 'Richard III and the Church of York', in *Kings and Nobles in the Later Middle Ages. A Tribute to Charles Ross,* ed. R. A. Griffiths and James Sherborne, Gloucester 1986, pp. 130–154.

Dowden, Bishop, 'Note on the foundation of Richard III at Queens' College Cambridge, 1477, illustrating the cult of St. Ninian', *Transactions of the Scottish Ecclesiological Society,* vol. 1 (1903), pp. 156–8.

Duby, Georges, ed., *A History of Private Life,* vol. 2, *Revelations of the Medieval World,* Harvard 1988.

The Dyson Perrins Collection, Part I. *Catalogue of Forty-Five Exceptionally Important Manuscripts ... the property of the late C. W. Dyson Perrins.* Introduction by Francis Wormald. Sotheby, London, 9 December 1958.

Egger, Gerhart and Hanna, *Schatzkammer in der Prälatur des Stiftes Altenburg,* Wien 1979.

English Book Illustration 966–1846, vol. 1 *Illuminated Manuscripts,* The British Museum, London 1965.

Farquhar, J. D., *Creation and Imitation, The Work of a Fifteenth-Century Manuscript Illuminator (William Vrelant),* Fort Lauderdale, 1976.

Fleming, P. W., 'Charity, Faith and the Gentry of Kent 1420–1529', in *Property and Politics: Essays in Later Medieval English History,* ed. Tony Pollard, Gloucester, 1984, pp. 36–58.

Friedman, John B., 'John Siferwas and the Mythological Illustrations in the *Liber Cosmographiae* of John de Foxton', *Speculum,* vol. 58 (1983), pp. 391–418.

Gaspar, C., and F. Lyna, eds., *Les principaux manuscrits à peintures de la Bibliothèque Royale de Belgique,* 2 parts, Brussels 1984.

Gaultier, L., *La Chevalerie,* Paris 1895.

Genet, J.-P., *Four English Political Tracts of the Later Middle Ages,* Camden Society 4th Series, vol. 18, 1977.

Gjerløw, L., *Adoratio Crucis. The Regularis Concordia and the Decreta Lanfranci,* Norwegian Universities Presses 1961.

Goodman, Anthony, 'Henry VII and Christian Renewal', *Studies in Church History,* vol. 17 (1981), pp. 115–125.

Gougaud, L., 'Etude sur les *Loricae* celtiques et sur les prières qui s'en rapprochent', *Bulletin d'ancienne littérature et d'archéologie,* vol. 1 (1911) pp. 265–91.

——, 'La prière dite de Charlemagne et les pièces apocryphes apparentées', *Revue de l'histoire ecclésiastique,* vol. 20 (1924), pp. 211–38.

——, *Devotional and Ascetic Practices in the Middle Ages,* English edition prepared by G. C. Bateman, London 1927.

——, 'Etude sur les "Ordines Commendationis Animae"', *Ephemerides Liturgicae,* vol. 49 (1935), pp. 3–27.

Gray, Douglas, 'The Five Wounds of Our Lord', *Notes and Queries,* vol. 208 (1963), pp. 50–1, 82–9, 127–34, 163–8.

——, 'Books of Comfort' in *Medieval English Religious and Ethical Literature: Essays in honour of G. H. Russell,* ed. G. Kratzmann and James Simpson, D. S. Brewer, Cambridge 1986, pp. 200–21.

Haimerl, F. X., *Mittelalterliche Frömmigkeit im Spiegel der Gebetbuchliteratur Süddeutschlands,* München 1952.

Halsted, C. A., *Richard III as Duke of Gloucester and King of England,* 2 vols, London 1844.

Hammond, P. W. and Sutton, Anne F., *Richard III. The Road to Bosworth Field,* London 1985.

Hammond, P. W. 'Richard III's Books: III. English New Testament', *The Ricardian,* vol. 7 (1987), pp. 479–485.

Die Handschriften der Hessischen Landes- und Hochschulbibliothek Darmstadt: vol. 2, ed. L. Eizenhöfer and H. Knaus, *Die liturgischen Handschriften der Hessischen Landes- und Hochschulbibliothek Darmstadt,* Wiesbaden 1968; vol. 3, ed. G.

Achten, L. Eizenhöfer and H. Knaus, *Die lateinischen Gebetbuchhandschriften der Hessischen etc.*, Wiesbaden 1972.

Die handschriftliche Ueberlieferung der Werke des heiligen Augustinus: I Italien, ed. M. Oberleitner, 2 vols; *II Grossbritannien und Irland*, ed. F. Roemer, 2 vols; *III Polen*, ed. F. Roemer; Oesterreichische Akademie der Wissenschaften, Phil.-Hist. Klasse, Sitzungsberichte 263, 267, 276, 281, 289, Vienna 1969–1973.

Hanham, A., 'A Medieval Scots Merchant's Handbook', *The Scottish Historical Review*, vol. 50 (1971), pp. 107–20.

Heath, Peter, 'Urban Piety in the later Middle Ages: the Evidence of Hull Wills,' in *The Church, Politics and Patronage in the Fifteenth Century*, ed. Barrie Dobson, Gloucester 1984, pp. 209–234.

Herbert, J., *The Sherborne Missal*, Roxburgh Club 1920.

Hicks, M. A. 'Piety and Lineage in the Wars of the Roses: the Hungerford Experience', in *Kings and Nobles in the Later Middle Ages. A Tribute to Charles Ross*, ed. R. A. Griffiths and James Sherborne, Gloucester 1986, pp. 90–108.

——, *Richard III as Duke of Gloucester*, University of York, Borthwick Papers no.70, 1986.

——, 'The Piety of Margaret, Lady Hungerford (d.1478)', *Journal of Ecclesiastical History*, vol. 38 (1987), pp. 19–38.

Hilger W., ed., *Das Ältere Gebetbuch Maximilians I. Vollständige Faksimile-Ausgabe im Original Format des Codex Vindobonensis 1907 der Oesterreichischen Nationalbibliothek*, Graz 1973.

Hoskins, E., *Horae Beatae Mariae Virginis or Sarum and York Primers with kindred books and primers of the reformed Roman use*, London 1901.

Hughes, A., *Medieval Manuscripts for Mass and Office: A guide to their organization and terminology*, Toronto 1982.

Huizinga, J., *The Waning of the Middle Ages* (1924), Harmondsworth reprint 1982.

Hurnard, N. D., 'Studies in Intellectual Life in England from the Middle of the Fifteenth Century till the time of Colet', unpublished D.Phil. thesis, Oxford 1935.

James, M. R., *Catalogue of Illuminated Manuscripts in the Fitzwilliam Museum*, Cambridge, Cambridge 1895.

——, *A Descriptive Catalogue of the Manuscripts in the Library of Lambeth Palace: The Medieval Manuscripts*, Cambridge 1932.

Jolliffe, P. S., *A Check-List of Middle English Prose Writings of Spiritual Guidance*, Subsidia Mediaevalia II. Pontifical Institute of Medieval Studies, Toronto 1974.

Jones, Kathryn, 'A Study of Lambeth Palace MS 474: A Book of Hours belonging to Richard III', unpublished MA thesis, London 1981.

Jones, M. K., 'Sir William Stanley of Holt: politics and family in the late fifteenth century', *Welsh History Review*, vol. 14 (1988), pp. 1–22.

Julian, J., ed., *Dictionary of Hymnology*, London 1892.

Kendall, Paul Murray, *Richard III*, London 1955.

Koch, M. P., *An Analysis of the Long Prayers in Old French Literature with Special Reference to the 'Biblical–Creed–Narrative' Prayers,* Washington DC 1940.

Kuhn, Charles L., 'Herman Scheerre and English Illumination of the early Fifteenth Century', *Art Bulletin,* vol. 22 (1940), pp. 136–156.

La Marche, Olivier de, *Mémoires,* ed. H. Beaune and J.d'Arbaumont, 4 vols., Paris 1883–8.

Lander, J. R., *Government and Community, England 1450–1509,* London 1980.

Legg, J. Wickham, *The Sarum Missal,* Oxford 1916.

Leroquais, Victor, *Les Livres d'Heures manuscrits de la Bibliothèque nationale,* Paris 1927.

——, *Les Bréviaires manuscrits des bibliothèques publiques de France,* 6 vols, Paris 1934.

——, *Les Psautiers manuscrits latins des bibliothèques publiques de France,* 3 vols, Mâcon 1940–41.

Littlehales, H., ed., *The Prymer or Lay Folks' Prayer Book,* Early English Text Society, OS. vols 105, 109 (1895, 1897).

Loiseleur, J., 'Les jours égyptiens, leur variations dans les calendres au Moyen Age', *Mémoires de la Société nationale des Antiquaires de France,* vol. 33 (1872), pp. 198–253.

Lovatt, Roger, 'John Blacman: biographer of Henry VI', in *The Writing of History in the Middle Ages. Essays presented to R. W. Southern,* Oxford 1981, pp. 415–444.

Lyna, F., 'Un livre de prières inconnu de Philippe le Hardi (Bruxelles, ms. 11035–37)', in *Mélanges Hulin de Loo,* Brussels/Paris 1931, pp. 249–259.

McFarlane, K. B., *Lancastrian Kings and Lollard Knights,* Oxford 1972.

Manning, B. L., *The People's Faith in the Time of Wyclif,* Cambridge 1919.

Marks, Richard, and Nigel Morgan, *The Golden Age of English Manuscript Painting,* London 1981.

Maskell, W., *Monumenta Ritualia Ecclesiae Anglicanae,* 3 vols, London 1846–7.

Meersseman, G. G., *Der Hymnos Akathistos im Abendland,* 2 vols, Freiburg Schweiz 1958–60.

Meertens, M., *De Godsvrucht in de Nederlanden naar handschriften en gebedenboeken der XVe Eeuw,* parts I, II, III and VI, [Antwerp] 1931–4.

Meier-Ewert, Ch., 'A Middle English Version of the *Fifteen Oes',* *Modern Philology,* vol. 58 (1971), pp. 355–61.

Melhuish, Joyce, 'The Hours of Richard III', *The Ricardian,* no. 22 (1968), pp. 2–4.

——, *The College of King Richard III Middleham,* Richard III Society n.d.

Migne, J. P., ed., *Patrologiae cursus completus. Series Latina,* 221 vols, Paris 1844–64.

Millar, Eric G., *English Illuminated Manuscripts in the Fourteenth and Fifteenth Centuries,* London and Brussels 1928.

Mols, Roger, 'Emploi et valeur des statistiques en histoire religieuse', *Nouvelle revue théologique,* vol. 86 (1964), pp. 388–410.

Mone, F. J., *Lateinische Hymnen,* 3 vols, Freiburg im Breisgau 1853–5, repr. Aalen 1964.

Monitor, Hansgeorg, 'Frömmigkeit im Spätmittelalter und früher Neuzeit als historisch-methodisches Problem', in *Festgabe für Ernst Walter Zeeden zum 60. Geburtstag am 14. Mai 1976,* Reformations-geschichtliche Studiën und Texte 2, Suppl. 2, ed. H. Rabe *et al.,* Münster 1976.

More, Thomas, *The History of King Richard III,* ed. R. S. Sylvester, *The Complete Works of St. Thomas More,* vol. 2, Yale, New Haven 1963.

Pächt, Otto, and J. J. G. Alexander, *Illuminated Manuscripts in the Bodleian Library:* vol. 1, *German, Dutch, Flemish, French and Spanish Schools,* Oxford 1966; vol. 3, *British Isles and Icelandic Schools* (with addenda to vols. 1 & 2), Oxford 1973.

Panofsky, Edwin, *Early Netherlandish Painting,* 2 vols (2nd edn.), New York 1971.

Pantin, W. A., 'Instructions for a Devout and Literate Layman', *Medieval Learning and Literature. Essays presented to Richard William Hunt,* ed. J. J. G. Alexander and M. T. Gibson, Oxford 1976, pp. 398–422.

Pfaff, R. W., *New Liturgical Feasts in Later Medieval England,* Oxford 1970.

Pollard, A. J., 'St Cuthbert and the Hog: Richard III and the County Palatine of Durham, 1471–85,' in *Kings and Nobles in the Later Middle Ages. A Tribute to Charles Ross,* ed. R. A. Griffiths and James Sherborne, Gloucester 1986, pp. 109–29.

Prims, F., *Een Limburgsch Gebedenboek uit de XVe Eeuw,* Koninklijke Vlaamsche Akademie voor Taal en Letterkunde, 1926.

Raby, F. J. E., *History of Christian–Latin Poetry,* Oxford 1927 (2nd edn 1953).

Raine, J., 'The Statutes ordained by Richard, Duke of Gloucester, for the College of Middleham. Dated July 4, 18 Edw. IV (1478)', *The Archaeological Journal,* vol.14 (1857), pp. 160–70.

Raleigh, Sir Walter, *History of the World,* London 1677.

Rézeau, P., *Répertoire d'incipit des prières françaises à la fin du Moyen Age,* Genève 1986.

Richmond, Colin, 'Religion and the Fifteenth-Century English Gentleman', in *The Church, Politics and Patronage in the Fifteenth Century,* ed. R. B. Dobson, Gloucester 1984, pp. 193–208.

Rickert, Margaret, 'The Reconstruction of an English Carmelite Missal', *Burlington Magazine,* no. 67 (1935), pp. 99–113.

——, 'Herman the Illuminator', *Burlington Magazine,* no. 66 (1935), pp. 39–40.

——, chapter on 'Illumination' in John M. Manly and Edith Rickert (eds.), *The Text of the Canterbury Tales,* 8 volumes, University of Chicago 1940, volume 1, pp. 561–605.

——, *The Reconstructed Carmelite Missal. An English Manuscript of the late XIV Century in the British Museum (Additional 29704–5, 44892),* London 1952.

——, 'The So-called Beaufort Hours and York Psalter', *Burlington Magazine,* vol. 104 (1962), pp. 238–246.

——, *Painting in Great Britain: The Middle Ages,* The Penguin History of Art, Harmondsworth, 2nd ed. 1965.

———, 'New Herman Attributions', in *Festschrift Ulrich Middeldorf,* ed. Antje Kosegarten and Peter Tigler, 2 vols, Berlin 1968, vol.1, pp. 88–92.

Robbins, R. H., 'Levation Prayers in Middle English Verse', *Modern Philology,* vol. 60 (1942–3), pp. 131–46.

Rogers, N. J., 'Books of Hours produced in the Low Countries for the English Market in the Fifteenth Century', 2 vols, unpublished M.Litt. thesis, Cambridge 1982.

———, 'About the 15 "O"s, The Brigittines and Syon Abbey', *St Ansgar's Bulletin,* vol. 80 (1984), pp. 29–30.

Rosenthal, J. T., 'Richard, Duke of York: A Fifteenth-Century Layman and the Church', *Catholic History Review,* vol. 50 (1964–5), pp. 171–87.

Ross, Charles, *Edward IV,* London 1974.

———, *Richard III,* London 1981.

Salicetus, Nicolaus, *Liber meditationum ac orationum devotarum qui Ant[h]idotarius Anime dicitur,* Antwerp, G. Leeu 1490.

Salmon, P., Oratio S. Brandani, in 'Testimonia Orationis Chistianae antiquioris', *Corpus Christianorum, Continuatio Medievalis,* vol. 47, Turnhout 1977.

Sandler, Lucy Freeman, *Gothic Manuscripts 1285–1385,* 2 vols., Oxford 1986.

Saunders, O. Elfrida, *English Illumination,* 2 vols., Florence 1928.

Schmidt, Gerhard, 'Two Unknown English Horae from the Fifteenth Century', *Burlington Magazine,* vol. 103 (1961), pp. 47–54.

Scott, Kathleen L., 'A Mid-Fifteenth Century English Illuminating Shop and its Customers', *Journal of the Warburg and Courtauld Institutes,* vol. 31 (1968), pp. 170–196.

Searle, W. G., *History of Queens' College Cambridge,* Cambridge Antiquarian Society, Octavo Publications, No. 9 (1867), vol. 1.

———, *The Illuminated Manuscripts in the Library of the Fitzwilliam Museum, Cambridge,* Cambridge 1876.

Selmer, J., ed., *Navigatio Sancti Brendani Abbatis,* Notre Dame, Indiana, 1959.

Shailor, B. A., ed., *Catalogue of Medieval and Renaissance Manuscripts in the Beinecke Rare Books and Manuscript Library, Yale University,* 2 vols, New York 1984–7.

Simmons, T. F., *The Lay-folks Mass Book,* Early English Text Society, OS. Vol. 71 (1879).

Sinclair, K. V., *Prières en ancien français. Nouvelles références ... du répertoire de Sonet,* Hamden, Conn., 1978.

Sonet, J., *Répertoire d'incipit de prières en ancien français,* Genève 1956.

Sotheby's Catalogue, 12 December 1967, *Western and Hebrew Manuscripts and Miniatures.*

———, 19 June 1989, *Illuminated Manuscripts from The Celebrated Library of The Late Major J. R. Abbey. The Eleventh and Final Part.*

Spriggs, Gereth M., 'Unnoticed Bodleian Manuscripts illuminated by Herman Scheerre and his School', *Bodleian Library Record,* vol. 7 (1964), pp. 193–203.

——, 'The Nevill Hours and the School of Herman Scheerre', *Journal of the Warburg and Courtauld Institutes,* vol. 37 (1974), pp. 104–129.

Stadlhuber, J., 'Das Laienstundengebet vom Leiden Christi in seinem Mittelalterlichen Fortleben', *Zeitschrift für Katholische Theologie,* vol. 72 (1950), pp. 282–325.

Steele, R., 'Dies Aegyptiaci', *Proceedings of the Royal Society of Medicine,* vol. 12 Suppl. (1918–9), pp. 108–21.

Sutton, Anne F., 'Richard III's Castle of Care', in *Richard III, Crown and People,* ed. J. Petre, London 1985, pp. 303–306.

——, '"A Curious Searcher for Our Weal Public": Richard III, Piety, Chivalry and the Concept of the "Good Prince"', in *Richard III, Loyalty, Lordship and Law,* ed. P. W. Hammond, London 1986, pp. 58–90.

——, and P. W. Hammond, eds., *The Coronation of Richard III, the Extant Documents,* Gloucester 1983.

—, and Livia Visser-Fuchs, 'Richard III's books: I. The Booke of Gostlye Grace of Mechtild of Hackeborn', *The Ricardian,* vol. 7 (1985–7), pp. 278–92; 'II. A Collection of Romances and Old Testament Stories', pp. 327–32, 371–79, 421–36; 'IV. Vegetius' *De Re Militari',* pp. 541–52; 'V. Aegidius Romanus' *De Regimine Principum', ibid.,* vol. 8 (1988–90), pp. 61–73; 'VI. The Anonymous or Fitzhugh Chronicle', pp. 104–19; 'VII. Guido delle Colonne's *Historia Destructionis Troiae.* VIII. Geoffrey of Monmouth's *Historia Regum Britanniae* with the *Prophecy of the Eagle* and Commentary', pp. 136–48.

——, and ——, 'Richard III and St. Julian: A New Myth', *The Ricardian,* vol. 8 (1988–90), pp. 265–270.

Szöverffy, J., *Die Annalen der lateinischen Hymnendichtung. Ein Handbuch,* 2 vols., Berlin 1964–5.

Tanner, N. P., *The Church in Late Medieval Norwich, 1370–1532,* Pontifical Institute of Medieval Studies 66, Toronto 1984.

Thalhofer, V., and L. Eisenhofer, *Handbuch der Katholischen Liturgik,* 2 vols, Freiburg im Breisgau 1912.

Thomson, J. A. F., 'Piety and charity in late medieval London', *Journal of Ecclesiastical History,* vol. 16 (1965), pp. 178–195.

Thoss, D., *Flämische Buchmalerei, Handschriftschätze aus dem Burgunderreich,* (Catalogue of an exhibition at the National Austrian Library, Vienna, 1987), Graz 1987.

Thurston, H. H. C., *Familiar Prayers,* London 1953.

Tolley, Thomas, 'John Siferwas. The Study of an English Illuminator', unpublished Ph.D. Thesis, University of East Anglia 1984.

Tudor-Craig, Pamela, *Richard III* (Catalogue of the National Portrait Gallery Exhibition 1973), 2nd edn. 1977.

——, 'The Hours of Edward V' in *England in the Fifteenth Century, Proceedings of the 1986 Harlaxton Symposium,* ed. D. Williams, Woodbridge 1987, pp. 351–370.

Turner, D. H., 'The Prayer-Book of Archbishop Arnulph II of Milan', *Revue bénédictine,* vol. 70 (1960), pp. 360–92.

——, 'The Bedford Hours and Psalter', *Apollo*, no.76, June 1962, pp. 265–70.

——, 'The Wyndham Payne Crucifixion', *British Library Journal*, vol. 2 (1976), pp. 8–26.

——, *The Hastings Hours. A 15th-Century Flemish Book of Hours made for William, Lord Hastings, now in the British Library*, London 1983.

Underwood, M. G., 'Politics and Piety in the Household of Lady Margaret Beaufort', *Journal of Ecclesiastical History*, vol. 38 (1987), pp. 39–52.

Vale, M. G. A., *Piety, Charity and Literacy among the Yorkshire Gentry, 1370–1480*, University of York, Borthwick Papers no. 50, 1976.

Vaughan, R., *Charles the Bold, the Last Valois Duke of Burgundy*, London 1973.

Vergil, Polydore, *Three Books of Polydore Vergil's English History*, ed. H. Ellis, Camden Society 1844.

Von Euw, A., and J. M. Plotzek, *Die Handschriften der Sammlung Ludwig*, 4 vols, Cologne 1979–85.

Voragine, Jacobus de, *The Golden Legend*, trans, and adapted Granger Ryan and Helmut Ripperger, London and New York 1941.

Walther, H., *Initia carminum ac versuum Medii Aevi posterioris Latinorum*, Gottingen 1959.

——, *Proverbia sententiaeque Latinitatis Medii Aevi*, 5 vols, Göttingen 1963–7.

Warner, G. F., *Descriptive Catalogue of the Illuminated Manuscripts in the Library of C. W. Dyson Perrins*, 2 vols, Oxford 1920.

Webb, J. F., ed. and transl., *Lives of the Saints*, Harmondsworth 1981.

White, W. T., 'The Death and Burial of Henry VI, Part II', *The Ricardian*, vol. 6 (1982), pp. 106–17.

Wieck, R. S., *Late Medieval and Renaissance Illuminated Manuscripts 1350–1525 in the Houghton Library*, Cambridge, Mass. 1983.

Wieck, R.S., et al., *The Book of Hours in Medieval Art and Life*, London 1988.

Wilmart, A., 'La Prière à Notre-Dame et à S. Jean publiée sous le nom de S. Anselme', *La Vie Spirituelle*, Supplément, Mai 1923, pp. 165–92.

——, 'Prières mediévales pour l'adoration de la Croix', *Ephemerides Liturgicae*, vol. 46 (1932), pp. 22–46.

——, 'L'office du Crucifix contre l'angoisse', *Ephemerides Liturgicae*, vol. 46 (1932), pp. 421–34.

——, *Auteurs spirituels et textes dévots du moyen âge latin*, Paris 1932.

——, 'Le grand poème Bonaventurien sur les Sept Paroles du Christ en Croix', *Revue bénédictine*, vol. 47 (1935), pp. 235–78.

——, 'Le manuel de prières de St. Jean Gualbert', *Revue bénédictine*, vol. 48 (1936), pp. 259–99.

Woolf, Rosemary, *The English Religious Lyric in the Middle Ages*, Oxford 1968.

Wordsworth, Christopher, *Ceremonies and Processions of the Cathedral Church of Salisbury*, Cambridge 1901.

——, ed., *Horae Eboracenses. The Prymer or Hours of the Blessed Virgin Mary, according to the Use of the Illustrious Church of York ...*, Surtees Society, vol.132 (1920).

Wormald, F. and P. M. Giles, 'Description of Fitzwilliam Museum ms. 3–1954', *Transactions of the Cambridge Bibliographical Society,* vol. 4 (1964), pp. 1–28.

Wright, Sylvia A., 'The Big Bible, Royal I E ix in the British Library, and Manuscript Illumination in London in the early Fifteenth Century', unpublished Ph.D. thesis, University of London 1986.

Yates Thompson Collection. *A Descriptive Catalogue of the Second Series of 50 Manuscripts in the Collection of Henry Yates Thompson,* by various hands, Cambridge 1920.

Index of *Incipit* of Prayers

This index does not include the opening lines of the usual prayers of the Hours of the Virgin, nor those of the memorials in Lauds. See also the general index.

Index

Additional references on the same page have not been noted.

Aristotle, 106
Armagnac, John, Count of, 150
Ave Maria, 73, 75, 76, 134, 135

Bancroft, Richard, Archbishop of
Canterbury, 51 Barnard Castle, 53,
105, 126
Beauchamp, Anne, Countess of
Warwick, 124
——, Henry, Duke of Warwick, 24,
25, 130; his hours and psalter, see
New York, Pierpont Morgan Library
Ms. 893; and see Cecily Nevill
—— Hours, see London, BL.
Ms. Royal 2 A xviii
——, Margaret, Countess of
Shrewsbury, her book of hours, see
Cambridge, Fitzwilliam Museum
Ms. 41–1950
——, Margaret, of Bletsoe, Countess
of Somerset, 118; her hours, see
London, BL. Ms. Royal 2 A xviii
Beaufort, John, Earl of Somerset
(d.1410), 17, 118; his psalter, see
London, BL. Ms. Royal 2 A
xviii, and Rennes, Bibliothèque
Municipale Ms. 22
—— Hours and York Psalter, see
London, BL. Ms. Royal 2 A
xviii, and Rennes, Bibliothèque
Municipale Ms. 22
——, John, Earl of Somerset (d.1444),
118
——, Margaret, Countess of
Richmond, 50, 51, 119
—— Saints, Master of the, 119
Bede, prayer attributed to, 8, 67, 97,
126, 139, 145; his psalter, 130
Bedford, John, Duke of, 9, 20, 21; his
hours, 146; his psalter and hours, see
London, BL. Ms. Add. 42131
Berengar of Tours, 65, 131

Berkeley Castle, Nevill Hours, 19, 35,
45, 47, 120, 123; fig. 5
Berry, John, Duke of, 9, 139; his *Petites
Heures,* see Paris, BN. Ms. latin 18014
Bible, Vulgate, 52, 63; texts, 77, 83, 84,
92, 94, 114, 143; 'biblical deliverances'
(*exempla*), 79, 88, 94–5, 97, 98, 110, 142,
144; and see prayers, psalms, St. Paul
Big Bible, the (BL. Ms. Royal 1 E ix),
48, 116, 123, 124
Biondo, Giovanni del, 118
Blackburn, Museum and Art Galleries,
Ms. Hart 21018, 19, 20, 28, 35, 120,
123, figs. 7, 14, 21
Bohun, Eleanor de, Duchess of
Gloucester, 16; her psalter and hours,
see Edinburgh, National Library of
Scotland Ms. Advocates 18.6.5
books of hours, see hours, books of
Bosworth, battle of, 2, 50
Boucicaut Master, 17, 118, 122
Bradfort, Ysabel, 51
breviary, definition of, 114
Bridgettine Order, 69
Broederlam, Melchior, 16
Bruges, 11, 17, 28, 88, 99, 120, 139, 142
Brussels, Bibliothèque Nationale Albert
I, Ms. 11035–37, 139, 140, 142, 146;
see also Cambridge, Fitzwilliam
Museum Ms. 3–1954
Ms. IV 95, 99, 146
Buck, George, 148
Burgundy, Dukes of 89, 99, 142;
Charles the Bold, 108, 150; John
the Fearless, 89; Philip the Bold, his
hours, see Brussels, Bibliothèque
Royale Ms. 11037–37, and
Cambridge, Fitzwilliam Museum
Ms. 3–1954; Philip the Good, 89,
140; and see Margaret of York
burial, as illustration of the Vigil of the
Dead, 25